SOCIAL POLICY IN AN ERA OF COMPETITION

From global to local perspectives

Edited by Dan Horsfall and John Hudson

First published in Great Britain in 2017 by

Policy Press
University of Bristol
1-9 Old Park Hill
Bristol
BS2 8BB
UK
t: +44 (0)117 954 5940
pp-info@bristol.ac.uk
www.policypress.co.uk

North America office:
Policy Press
c/o The University of Chicago Press
1427 East 60th Street
Chicago, IL 60637, USA
t: +1 773 702 7700
f: +1 773-702-9756
sales@press.uchicago.edu
www.press.uchicago.edu

© Policy Press 2017

British Library Cataloguing in Publication Data
A catalogue record for this book is available from the British Library

Library of Congress Cataloging-in-Publication Data
A catalog record for this book has been requested

ISBN 978 1 4473-2627-4 hardcover
ISBN 978-1-4473-2630-4 ePub
ISBN 978-1-4473-2631-1 Mobi
ISBN 978-1-4473-2629-8 ePdf

The rights of Dan Horsfall and John Hudson to be identified as editors of this work has been asserted by them in accordance with the Copyright, Designs and Patents Act 1988.

Cover design by Hayes Design
Front cover image: istock
Printed and bound in Great Britain by CPI Group (UK) Ltd, Croydon, CR0 4YY
Policy Press uses environmentally responsible print partners

Contents

List of figures, tables and boxes

Figures

Tables

Boxes

List of contributors

Kate Brown is a Lecturer in Social Policy and Crime in the Department of Social Policy and Social Work, University of York, UK.

Peter Dwyer is Professor of Social Policy in the Department of Social Policy and Social Work, University of York, UK.

Kevin Farnsworth is a Reader in Comparative and Global Social Policy in the Department of Social Policy and Social Work, University of York, UK.

Naomi Finch is a Lecturer in Social Policy in the Department of Social Policy and Social Work, University of York, UK.

Chris Holden is a Reader in International Social Policy in the Department of Social Policy and Social Work, University of York, UK.

Dan Horsfall is a Lecturer in Comparative Social Policy in the Department of Social Policy and Social Work, University of York, UK.

John Hudson is Professor of Social Policy in the Department of Social Policy and Social Work, University of York, UK, where he is Co-Director of the Centre for Research in Comparative and Global Social Policy (CRCG).

Zoë Irving is a Senior Lecturer in Comparative and Global Social Policy in the Department of Social Policy and Social Work, University of York, UK, where she is Co-Director of the Centre for Research in Comparative and Global Social Policy (CRCG).

Stefan Kühner is an Assistant Professor in Social Policy at Lingnan University, Hong Kong and an Honorary Fellow of the Department of Social Policy and Social Work, University of York, UK; until 2016 he was a Senior Lecturer in Social Policy in the Department of Social Policy and Social Work, University of York, UK.

Stuart Lowe is an Honorary Fellow of – and until 2015 was Senior Lecturer in Social Policy in – the Department of Social Policy and Social Work, University of York, UK.

Neil Lunt is Professor of Social Policy and Public Sector Management in the Department of Social Policy and Social Work, University of York, UK.

Theo Papadopoulos is a Lecturer in Social Policy at the University of Bath, UK.

Antonios Roumpakis is a Lecturer in Comparative Social Policy in the Department of Social Policy and Social Work, University of York, UK.

Carolyn Snell is a Senior Lecturer in Social Policy in the Department of Social Policy and Social Work, University of York, UK.

List of abbreviations

ALMP	active labour market programme
CEE	Central and Eastern European
CMA	Competition and Markets Authority
CME	coordinated market economy
CPGC	centre of political gravity of the cabinet
CRCG	Centre for Research in Comparative and Global Social Policy
EC	European Commission
ECHR	European Court of Human Rights
ECJ	European Court of Justice
EES	European Employment Strategy
EPL	employment protection legislation
ESA	Employment and Support Allowance
ETUC	European Trade Union Confederation
EU	European Union
Fa-QCA	Fuzzy-Set Qualitative Comparative Analysis
FDI	Foreign Direct Investment
GDP	gross domestic product
ILO	International Labour Organization
IMF	International Monetary Fund
JSA	Jobseeker's Allowance
LME	liberal market economy
MBS	Mortgage Backed Securities
MIP	Macroeconomic Imbalance Procedure
MRG/CMP/ MARPOR	Manifesto Research Group/Comparative Manifesto Project
OECD	Organisation for Economic Co-operation and Development
PMR	product market regulation
R&D	research and development
SEZ	Special Economic Zone
SMOP	Surface Measure of Overall Performance
TNC	transnational corporation
UKTI	UK Trade and Investment
UNDP	United Nations Development Programme
VoC	varieties of capitalism
WEF	World Economic Forum
WTO	World Trade Organization

Introduction: social policy in an era of competition

Dan Horsfall and John Hudson

The competition state thesis and beyond

A quarter of a century ago Cerny (1990) outlined his 'competition state thesis', in which he suggested that neoliberal reform agendas, gaining traction because of the intensification of global economic competition, were sounding the death knell of the welfare state and the birth of the 'competition state', in which social policy is subjugated to the needs of economic competitiveness (Cerny, 1990; 1997; Cerny and Evans, 1999). With the benefit of hindsight we can say that Cerny's claim exaggerated the threat to the welfare state, but few dispute the central idea that welfare states across the Organisation for Economic Co-operation and Development (OECD) have been subjected to reform agendas that have stressed economic competitiveness (Horsfall, 2010).

Indeed, there is an increasing consensus that welfare states have been recalibrated and restructured in significant ways, with many arguing that neoliberal competition imperatives have permeated the fabric of welfare state institutions and altered perceptions of social rights (Bonoli and Natali, 2012). However, contributions to this debate are scattered across a wide range of literatures and, moreover, overlapping arguments in different disciplines are too often debated in isolation. This text fuses key insights from theoretical political economy, macro-sociology and empirical social policy analysis in order to shed new light on the ways in which global competition is reshaping welfare states in practice. Moreover, it does so from a cross-national and international perspective, on the basis that contemporary welfare reform processes must be located in a broader global context in order to be fully understood.

Much of Cerny's work on the competition state thesis was completed while he was based in the Department of Politics at the University of York between 1970 and 1995 and/or in collaboration with Mark Evans who was based in the same department from 1993 to 2009, eight of those years as its Head of Department. Their key works on the 'competition state thesis' have triggered international debates of some significance; for instance, Google Scholar records over 1,000 citations for Cerny's (1997) 'Paradoxes of the competition state' article and around 1,000 citations for his 1990 book *The Changing Architecture of Politics*. Evans and Davies' 1999 article in which they outline a multi-level understanding of policy transfer processes, with the competition state as the key macro-level driver of the international movement of policy ideas, has been cited over 600 times, according to Google Scholar.

But their arguments also triggered a very *local* debate among social policy scholars based in the Department of Social Policy and Social Work at the University of York. The core arguments advanced by Cerny and Evans chimed with the conclusions that many of us specialising in social policy research had come to about the nature and direction of welfare state reform agendas, but our research agendas often also highlighted contrary and contradictory processes too. As the welfare state dimensions of the competition state thesis became sharper in the work of Cerny and Evans in the early 2000s, a fruitful cross-disciplinary dialogue began to emerge in both the teaching and research of the Department of Social Policy and Social Work. Some of the questions Cerny and Evans raised about the likely impact of globalisation and intensified economic competition on the shape and nature of welfare states moved from the periphery of our work to the core. This meant that questions informed by the political economy literature began to be placed more firmly alongside the empirically rooted social policy analysis that had long been the core of the Department of Social Policy and Social Work's research. Indeed, today, much of our teaching and research approaches social policy analysis from a comparative and international perspective and in 2015 we established the Centre for Research in Comparative and Global Social Policy (CRCG) to drive work forward in this area.

This book draws together arguments and evidence from a wide range of projects that are ongoing or have been recently completed by staff connected to the CRCG at the University of York. Although it is not a book about the competition state thesis per se, it is fair to say that, in many respects, it represents a long-gestating response to the questions that the Cerny and Evans competition state thesis raised for social policy analysis. Throughout the book we underline the value that is added to debates on the impact of intensified global economic competition on welfare states when they are approached from a perspective that fuses the applied empirical concerns of traditional social policy scholarship with the broader theoretical perspectives found in comparative political economy and macro-sociology. It is in this sense that the book is a response to the competition state thesis debate: while the theoretically rooted arguments of Cerny and Evans triggered new lines of investigation in our work, we hope that the empirical traditions of social policy analysis in which we are rooted help us in turn to push forward theoretical agendas in comparative political economy and macro-sociology.

Key focal points

To do this, the book addresses some of the major theoretical debates in the social sciences about how the intensification of global economic competition has influenced the direction of welfare state reform processes across the OECD in recent decades and vice versa. But, at the same time, it aims to offer some more nuanced, empirically rooted alternatives to the 'competition state thesis' perspective that can better account for how welfare states have responded to the intensification of global economic competition in reality. The individual chapters draw on a wide range of examples that speak to these themes, with all chapters having either: (i) an explicitly cross-national focus (drawing on data relating to multiple countries); or (ii) an explicitly international focus (examining local cases, but in order to shed light on the impact of international forces); or (iii) a conceptual basis that has resonance for welfare states across high-income countries generally. Indeed, some chapters have all three. In addition, three broad umbrella terms capture key dimensions of change that connect the arguments made across the book as a whole: competition, conditionality and cognition.

Competition represents the starting point of our analysis, it being at the heart of debates around globalisation. The notion of competition impacts on and permeates welfare states in many ways. For instance, we explore: how intensified economic competition creates pressure for fiscal constraint or the redirection of social expenditures; how competition is increasingly embedded within public services, major utilities and transnational regulatory frameworks, often compromising key social agendas as a consequence; and how structures of governance are being reconfigured and rescaled in order to enhance economic competiveness, often with profound implications for welfare.

One of the ways in which welfare states have been reconfigured in response to perceived competition pressures is through a rewriting of social contracts in order to de-emphasise social rights and place a stronger emphasis on individual responsibilities. Not only have such interventions been used in an attempt to scale back welfare state expenditures, they have also been deployed in order to underline the prioritisation of work obligations over social rights. Conditionality forms our second theme, therefore. We explore, for instance: how services in a range of different policy sectors have been affected by conditionality; how social citizenship has been redefined by it; how the delivery of services is being reshaped by it; and how new concepts such as vulnerability are coming to the fore in justifying a narrower targeting of entitlements as the social policy agenda moves away from a social rights-based approach.

Arguably the most profound impact of the rise of both conditionality and neoliberal competition discourses has been on how the social role of the state is conceived and understood. Cognition therefore forms our final theme. Among other issues, we explore here: how the campaigning platforms of political parties across the OECD have shifted on welfare state issues since the 1970s; how societal values relevant to key social policy agendas have altered over recent decades; and how social citizenship and, ultimately, the welfare state itself, have been reconceptualised by governments and international organisations such as the OECD over the course of the past quarter of a century or so.

Using these three themes a new narrative that goes beyond the 'competition state' model emerges, one that captures the complexity of social policy reform processes that have taken place over the past quarter of a century or so. While some chapters (necessarily) speak more fully to one of the themes rather than all three, many speak to two or all three. To this end, the book is not presented in three distinct parts dealing with each theme, as this would create an artificial trichotomy between what are three interrelated and overlapping themes. Instead we break the book into three core parts capturing different aspects of change: Part One examines 'Global competition as the context for welfare'; Part Two examines 'The impact of intensified competition on local governance'; Part Three examines 'The reframing of welfare discourses in an era of competition'.

Global competition as the context for welfare

In Part One of the book we focus primarily on macro-level arguments about the changing shape of the welfare state in the face of intensified global economic pressures. Horsfall's Chapter One draws together arguments from comparative political economy and macro-sociology that suggested that the traditional welfare state would wither in the face of globalisation, but crucially he then exposes these theoretical arguments to detailed empirical analysis using quantitative comparative data. Not only does this allow him to challenge the veracity of some of the more fatalistic models of change, he is also able to offer a more nuanced account that shows different ways in which different countries have responded to global competition pressures. The chapter also serves as a foundation on which many other chapters will build, scoping out key contextual theories about the modernisation of the welfare state.

One of the core arguments made in Chapter One is that we can identify both neoliberal and more 'progressive' models of 'competition state'; in Chapter Two Finch et al examine in more depth one of the attempts to develop a 'progressive' modernisation of welfare: the social investment model. They too combine a review of key theoretical arguments with analysis of comparative quantitative cross-national data, reviewing how far reform agendas match the reality of the social investment model theory and, moreover, probing the effectiveness of the approach in reconciling social and economic pressures. Crucially, they argue that, irrespective of the virtues of the social investment model, the role of international actors in encouraging its diffusion – especially the OECD and European Union (EU) – tells us much about contemporary politics.

The latter theme is pursued in more depth in Chapter Three by Roumpakis and Papadopoulos, who explore the often conflicting social and economic agendas pushed by the EU. Via a detailed analysis of regulatory frameworks, policy directives and court rulings, they carefully unpick the changing international policy framework within which EU member states operate. In so doing, they point to important but rarely explored shifts in governance frameworks that have acted to prioritise economic goals over social goals. Moreover, they suggest that such shifts have been hastened by the response to the financial crisis. Ultimately, they argue that the old common project of 'Social Europe' is increasingly giving up its place to a global-market project of 'Competition Europe' as a consequence of these changes.

Chapter Three ties in with one of the core themes of Lowe's Chapter Four, for he too stresses the ways in which international regulatory frameworks have restricted the space in which social policy operated, particularly so since the financial crisis. However, Lowe's argument is broader still, focusing on the globalisation and liberalisation of mortgage markets. He argues that not only has the exposure of nations to intensified global capital flows exposed national economic policies to global risks and surveillance, and financialised housing to an unprecedented degree, but that the growth in homeownership and mortgage debt that it facilitates has impacted on the social policy priorities of many governments. In particular, he suggests, it has undermined public provision in key areas such as pensions and social care, as private households increasingly view equity stored in housing as a resource for their welfare needs. Using comparative data he argues that we are seeing the rise of a low tax/low spend 'asset-based welfare state' in many countries.

The impact of global competition on local governance

While the Part One focuses primarily on macro-level arguments and how national welfare states have been repositioned to respond to competition pressures, Part Two explores the impact of intensified competitive pressures and processes through case studies of local responses. In so doing, it demonstrates how specific policy sectors in specific localities are being reshaped by the competition logic, and rises to the challenge set by Fiona Williams (2015, p 103) of 'forging of *conceptual alliances* through vertical connections between scales'.

It has long been recognised that one of the major global policy challenges shared by all countries is adapting to climate change. Reduction of energy consumption is a key part of this challenge but, as Snell's Chapter Five shows, this brings challenges for social policy, particularly given that rising energy costs have resulted in increasing levels of fuel poverty. The potential conflict between social and environmental policy objectives has been noted by scholars in the field, but that these objectives also interact with increasingly global and competitive energy markets (and how they do so) is less well understood. Snell explores the contradictions and tensions in this area, using UK policy as an example, but where the context is one of an internationalised private energy market and strong EU and World Trade Organization (WTO) policy frameworks hollowing out local governance. As she notes, this makes it increasingly difficult for government policy frameworks to address fuel poverty agendas effectively.

Once regarded as unthinkable, the private ownership of the energy sector and the transfer of key national assets to multinational corporations is now an established aspect of the contemporary policy landscape. Lunt's Chapter Six explores aspects of change in the healthcare sector that have similar parallels but where many processes of change are at a relatively early stage. More specifically, he examines the nature of national strategies aimed at promoting the export of health services as part of a broader economic growth strategy. Much of this activity involves public and private partnerships, with state support crucial in supporting economic conditions that are favourable for exporting health services. One particular example of health service export is that of medical tourism: the travel of patients for treatment abroad. While much of the popular debate here has focused on the increased mobility of people facilitating access to cheap cosmetic surgery, an overlooked dimension is that some countries have actively promoted medical tourism alongside wider health service export as way of generating significant revenues from foreign citizens in order to boost national economic output and/or subsidise the cost of national healthcare policies. Lunt explores these processes in three countries with different economic and social policy contexts. The example of medical tourism underlines not only how welfare services are increasingly being viewed as sources for export growth in the face of declining economic growth, but also that states are beginning to act as (internationally) competing providers of welfare services, contributing further to the hollowing-out of social policy governance processes.

In Chapter Seven Holden and Hudson explore in more detail the ways in which governance is being reframed by globalisation processes. More specifically, they explore how governance is being rescaled by globalisation, arguing that some nation-states have tried to circumvent globalisation pressures by injecting small slices of their territory more deeply into the global economy. They argue that this has been through establishing policy frameworks for specific localities that deliberately vary from those of the nation-state as a whole. They focus on two examples – global cities and Special Economic Zones – the former being more common in high-income countries, the latter more common in lower-income countries. In both instances, the intensification of globalisation processes in these zones has significant implications for welfare, although the authors suggest that the effects are by no means straightforward to analyse. Moreover, they note that the two are often connected by global economic processes, SEZs and global cities often being key sites but serving different functions in the global production chains employed by multinational corporations.

The reframing of welfare discourses in an era of competition

Part Three explores an aspect of change that is more nebulous than those covered in the earlier sections but arguably the deepest of all: the shifting conceptualisation of welfare.

While early theories such as Cerny's competition state thesis suggested the welfare state would wither in the face of global economic competition, the broad consensus today is that welfare has been recalibrated rather than merely retrenched. Central to this recasting of welfare has been the rise of conditionality across a wide range of social interventions. Dwyer's Chapter Eight addresses this, exploring how conditionality has reshaped notions of social citizenship in a fundamental manner. The language of conditionality has been key in selling diminished social rights to electorates, emphasising responsibilities alongside rights as a much-needed reform process. Indeed, the rise of conditionality discourses is such that few key political actors seem prepared to challenge what were once contentious alternatives to the traditional social rights model of welfare.

Brown's Chapter Nine follows in a similar vein to Dwyer's, exploring the increasingly strong targeting of welfare provisions on the most 'vulnerable' groups. In the current era of heightened pressure on resources and often increasing social polarisation, focusing resources on more intensive support for the most vulnerable is an inviting option for policy makers. Indeed, key international organisations such as the OECD and United Nations Development Programme (UNDP) have begun to adopt the language of vulnerability to this end. Brown explores the rise of this vulnerability rationale, but probes its application in practice to demonstrate that a heightened focus on the most 'vulnerable' can contribute towards an intensified competition for resources among the least well-off, obscuring questions about the distribution of resources and opportunities across the whole of society. In such a context, debates about who is vulnerable become increasingly key, with attempts to define and classify people accordingly often serving to exclude groups not seen as vulnerable in the popular imagination.

While Dwyer and Brown focus very much on how policy rules and frameworks have been reconceptualised, Kühner's Chapter Ten uses data on the manifestos of political parties across OECD countries to capture how political actors have reframed their perspectives on welfare in light of the intensification of global economic competition since the 1970s. In particular, he focuses on how – and how far – left- and right-wing parties have converged in terms of their social and economic policy agendas and, relatedly, to what degree perceived intensification of global economic pressures has driven partisan convergence.

The final chapter of Part Three is by Farnsworth and Irving (Chapter Eleven). Building on their extensive work on welfare states and the global financial crisis, they examine how economists, governments, international organisations and various other political and financial interests have exploited the economic crisis to assert the argument that the welfare state is unsustainable and that major social policy reforms are essential if nations affected by the crisis – particularly in Europe – are to become competitive in the world system. They argue that discourse has been powerfully reframed, the neoliberal orthodoxy being reinvigorated with a strengthened mission to shrink the (welfare) state. However, while they survey developments since the financial crisis, they also offer a critique, noting that welfare states underpin capitalist productivity and competitiveness during boom times and periods of economic crisis.

Welfare states, global competition: towards new agendas

Although the book draws together arguments and evidence from a wide range of projects undertaken by staff connected to the CRCG at the University of York, it does so in a way that creates major synergies between the projects, connecting together their separate foci into an integrated whole. As such the aim of the book is to set out an integrated agenda for future research and to underline the value added to debates around the intensification of global competition when they are approached from a perspective that fuses the applied empirical concerns of traditional social policy scholarship with the broader theoretical perspectives found in comparative political economy and macro-sociology.

The final chapter of the book, Chapter Twelve, fleshes out this agenda, looking back across the chapters of the book while also glancing forward to future research agendas. In so doing, we scope out a series of key hypothesis and exploratory research questions that the book points towards. As such, the book does not aim to represent a final word in the 'competition state' debate, but merely a step in the fruitful ongoing dialogue between empirically rooted social policy analysis and theoretically rooted comparative political economy and macro-sociology.

Part One
Global competition
as the context for welfare

The competition state thesis in a comparative perspective: the evolution of a thesis

Dan Horsfall

Introduction

The competition state thesis describes a product of globalisation and as such has not remained static since its conception some 25 years ago. The core ideals have held, although the emphasis placed by the authors on certain aspects of the competition state thesis has strengthened over time while other aspects have become comparatively muted. In part this is a natural consequence of the passage of time and increasing understanding of globalisation, as well as the perhaps unexpected level of complexity that has marked an increasingly interconnected world.

This chapter seeks to introduce the competition state thesis, serving the dual purpose of framing the chapter and providing an overall context for the remainder of the book. It then summarises and subsequently extends previous empirical work undertaken using the competition state framework in order to assess the extent to which the core thesis is still relevant today. The competition state may appear a little dated now and its more contentious assertion can be dismissed. However, the core processes identified by Cerny and Evans have clearly influenced welfare policies and ultimately played a part in reshaping welfare states, if not killing them off completely.

The competition state thesis

The key pressures that first Cerny (1990; 1997) and, later, Cerny and Evans (1999; 2003; 2004) and others such as Jessop (2000; 2002) and Fougner (2006) insisted were being faced by national welfare states have indeed come to pass. And yet, many of the assumptions made with regard to the consequences of globalisation, so contentious when first given voice, now seem a little dated. Despite this, many of the predictions made by Cerny and Evans, while both bold and controversial at the time are now taken for granted to such an extent that, with the benefit of hindsight, they appear as statements of the obvious rather than as prescient observations about the evolving nature of the political economy of welfare states.

Globalisation, the decline of the Fordist model of production and the rise of the global knowledge economy have all played their role in producing a more competitive environment in which welfare states operate. As Lunt notes in this collection (Chapter Six), there is an acceptance that not only has competition grown within welfare states but welfare states themselves now compete. As Cerny and Evans have maintained, competition is perhaps the 'only game in town' (2004), and while forging a consensus around the implications for welfare services of shifting to a more competitive arrangement is unlikely, a more competitive arrangement certainly exists.

But what exactly is the competition state? According to Cerny and Evans, it is the 'successor to the welfare state, retaining many of its features but reshaping them, sometimes quite drastically to fit a globalising world' (2003, p 24). Crucially, the emphasis is different; where the welfare state seeks to use the tools of the economy to further the public interest and promote social justice, the competition state seeks only economic success, with welfare provisions not only secondary, but offered only when they support the primary goal of economic success. This, Cerny and Evans insist, draws the nation-state into the conflict between the contrasting goals of the welfare state and the competition state, with its pursuit of greater economic efficiency and success, undermining the ideals of the traditional welfare state, especially in terms of safeguarding social rights and promoting social justice. Moreover, it is this reshaping that Cerny and Evans believe locks in the competition state, with each pro-competition state policy or decision that is made increasing the returns of the competition state and at the same time weakening the institutions of, support for and, ultimately, viability of the welfare state. All of this produces an economy, a state and, consequently, policies geared towards the pursuit of economic efficiency and competitive advantage. Cerny and Evans allow for some culturally or institutionally rooted variations but argue that the new economic realities wrought by globalisation invariably lead to a quantitative downsizing and qualitative disempowering of the welfare state.

Cerny and Evans contend that the core features (the following discussion draws on Cerny and Evans, 1999; 2004; Evans, 2010; and Horsfall, 2010) of the competition state are largely shaped by the adoption of the tools of New Public Management in the early 1990s. They argue that this marketisation of public service production precipitated a shift from inefficient models of government to a governance approach marked by arm's-length relationships and service delivery marked by contractualism. As a consequence, competition states seek to actively curtail the size of the state, in particular the welfare state, and, as such, a core feature of competition states is lower social expenditure than is exhibited by traditional welfare states; moreover, as part of what Cerny and Evans label the 'post-welfare contracting state', social expenditures are focused on active measures such as active labour market programmes (ALMP) rather than passive programmes of support. Competition states are also marked by low levels of regulation in industry and legislative protections for employees. Perhaps not unexpectedly, taxation is also a key feature of the competition state model (Genschel, 2002; Hay, 2004; Genschel and Seelkopf, 2015), with higher rates of taxation seen as indicative of not only a large, bureaucratic state, but also one that is particularly burdensome for industry. Indeed it is held that it is in the arena of corporation tax that the competition state finds its earliest traction, and through the global race to reduce corporation taxes the competition state is effectively 'locked in'.

This vision of competition-state social policy reads very much like a description of neoliberal ideals. Indeed Hay's (2004) key criticism of Cerny's competition state thesis is that it is little more than a stylised moniker for a particular variety of capitalism. While Cerny and Evans are keen to stress that the competition state may in some way reflect the variety of state forms or political economies of welfare that it encounters, thus allowing for some variation between different countries, their core thesis is built upon the notion that the competition state has seen the embedding of a neoliberal financial orthodoxy and it is realistically only through this that states can compete. In essence they attempt to sidestep a key criticism by ignoring it, failing to assimilate divergent approaches to both the economy and the welfare state into the competition state thesis, or to explain them, rather asserting that such differences harm comparative advantage, with the implication being that at some stage they will disappear.

This notion of neoliberal determinism and convergence stands in contrast to the notion of divergence being the natural consequence of the need to chase the comparative advantage as suggested in the varieties of capitalism (VoC) literature. In the works of Hall and Soskice (2001) and those who follow (see Hancké, 2009) it is argued that the very pressures outlined by Cerny and Evans reinforce the need for economies to differ. That said, while others have extended their work and suggested other models, Hall and Soskice (2001) themselves outline only two models of capitalism: the liberal market economy (LME) and the coordinated market economy (CME). The VoC thesis places the traditional 'firm' at the heart of its analysis and argues that firms in these two types of economies experience very different forms of capitalism and indeed are attracted to or emerge within different countries largely as a consequence of the nature of capitalism found there. In the coordinated market economies the state plays an important role in supporting slow-burn innovation, or innovation that builds on industrial memory and, as such, lends itself to the manufacturing sectors. It is this form of capitalism that Hall and Soskice believe is evident in much of Europe, particularly the countries that Esping-Andersen (1990) labelled either corporatist or social democratic. In the liberal market economies, which are primarily the Anglophone nations, the role of the state is subordinated to that of the market and consequently here we find 'radical' innovators among firms (Hall and Soskice, 2001). Such divergent approaches to capitalism are also reinforced by welfare arrangements, with approaches to labour market policy and even social protection, especially with regard to skill formation, playing a role in the nature of firm that locates in certain territories (Estevez-Abe et al, 2001).

The simplicity of the VoC model has been widely debated, with some criticising the distinction between radical and incremental innovation, others pointing to apparent contradictions such as the burgeoning mobile communications technologies (reliant on radical innovation) found in CMEs such as Sweden, and many suggesting third, fourth and fifth varieties of capitalism (Casper et al, 1999; Schmidt, 2002; Molina and Rhodes, 2007; Taylor, 2007). However, it is worth discussing the VoC literature as it is in many ways built on a fundamentally contrary position to the competition state with regard to the impact of globalisation. Where Cerny and Evans contend that the process of globalisation embeds a neoliberal financial orthodoxy, the VoC standpoint is that, rather than diversity being flattened by globalisation, such diversity channels globalisation, with globalisation reinforcing the comparative advantage of different varieties of capitalism.

The competition state seems in many ways to mirror the LME described by Hall and Soskice; however, it is perhaps unreasonable to characterise the competition state thesis as merely a stylised moniker for this variety of capitalism, for while the LME is viewed as one variety of capitalism, it can be argued that the competition state represents an end to varieties of capitalism. Given that the implications of this are often portrayed to be rather bleak with respect to the welfare state (not only from Cerny and Evans), the competition state thesis has been met with much hostility. One particularly noteworthy criticism is that the competition state thesis was advanced with almost no empirical corroboration of its core claims (Hay, 2004; Genschel and Seelkopf, 2015, p 244). Given that the forecasted race-to-the-bottom of public spending, so often intertwined with neoliberal accounts of welfare state change (Hay, 2004; Genschel and Seelkopf, 2015), never emerged, the competition state has largely been dismissed in recent literature. In many respects this is understandable; a more nuanced understanding of what the welfare state does in terms of productive and protective functions, as well as social investment strategies has replaced tired debates around simple retrenchment (see Hudson and Kühner, 2009; Morel et al, 2012a). However, a rush to dismiss the competition state thesis on the grounds that the welfare state has not died risks throwing out the baby with the bathwater. Where empirical exploration has taken place, there appears to be much of value in revisiting the arguments at the heart of the competition state.

Competition state models

Empirical exploration of the competition state has been limited to two main bodies of work, that of Genschel, who focuses on taxation (2002; and Genschel and Seelkopf, 2015) through the lens of the competition state, and of Horsfall, who has operationalised and measured the competition state as a whole (2010; 2013a; 2013b). Initial analysis that utilised an additive index to measure competition the comparative behaviours of countries with regard to the key dimensions of the competition state[1] suggested that there were two empirically identifiable approaches to the competition state, along with a number of countries that seemed to have resisted the competition state (Horsfall, 2010). The countries that appeared (in 2002) to have either resisted or not yet capitulated to the rise of the competition state were those that Esping-Andersen (1990) labelled as corporatist and included many of those coordinated market economies detailed in the VoC literature. Notably, Germany appeared in 2002 to soundly reject the competition state, exhibiting comparatively high levels of social expenditure, low levels of activation, high levels of product market regulation, strong employment protections and relatively high levels of corporation tax (and other forms of taxation). Predictably, the opposing model was dominated by Esping-Andersen's liberal or

Hall and Soskice's LME countries. Not even here, however, were extremely low levels of social expenditure witnessed, nor, counter to expectations, were high levels of activation apparent. Rather, these countries had low levels of taxation and regulation as well as rather weak employment protections. The third group of countries was largely populated by social democratic countries (also categorised in the VoC debate as CMEs alongside Germany) and was driven by reasonably low levels of market regulation and high levels of activation.

The findings of this first exploration provoked a number of questions, but because they related to only one time point they were unable to answer questions relating to the nature of change. A second study used the same basic method to compare countries' competition state behaviours at three time points (1997, 2002 and 2007). Data from the first time point was used to 'anchor' the data so as to not only highlight shifts in relative behaviours but also enable a comparison over time. Three key findings emerged from this work: first, all countries studied became more 'competitive' over the course of time, to the extent that only Germany would have been classed in 2007 as not a competition state in the original study. Second, while the countries that are categorised as liberal (Esping-Andersen, 1990), LME (Hall and Soskice, 2001) or archetypal neoliberal competition states (Cerny and Evans, 1999; Horsfall, 2010; 2013b) remained coherent, the burgeoning second group began to consist of countries whose approach was not 'active'; indeed, activation weakened in general across the decade. Third, it was clear that the methodology used could not cope with the multi-dimensional nature of the competition state (or any welfare state theory). It was clear that countries were arriving at similar overall scores (and consequently classifications or labels) from rather different pathways.

To accommodate and better understand the multi-dimensional nature of the competition state this empirical strand of work adopted a Fuzzy-Set Qualitative Comparative Analysis Fs-QCA[2] approach, subjecting behaviours on different dimensions of the competition state to Boolean algebra in order to better categorise countries as to the nature of their engagement with the competition state. Table 1.1 shows country memberships of four categories into which countries fell in 2007 using the Fs-QCA approach.

In short, three relatively stable forms of the competition state seemed to exist as of 2007, alongside Germany, which remained 'resistant' to the competition state regardless of the different methodology. As with previous work there appeared to be identifiable 'neoliberal' and 'active' models. To be categorised as broadly neoliberal a country simply had

Table 1.1: Competition state types (2007)

Broadly neoliberal	Active	Welfare/competition state mix	Conservative welfare
Australia	Austria	New Zealand	Germany
Canada	Belgium	Czech Republic	
Ireland	Denmark	Finland	
Korea	Netherlands,	France	
Slovak Republic	Norway	Greece	
USA	Sweden	Italy	
	Switzerland	Japan	
		Poland	
		Portugal	
		Spain	
		UK	

Source: Horsfall, 2013b.

to exhibit low social expenditure as well as not exhibiting high levels of activation. To be considered as active a country needed to exhibit high levels of activation but not low levels of social expenditure. The strength of countries' respective memberships (that is, + or strong +) was then determined by whether they had low levels of corporate taxation and/or employment protection, with low scores on either producing a + membership and low levels on both producing a strong + membership. The third type of competition state bypasses the welfare elements of the thesis, with countries in this category having neither low levels of social expenditure nor high levels of activation, but crucially low levels of corporation tax and/or employment protection legislation. Not only does this third type appear across time (1997, 2002 and 2007), but it appears to be the biggest 'growth' group, with many countries that conformed to no dimensions of the competition state in 1997 and/or 2002 transitioning to this type by 2007. Despite increasing pro-business behaviour, countries in this group did not appear to be on a pathway to either the active or neoliberal model, with activation spending and overall spending remaining stable in the case of the former and even increasing with regard to overall expenditure.

Previously published empirical work charts only to 2007, however, and it could be argued that the global financial crisis that was then in its infancy created the perfect conditions for the further embedding of the competition state model. In particular, the seemingly widespread acceptance of the need to reduce government expenditure and the similarly common roll-out of austerity programmes (Farnsworth and Irving, 2011a,b; Farnsworth, 2012; Crouch, 2015; Mason, 2015) in order to achieve this end would seem to point to an era of 'small government'. As many have noted, however, what actually happened was that social expenditure increased. In the sample of countries shown in Table 1.1 the average level of public social expenditure increased from 20.5% of gross domestic product (GDP) in 2007 to 23.7% in 2014, with no country presenting lower levels in 2014 than in 2007 (OECD, 2015a). It is worth noting that this expansion of expenditure continued beyond the initial stages of the crisis, beyond the point when countries were, at least in terms of rhetoric, abandoning fiscal stimulus in favour of austerity measures (Farnsworth, 2012). With the exception of the UK, Ireland and Canada, none of the countries charted here had lower public social expenditures in 2014 than in 2011, although data for 2014 shows a slight decrease in the sample average from 2013 (OECD, 2015a). Analysis of more up-to-date data tells us that by 2014 only Canada and Korea are identified as pursuing a broadly neoliberal approach to the competition state (Table 1.2).

In much the same fashion, membership of the active type shrinks from 2007 to 2014 although it includes the notable addition of Germany. It is difficult to assess what this tells us about this form of the competition state. Cerny and Evans initially argued that central to the competition state would be a shift towards more active approaches to welfare (1999), accepting the notion that this would be captured by investment in or use of ALMP (Evans, 2010). It became clear, however, that in the archetypal competition states activation

Table 1.2: Competition state types (2015/most recent year)

Broadly neoliberal	Active	Welfare/competition state mix	Conservative welfare
Canada	Denmark	Australia	
Korea	Germany	Austria	
	Norway	Belgium	
	Sweden	Czech Republic	
		Greece	
		Finland	
		France	
		Italy	
		Ireland	
		Japan	
		Netherlands	
		New Zealand	
		Switzerland	
		Poland	
		Portugal	
		Slovak Republic	
		Spain	
		UK	
		USA	

Note: Produced using Horsfall's 2013b methodology with more recent data.

was better characterised by the withdrawal of protection than by an investment in activation, especially the human capital investment schemes synonymous with social democratic countries (Jonasson et al, 2004). For the social democratic countries it might well be that high levels of ALMP expenditure per unemployed person reflected a long history of ALMP use, one that was unrelated to the rise of the competition state. Increasing ALMP expenditure in countries such as Austria and Belgium proved to be fleeting (both were categorised as adopting broadly active approaches in 2007 only) and may have been a consequence of lags between fluctuating unemployment levels and ALMP expenditure. This issue might go some way to explaining both Germany's inclusion and Netherland's exclusion of the active group in the most recent data; rather than signifying a more active approach in Germany and less active in the Netherlands, it may well be that unemployment has fallen rapidly in Germany and risen in the Netherlands, with the subsequent ALMP expenditure adjustment still lagging. Indeed, while ALMP expenditure has remained stable since the mid-1990s Germany's unemployment rate dropped from 8.54% in 2007 to 5.83% in 2011 and 4.99% in 2014, whereas the Netherlands saw increases from 4.1% in 2007 to 4.99% in 2011 and 7.43% in 2014 (OECD, 2015b). Both Germany and the Netherlands were extremely close to the thresholds set for inclusion in the active group and, as such, small fluctuations in unemployment rates coupled with a lag in ALMP expenditure changes might hold more explanatory power than the notion of an activation turn in Germany and a less active approach in the Netherlands.

The group that is perhaps most interesting is the welfare/competition state mix model. As Table 1.2 shows, by 2015 (or the most recent year for which data was available), it is this model that is most densely populated. Those countries in this category not only demonstrate competition state behaviours in either the sphere of corporate taxation or employment protection (or both, in the cases of the strong pro-business countries), but also do *not* demonstrate either the neoliberal trait of low social expenditure or the activation approach found among the social democratic countries.

This welfare/competition state mix grouping is interesting for three main reasons: first, it implies that competition state behaviours can be demonstrated by countries that are also resistant to retrenchment in terms of public spending. This in itself presents a challenge for Cerny and Evans' original (1999) thesis, which held the quantitative reduction of the welfare state at its core.

Second, this grouping exhibits the largest growth in membership over time. In 1997 nine countries demonstrated no 'pro-business' behaviour at all, with high corporation tax rates and strong employment protections. By 2007 only Germany maintained its complete lack of 'pro-business' engagement and by 2011 even Germany was demonstrating much lower levels of corporation tax. This is not to say, of course, that Germany was previously anti-business; as Hall and Soskice (2001) posit, Germany's approach is simply different, with its coordinated market economy, built around incremental expansion within manufacturing, offering different comparative advantages to the low-tax, low-regulation model. Indeed it is worth noting that Germany has consistently ranked high in the World Economic Forum's (WEF) Global Competitiveness Index, especially in terms of its innovation indicators, with the WEF noting in 2007 that the sophistication of the German business community 'knows no peers' (WEF, 2006). Despite this, tax rates, tax regulations and labour regulations have been identified as key barriers to Germany's competitiveness (WEF, 2008; 2014), although the extent to which tax rates are seen as a barrier has declined since 2007.

Indeed, corporation tax decreases have been the core driver of the burgeoning membership of this competition state/welfare state mix model, rather than weakening employment protections. Across the sample explored here the average corporation tax rate has fallen from just under 50% at the beginning of the 1980s to around 34% in 2000 and 26% by 2015. Corporate tax has been highlighted as burdensome by a number of individuals (Genschel, 2002; Genschel and Seelkopf) and organisations (OECD, WEF) and is seen as a key barrier to competition, with high rates risking capital flight and business relocation.

The consistent and relatively steep decline in corporate tax rates over time suggests that governments have accepted the notion that high corporate tax rates are at least perceived as anti-business. Genschel and Seelkopf (2105) accept that we have witnessed a convergence towards lower levels of corporate taxation, largely because countries and organisations such as the OECD accept the notion that high levels of corporate tax are burdensome (2015, p 243). Interestingly, though, they note that other seemingly logical implications of declining corporate tax rates have not presented. First, as Figure 1.1 shows, the neither the average nor the top rate of tax have altered much, and certainly they have not increased. This is important, as theories of tax competition would hold that while a decline in taxation aimed at mobile corporations or capital is likely to be offset with an increased

Figure 1.1: Sample average top, average and corporate tax rate alongside sample average tax revenue as a proportion of GDP over time

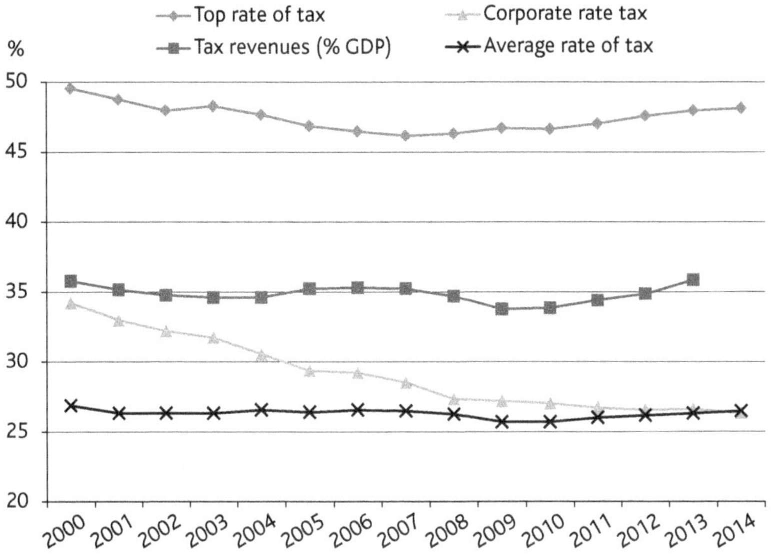

Notes: Tax rates are 'all-in' and includes social security contributions. The average tax rate is for a single person with no children.

Source: OECD, 2015c Tax Database

burden on less-mobile revenue streams – notably workers (Genschel and Seelkopf, 2015, p 244). Second, despite downward convergence in terms of corporation taxes, with no counterbalancing increase in the average tax wedge, tax revenues as a proportion of GDP have increased slightly since the late 1980s (with the increase being more marked in the Southern/Mediterranean countries) and revenues from corporate taxes have also increased from an average of 2.7% of GDP in the late 1980s to 3.8% in the period 2005–09, while at the same time budget deficits declined (Genschel and Seelkopf, 2015, pp 245–6). The implications of this for the welfare state are clear; even acceptance of the competition state rationale for declining corporate tax rates need not increase budgetary pressure on the welfare state.

While corporate tax rates have declined, the protectiveness of employment legislation has remained rather stable since the mid 1980s,[3] with some countries even strengthening protections (OECD, 2015b). Germany in particular has strengthened its employment protection legislation to such an extent that the WEF described its business community as 'saddled with sclerotic labor regulations' (WEF, 2006, p 31). This is perhaps surprising, given the centrality of labour market flexibility to many if not most prescriptions for efficient and competitive economies.

With respect to employment protection legislation (EPL), the LME/CME dichotomy found in the VoC literature is more evident than Esping-Andersen's three worlds. While there is a distinct neoliberal/Anglophone/archetypal competition state grouping where EPL is weakest, there is no discernible difference between corporatist and social democratic countries. This chimes not only with the VoC categorisations of countries but also the work of others such as Kemeny who insist that social democracy is actually a form of corporatism and not a distinct 'regime' (Kemeny, 2006).

All this is not to say that this welfare state/competition state mix model is simply an overblown assessment of decreasing corporation tax. While corporation tax accounts for the transition of countries that have shifted away from a rejection of or resilience to the competition state and towards some pro-business behaviours, seven of the nine countries in this grouping have weak employment protections, with the transition of countries with weak EPL being driven by increasing public expenditure.[4]

The third reason why this model is particularly noteworthy is that engagement with some element of pro-business policy as captured here is reflected in a general shift towards other pro-business behaviours not captured by Horsfall (2013b). In particular, product market regulation (PMR), which was not included in the Fs-QCA analysis undertaken by Horsfall[5] (2013b), has seen a steady decrease over the near 20 years that the OECD has measured it. PMR is a composite indicator of the degree to which regulatory burdens are placed on business (Nicoletti et al, 2000, p 2). Seen by some as the most burdensome form of regulation (Conway et al, 2005, p 4), the reduction of PMR has been seen as a priority for governments and by bodies such as the OECD (Nicoletti and Scarpetta, 2006, p 83; Schiantarelli, 2008, pp 46–8). The fall in PMR has been steady and substantial, with the average level of PMR among the countries studied here 35 percentage points lower in 2013 than when the OECD first started measuring it in 1998, with all its member countries witnessing a decrease during that time, some as much as nearly 50 percentage points (OECD, 2013a).

These decreases in PMR reflect changes in other indicators of competitiveness such as the diverse range of data collected by the WEF and organised under what it calls the 12 pillars of competitiveness (WEF, 2014). Similarly, while EPL rates have held reasonably steady, the measure used is one that looks at regular contracts. An exploration of increasingly common temporary contracts shows not only much weaker protections in general, but also a substantial weakening of these protections over the last decade. These relatively stable levels of EPL in regular contracts mask much weaker forms of protection for increasingly common forms of employment, ranging from zero-hours contracts to part-time and flexible work (OECD, 2014a).

It may seem a little grand to label countries as being pro-business and belonging to a welfare state/competition state model of political economy largely on the basis of declining rates of corporation tax. However, not only do other indicators of pro-business behaviour also seem to support this pro-business categorisation, but the welfare/competition mix model rests not only on pro-business policies but also on a traditional approach to social expenditure levels. There is, then, a theoretical coherence to the model that is also supported by empirical evidence.

So, what does the existence and apparent dominance of this model of the competition state tell us? At first glance it seems to confirm the predictions made by Cerny and Evans as to the extent to which the pressures of competition in the global economy would be felt. The policy elites they identified as holding extreme power have become firmly entrenched and firms have become increasingly central to government policy (Farnsworth, 2012). However, the demise of the welfare state of which they were so convinced has not come to pass. In many respects it is not a particularly ground-breaking finding. For critics of the competition state and theories that foretell the end of the welfare state more widely, it is proof that institutional differences persist,

Figure 1.2: Sample average EPL scores (0–6 scale) over time for regular and temporary contracts

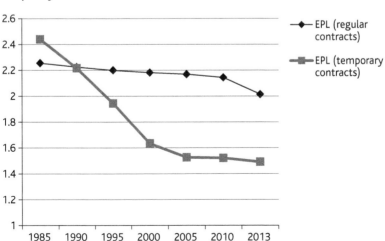

even in a globally more connected and competitive marketplace. Even among countries actively chasing comparative advantage, decisions regarding welfare arrangements are not predetermined by this pursuit of economic success. The competition state thesis as crafted by Cerny and Evans held at its core a neoliberal orthodoxy. This orthodoxy was built around a state that was quantitatively smaller, spent less and had no welfare state that promoted the needs of citizens above those of the economy. The implications of neoliberal economics were a key selling point of the thesis; the competition state was identified by Cerny and Evans as a successor to a welfare state that had died. As this chapter demonstrates, we have not seen such shifts and, as such, the thesis can in many respects be dismissed. The dismissal of the competition state thesis as penned by Cerny and Evans should not, however, be taken as the dismissal of neoliberalism or of the importance of competition in a global marketplace. First, social expenditure is a crude measure by which to judge welfare state retrenchment, one that does not take into account the nature of expenditure. Is expenditure primarily protective or productive? Can it be considered social investment? There is some evidence that protective policies have weakened. For example, average net replacement rates over 60 months of unemployment for four family types at two earning levels have fallen by six percentage points between 2000 and 2013 (OECD, 2015). However, it is unclear whether this is reflected in a wider weakening of protective policies. Indeed one study suggests that not only is a mix of productive and protective policies the most common, but many of the shifts over time that have been witnessed have tended to be from productive to protective policy (Hudson and Kühner, 2009). Similarly, while the social investment state model holds much persuasive power, as Finch et al show in this collection (Chapter Two), accurately measuring and charting it is neither easy nor completely convincing.

A second issue is the need to consider the extent to which the competition state, or neoliberalism as an economic imperative (rather than an ideological construct), even notices the welfare state. By this I mean, might laying the conditions for a competitive economy be achieved largely independent of welfare expenditure? Hall and Soskice (2001) put firms at the heart of capitalism, making them their primary unit of analysis in their VoC framework. To what extent are businesses (or the super-wealthy) and their ability to compete truly affected by a protective welfare state, especially one in which corporate taxes are low?

In some quarters it has even been suggested that businesses rely on the state not only for its ability to foster a healthy economic environment but also as a source of 'corporate welfare'. This is a point advanced by Farnsworth, with his recent work suggesting that 'welfare' payments to firms outstrip those to citizens (Farnsworth, 2012; Farnsworth and Fooks, 2015 – see also Chakrabortty, 2015). Pierson, sceptical of those who foresaw the demise of the welfare state, argued that it was a much-hardy perennial, deeply embedded with a 'constituency of its own' (1994, p 2). It can be argued that business, alongside individual welfare recipients, actually make up this constituency, with an embedded interest in its survival. Additionally, as Crouch notes, capitalism is increasingly relying on less-secure, lower-paid workers being confident, high-spending consumers (2015, p 2). A welfare state offering some level of protection is not only one of the bedrocks of capitalism, offering a check on the revolutionary urges of labour/production (Polanyi, 1944; Crouch, 2015, p 256); in more practical day-to-day terms it shifts the burden of providing a living wage away from business and towards citizens themselves (through the state) as corporations pay ever-lower rates of tax.

Perhaps more importantly, not only does neoliberalism refuse to die (Crouch, 2011), it never really existed in the manner in which Cerny and Evans, among others, conceptualised it. Neoliberalism is not the retreat of the state, it is built upon an active, innovative state. Not even Cerny and Evans suggest that neoliberalism is truly laissez faire; however, their vision of the state, regardless of the importance they place on it, is one of a business enabler and little more: there to regulate on issues of anti-trust and promote business, but otherwise to get out of the way of individuals and businesses, the real entrepreneurs, innovators and risk takers. Others would add to this that the state has a crucial role as the financier of last resort. Mazzucato is scornful of such positions, insisting that 'the characterization of the state as inefficient is an ideologically driven discursive tool' (2013, p 2). Mazzucato's *The entrepreneurial state* outlines six 'myths' about innovation, all of which are underpinned by what she sees as the false dogma of neoliberalism – that the state is inefficient. In her work she highlights the role governments have played not only in propping up free markets but also in creating and shaping them, and the ignored or often purposely obscured leadership that the state has played in taking risks or supporting risk takers at the very beginning of some of the most famous examples of innovation. Citing the technology company Apple, Mazzucato describes how the company has benefited from the state throughout its history, from initial funding made possible the Small Business Administration (a US federal agency) right through to the adoption and advancement of core technologies developed either by the US government or through public funding of research. It is Mazzucato's contention that 'there is not a single key technology behind the iPhone that has not been state funded' (Mazzucato, 2013, p 11).

The most relevant of Mazzucato's charges against neoliberalism and the 'myth' of the free market is that neoliberal measures aimed at supporting a prosperous, innovative economy have actually very little to do with inspiring innovation. Mazzucato is particularly critical of the 'gold standard' of pro-business, innovation-inspiring policy, namely the reduction of corporate taxes, noting that 'the business sector might talk about tax but walks to where there are new technology and market opportunities – and that this is strongly correlated with areas characterized by major public sector investments' (2013, p 8). Reducing corporate taxes, she contends, does not stimulate innovation or investment in research and development (R&D); instead it simply provides 'a welcome cash transfer to firms that have already done so' (2013, pp 53–4) and may not truly even be rewarding it, as in many cases it is not possible to distinguish between genuine innovation and more routine forms of product development (2013, p 54). Ultimately, Mazzucato argues that the discursive battle that has seen the state painted as inefficient has facilitated and hidden from view an arrangement in which the state is being used to socialise the risks of capitalism while the rewards are being privatised (2013, p 181).

The persistence of neoliberalism owes less, then, to market efficiency and more to entrenched business interests, relationships between industry and policy elites and, ultimately, corporate power (Crouch, 2011; Farnsworth, 2012). Moreover, this neoliberalism, while painted as thriving in free markets, liberated by small, hollow governments, actually relies on a strong state. A strong state is needed not only as a bank of last resort, or even a facilitator of a buoyant innovative economy, but as an entrepreneur that creates and shapes markets. The implications of this for the welfare state are that decisions regarding welfare policies, however they are presented, are informed by what policy elites believe welfare states *should* do, rather than some inexorable economic imperative that limits what welfare states *can* do.

Theories of welfare state demise or retrenchment that emerged throughout the 1980s and 1990s were often countered with an assertion that welfare states were actually continuing to grow, and that where cutbacks could be identified, they owed almost all to ideological decisions rather than economic realities. As implied above, welfare states were being shaped by what it was thought they *should* do. Competition in the global economy has fed into this discourse; the transition towards a knowledge economy, or at least the supplanting of manufacturing with a now-dominant service sector, has undeniably altered labour practices and even, as Cerny and Evans suggested, weakened the bonds of worker solidarity. This has helped to alter the way in which the welfare state is now viewed. Today's and tomorrow's welfare states are likely shaped by a combination of their long histories, culture, path-dependency and the stickiness of institutions, the need to compete in a global economy, events such as global financial crises and, in no little measure, by powerful elites that are increasingly intertwined with corporate interests. But perhaps most important is the issue of how all this affects cognition; how the welfare state is viewed by all citizens. There is evidence that public opinion in many countries has hardened against some forms of welfare even throughout periods of austerity (Clarke and Newman, 2012; Krugman, 2012; Clarke et al, 2013), but a counter movement has emerged, driven by the issue of inequality (Piketty, 2013; Crouch, 2015, p 256). Inequality has come to represent the unacceptable consequence of neoliberalism,[6] and austerity in particular (Mason, 2015), but importantly not only among the usual champions of the welfare state. Increasingly the case is being made that inequality is actually harmful for economic growth (Mazzucato, 2013, p 31; Piketty, 2013; OECD, 2014b).

These concerns with regard to inequality and changing notions of what the welfare state should do chime with many of the core features of the social investment state, or social investment approaches to social policy. Finch et al discuss the social investment state in Chapter Two in this collection, highlighting that the persuasive power of the model is such that it has been adopted and championed by the OECD. Whether social investment has truly been witnessed is a key consideration of Finch et al's chapter, but Morel et al's (2012a) attempt to assimilate core features of welfare states, respecting their historical and often culturally driven differences, into a model that considers the challenges of a competitive global economy offers much more nuance than theories of welfare state collapse such as the competition state thesis. Indeed Mazzucato, without directly mentioning the social investment state, seems to be outlining the core of it when she envisages the future of the successful entrepreneurial state being one that creates and shapes markets, invests in training and education, provides high-quality core services and is mindful of inequality (Mazzucato, 2013). It is a stretch to suggest that the welfare/competition state mix model discussed in this chapter captures all of what Mazzucato discusses, but it does suggest that countries are indeed blending approaches to competition with the provision of welfare.

Concluding thoughts

We are not seeing the quantitative reduction of governments or welfare states. It is also unclear whether we are genuinely witnessing a shift towards more productive forms of welfare or the rise of a true social investment state. What we are seeing is a refocusing of welfare provision alongside the pursuit of the competitive advantage. The primary strategies adopted involve tax measures alongside the cutting of red tape and some weakening of employment protections. These approaches accept one of the central dogmas of neoliberalism: that the state should get out of the way of business. However, not only has this not been accompanied by a wholesale acceptance that the state should also get out of the business of welfare, but there are those who reject this neoliberal dogma and argue that the state has an important role to play in supporting, shaping and even creating markets. Such an approach involves not only investment in research and development, but also risk taking on the part of the state; it requires investment in human capital through education and training and redistribution so as to ameliorate the negative consequences of a balance that has increasingly shifted in the favour of businesses – notably inequality.

At a time when many welfare states were first taking shape, economists such as Keynes and Polanyi advanced convincing arguments that global markets were not truly laissez faire and that they relied heavily on the state (Polanyi, 1944). Polanyi extended this by highlighting the importance of the welfare state, or at least welfare provision for those who would always be at the greatest risk of losing out in the free market (the workers). Some 70 years later we see that the free market is still reliant on the state, not only as a lender of last resort but also as an innovator, a risk taker, a source of corporate welfare and a protector of the citizenry on which the success of the 'free market' ultimately relies. As Crouch noted recently (2015, p 2), capitalism is now reliant on increasingly low-paid, insecure workers being confident, high-spending consumers. Businesses need the welfare state perhaps now more than ever.

Notes

[1] Low social expenditure, strong activation policies, pro-market regulation, weak employment protection and low taxation.

[2] Full details of the methodology can be found in Horsfall, 2013c.

[3] There has been some weakening, although it is insufficient to characterise as major change.

[4] All countries classified in Table 1.2 as being strong pro-business, and the USA, which actually has high corporate tax rates.

[5] Although Horsfall (2010) explores the relevance of PMR to the competition state.

[6] Milanovic, one of the leading scholars concerned with global inequality, recently recounted having a paper rejected only 20 years ago because 'inequality is not an important topic' (Milanovic, 2015).

TWO

Changing labour markets, changing welfare across the OECD: the move towards a social investment model of welfare as a response to competition

Naomi Finch, Dan Horsfall and John Hudson

The rise of the social investment model in the OECD?

The notion of a 'social investment welfare state' has gained increasing ground over recent years (Morel et al, 2012a), playing an important role in the discourse of international organisations such as the OECD and EU (Mahon, 2013; Deeming and Smyth, 2015). As Taylor-Gooby et al (2015, pp 83–4) note, it forms of one a number of concepts – others include 'active social welfare', the 'new welfare state' and 'new risk welfare' – that might be grouped under the label 'new welfare'. All are based around a shared view that developed welfare states have begun to place less emphasis on income protection and more emphasis on investing in human capital. Put differently, they stress the growing importance of the 'productive' (as opposed to 'protective') elements of social policy (compare Hudson and Kühner, 2009), chiefly on the basis that this may square the circle of maintaining social expenditures while responding to increased economic competition. Indeed, as Deeming and Smyth (2015, p 298) put it '"Social investment" arguably represents the very latest justification for social policy to guide the development of the economy and society in the twenty-first century.'

Jenson (2010, p 62) argues that the social investment perspective breaks with past understandings, 'represent[ing] an approach to social policy different from the social protection logic of post-1945 welfare regimes as well as the safety-net stance of neoliberals', but notes rather different models have been advocated and implemented in practice, such as Giddens' (1998) Third Way-rooted 'social investment state' and Esping-Andersen's (2002) more expansive Nordic child-centred social investment model. Other scholars have made similar observations. For instance: Deeming and Smyth (2015) draw a distinction between a liberal 'light' and Nordic 'heavy' social investment strategy; Morel et al (2012c) differentiate between social investment strategies that are matched with strong social protection and those that are not; and Mahon (2103) identifies a 'neoliberal variant' along with 'inclusive liberal' and 'social democratic' versions of social investment.

In delineating these variants, Mahon traces the evolution of social investment discourse in the OECD, suggesting that the notion has become increasingly central to the OECD's 'long term project of modernizing social policy' (Mahon, 2013, p 157), allowing it move beyond the neoliberal view of social policy as a burden on economic competitiveness. More specifically, it has allowed the OECD Social Policy Division to tie together social policy and economic competitiveness agendas through emphasis on boosting the number of 'dual worker' households, the need to address work/life balance as part of this – including greater emphasis on the need for expanded childcare provision – and a connection of this with arguments that more spending on children will serve as an investment for the future, ultimately leading to a 'child centred' approach in the OECD's work. Jenson (2010, p 72) similarly traces the diffusion of the social investment perspective across different international organisations, arguing, for example, that 'Following the OECD's key notion that social spending is not a burden but an investment in economic growth, the European Union could quickly move towards its own version.' Importantly, she notes that ambiguity in social investment discourse – its 'polysemic character' – aided its diffusion, allowing proponents of the concept to appeal to those holding relatively diverse views.

Of course, the polysemic character of social investment also makes it difficult to define, but in what Crouch (2015a) describes as 'the main collected volume on [the] Social Investment Welfare State', Morel et al (2012b, p 12) attempt to draw together these diverse debates, suggesting that the key policy instruments of the social investment state are 'human capital investment policies to increase competitiveness and job creation'. More specifically, they place a particular stress on social policies connected to the labour market, such as: early childhood education and care; higher education and life-long learning/training; active labour market policies (ALMPs); policies that support women's employment; and flexicurity (2012b, p 12). Mahon's (2013) analysis sees an important dividing line between what she terms the 'inclusive liberal' and 'social democratic' versions of social investment, with the latter focused on gender equality and the former merely 'gender aware' (both contrasting with what she sees as the normally 'gender blind' orientation of the neoliberal variant).

As the above hints, a factor complicating attempts to define social investment states is that debates about what the social investment should comprise in practice are very much ongoing and, relatedly, governments across the OECD having varied in how and how far they have adopted these ideas. Consequently, rather than using phrases such as 'social investment state', Morel et al (2012b, p 14) prefer to talk about social investment as an 'emerging paradigm', and choose to use the expression 'social investment perspective or "social investment strategy"' to reflect this. Indeed, they suggest that such strategies have not yet reached a mature phase across the OECD, for 'only a few countries can be said to have implemented [social investment] policies in a comprehensive fashion' (Morel et al, 2012c, p 356). To this end, they suggest that we might draw a distinction between 'four worlds of social expenditure' (Morel et al, 2012c, p 358) on the basis of the varying strength of (protective) compensatory expenditures and (productive) social investment expenditures found in OECD welfare states (Table 2.1). In this model, Type I and Type II welfare systems (as we label them) fall outside the realm of social investment states, while Type III and Type IV fall within but bifurcate into rough equivalents of the 'light' and 'heavy' models that Deeming and Smyth (2015) identify (and we add these labels to Table 2.1 accordingly).

Writing in the same collection as Morel et al, Nikolai (2012), broadly speaking, operationalises their typology for OECD members in 2007 by plotting the percentage of GDP allocated to investment-based social policies (using the categories education, ALMPs and

Table 2.1: Morel et al's four worlds of social expenditure

		Social investment expenditure	
		Low	High
Compensatory expenditure	Low	Type I Hidden welfare state (example: USA)	Type III (Light social investment model) Investing in human capital and low protection (example: UK)
	High	Type II Traditional compensatory welfare systems (example: Southern Europe)	Type IV (Heavy social investment model) Social investment with double liability: protection and promotion (example: Nordic countries)

Source: Adapted from Morel et al, 2012c, p 358.

family policy from OECD databases) against the percentage of GDP allocated to compensatory expenditures (using the categories old age, incapacity, survivors and unemployment from OECD databases). Average spending on each axis is then used to create dividing lines between high and low spenders, creating a four-way matrix similar to that in Table 2.1. She then uses the 2007 averages as benchmarks for high and low spending at different time points in order to track broad shifts in membership of types over time. In Table 2.2 we adopt a similar approach for similar reasons, but with some important differences: we use 2011 as our baseline year to reflect the availability of more recent data; we use median (rather than mean) scores to divide countries into high and low spenders in each category; rather than plotting scores graphically, we instead perform a simple fuzzy set ideal type analysis (Hudson and Kühner, 2010) to divide countries into one of the four types in Figure 2.1, using the 2011 median scores as break points dividing high and low spending for both compensatory and investment spending. We do so for all long-term members of the OECD for which there is data except those with transitional economies.

As Table 2.2 shows, using the classificatory approach countries are split fairly evenly across the different types in 2011 but that is, of course, in large part a reflection of the fact that median scores for each dimension are used to determine 'high' and 'low' spenders. What is more surprising, perhaps, is that there is not a great deal of dynamism in the membership of the types from 1995 (when social investment discourses begin to gain significant traction in the OECD) through to 2011. Notably, all those countries that are members of Type IV (Social investment with double liability) in 2011 are members also at the other time points we examine (1995, 2000 and 2005). Similarly, all countries that are members of Type I (Hidden welfare state) in 2011 are members of this type throughout. While there is some dynamism in Type II (Traditional compensatory welfare systems), this does not reflect a move towards social investment but, instead, captures that some countries (Greece, Japan and Portugal) increase their compensatory expenditures. More pertinent to the social investment debates is Type III (Investing in human capital and low protection), which shows the most dynamism of any type. Two of the Nordic countries, despite being identified by Morel et al (2012c) as home to Type IV, show as largely stable members of Type III, Iceland being a member throughout and Norway moving from Type IV between 1995 and 2000 following a drop in compensatory spending. By contrast, three Anglophone countries – Ireland, New Zealand and the UK – 'upgrade' their systems from a low-spending Type I to a social

Table 2.2: Capturing Morel et al's four worlds of social expenditure over time (2011 median base line)

	1995	2000	2005	2011
Type I (Hidden welfare state) in 2011				
Australia	I	I	I	I
Canada	I	I	I	I
Korea	I [a, b]	I	I	I
Switzerland	I	I	I	I
United States	I	I	I	I
Type II (Traditional compensatory welfare systems) in 2011				
Germany	II	II	II	II
Greece	I	I	II [b]	II [b]
Italy	II	II	II	II
Japan	I	I	I	II
Portugal	I	I	II	II
Spain	II	II	II	II
Type III (Investing in human capital and low protection) in 2011				
Iceland	III [b]	III	III	III
Ireland	I	I	I	III
Netherlands	II	I	I	III [d]
New Zealand	I [c]	III	III	III
Norway	IV	III	III	III
United Kingdom	I	I	I	III
Type IV (Social investment with double liability) in 2011				
Austria	IV	IV	IV	IV
Belgium	IV [b]	IV	IV	IV
Denmark	IV	IV	IV	IV
Finland	IV	IV	IV	IV
France	IV	IV	IV	IV
Sweden	IV	IV	IV	IV

Notes: [a] Unemployment data 1996 (nearest year); [b] education data 2000 (nearest year); [c] close to membership of Type III; [d] close to membership of Type I.

Source: All calculated from OECD SOCX and OECD Education at a Glance data.

investment-focused Type III, perhaps reflecting the influence of EU and Third Way social investment-rooted discourses. The Netherlands appears to follow a similar route, although only after having retrenched its Type II compensatory system first.

There are strengths and weaknesses of the methods and measures used in this approach to classifying countries. In particular, more might be done to root the breakpoints in conceptual discussions rather using median spending in 2011 as the dividing line and, similarly, more might be done to capture 'high' and 'low' spending rather than looking at percentage of GDP allocated to broad areas of spending that cannot (for example) account for different levels of unemployment across time and place. We reflect on these limits in the final section of the chapter, but, given that we build on Morel et al's classification, it makes sense to broadly follow Nikolai's approach. Moreover, most countries in Table 2.2 are clear members of a specific type at each time point (exceptions highlighted in the table notes) and membership of the types is broadly stable over time. This suggests that they are good enough for the purpose we have mind here, which, rather than focusing overtly on the question of classification, is to explore how far social investment strategies deliver the improved outcomes anticipated by their advocates. It is to exploration of this that we now turn.

Outcome indicators for social investment strategies

Given the ambiguity of social investment strategies, systematic empirical exploration of their efficacy is a challenging task. Limitations in the availability of comparative outcome indicators relating to key dimensions of the social investment model compound this challenge (Crouch, 2015b). With these limitations in mind, in this section we provide a rationale for six outcome indicators selected to represent the six components of social investment strategies highlighted above: policies to support women's employment; (quality) early childhood education and care; gender equality; higher education and life-long training; active labour market policies; and 'Flexicurity'. We briefly justify our chosen indicators before, in the next section, evaluating the performance of OECD states in these domains.

Women's employment

Supporting female employment is a key focus of the social investment state, departing from the male breadwinner model towards support for the dual-earner, gender-equal family (Mahon, 2013). To this end, an ideal outcome measure would capture maternal, rather than female, employment, given that, in the absence of supporting social policies, childcare commitments make it difficult for mothers to (return to) work, especially those with very young children. The social investment strategies advocated by the OECD recognise this (Mahon, 2013) with work–family balance policies such as parental leave, support for part-time work and early childhood education and care introduced in order to support mothers with young children to take up paid work. However, due to data constraints – mainly out-of-date maternal employment data for certain countries – we have used the female employment rate for 15- to 64-year-olds as a second-best measure for this domain.

Early childhood education and care

Early childhood education and care is a key social investment strategy for two reasons. On the one hand, low-cost quality childcare is important to activate mothers with young children into paid work. On the other hand, good-quality early childhood education and care is important for child development, which reflects the social investment state's aim of investing in human capital early so as to manipulate outcomes and the nation's future workforce (Morel et al, 2012c; Mahon, 2013). At the same time, parental care in the child's first year is also argued to be beneficial from a child-development perspective (Waldfogel, 2006). Thus, parental leave needs to be balanced with formal childcare for very young children – low enrolment in formal care may reflect longer periods out of the labour market for mothers. Indeed, it has been argued that long leaves undermine maternal labour market activation and so run counter to the social investment state's dual-earner model (Hegewisch and Gornick, 2011). Given the nuances of this debate, we have chosen formal childcare for those under 3 years (as opposed to 3–5 years) as our outcome, high enrolment here better capturing both extensive childcare provision and shorter parental leaves.

Gender equality

The social investment state marks a shift away from a 'gender blind' policy outlook towards one that encompasses 'gender equality', supported primarily by enabling women into paid work. Arguably, however, female employment is considered a means to an end – to reduce child poverty or to pay for an ageing population – rather than for the purpose of gender equality itself (Morgan, 2012). To really embrace gender equality, a change in men's participation in unpaid work is crucial, not least because how unpaid work is shared between partners enables female employment by sharing the care burden and moving away from the assumption of care work as 'women's work', and the associated negative impact this has on female employment. Without such change, a 'glass ceiling' effect for women, gender segregation in the labour market, gender pay gaps and generally constrained career prospects will remain. Our third indicator is therefore a measure of gender equality. We have used the gender pay gap (the difference in percentage terms between the mean[1] earnings of women and men working full time) for those in full-time employment with tertiary education. Not only does a gender pay gap reflect the negative impact of gender inequality in the division of labour, but it can also serve to reinforce this division – if fathers earn more than mothers it makes economic sense for fathers rather than mothers to take up paid work (Finch, 2006). We focus on the pay gap for those with tertiary education firstly to account for gender differences in the level of education achieved and the associated impact this could have upon gender pay differences, and also because the human capital dimension of the social investment approach is undermined if highly educated women are experiencing a 'glass ceiling' effect in the labour market (Mahon, 2013).

Higher education

Boosting skills is central to the social investment state, indeed it is a constant within all forms of the social investment state (Morel et al, 2012c; Nikolai, 2012; Mahon, 2013) Operationalising this is not straightforward, given the availability of numerous variables ranging from enrolment in non-tertiary 'vocational' education, participation in up-skilling elements of active labour market programmes and graduation from tertiary education. To underscore the importance of education broadly as an investment strategy and reconcile this with the emphasis placed on the high skills-based knowledge economy in social investment rhetoric, we focus on tertiary education, selecting the graduation rates of 'home' students with first or 'type A' degrees. This is not without flaws. Mahon (2013, p 156) points out that investment in tertiary education is simply an investment in those who have already succeeded and so may deliver lower returns than investment at earlier stages of education. Similarly, Lundvall and Lorenz (2012) place much more emphasis on further education, vocational training and in-work learning. However, counting the number of people achieving tertiary education provides a sensible barometer of how well equipped they are for the knowledge economy.

Activation

Measuring activation outcomes is particularly tricky, for conceptual as well as methodological reasons. Activation features heavily in social investment debates (Morel et al, 2012a), but while the notion that passive out-of-work security should give way to more active forms of support aimed at reintroducing the unemployed to the labour market is at the core of the notion, whether an activation approach extends beyond the 'bottom line' of labour force participation is a moot point. Bonoli (2012) explores what he sees as four 'types' of active labour market policy that differ in the emphasis they place on human capital creation. Capturing this nuance is difficult, as it is hard to discern both whether a person has been 'activated' and how they have been activated While data exist on relevant inputs (for example, on expenditure ALMPs or particular forms of ALMPs – see Bonoli, 2012, 2013) and outputs (such as participant stocks on particular programmes – see OECD, 2014c), establishing what is an outcome of activation is more complex. Ideally, data illustrating who has been activated and the route through which they were activated would exist, but it does not. To reflect the fact that all countries will have transitional unemployment but that effective ALMPs will seek to remove people from unemployment, it can be assumed that any country adopting an active approach would have low levels of long-term unemployment. Of course it is not possible to say that those in employment have been activated, but it is possible to suggest that those who have been out of work for over 12 months have not. Consequently we have used the long-term unemployment rate (those unemployed for longer than 12 months) as a proportion of the labour force as our key activation indicator.

Flexicurity

Lundvall and Lorenz (2012) suggest that flexicurity – the combination of greater flexibilisation of labour markets with protection for those who find themselves out of work – is a rational response to the demands of the knowledge economy where research and other knowledge-based forms of employment are often shorter term and more contractual in their nature than traditional forms of employment. Identifying suitable indicators of flexibility and security is not difficult, with established measures of the strength of employment protection legislation and generosity of social security payments to unemployed workers speaking neatly to the respective concepts (see also Lundvall and Lorenz, 2012; and Tangian, 2007; 2010). How to combine them is perhaps a little more complex. Drawing on Boolean logic, one can posit that regardless of how flexible a system is, without sufficient security it does not exhibit flexicurity. Nor does an inflexible yet secure system exhibit flexicurity. What is needed is both flexibility and security. The replacement rate of unemployment benefits (factoring in housing benefit) for a long-term unemployed married couple with two children (OECD, 2015), alongside employment legislation (OECD, 2015b) scores, are therefore standardised and the lowest score on these two measures becomes a country's flexicurity score. The logic here is that the indicator score can be only as strong as its weakest component.

Evaluating social investment strategies across the OECD

Having outlined our social investment outcome indicators, we now move on to an examination of the data, with a view to understanding the extent to which welfare states are achieving the aims of the social investment model. We do this using Surface Measure of Overall Performance (SMOP), with radar charts illustrating the performance of each country. This approach has been used to measure performance in relation to the labour market (Schutz et al, 1998; Mosley and Mayer, 1999) and equal opportunities in the labour market (Plantenga and Hansen, 1999). The method is useful because it enables performance to be compared on multiple dimensions and offers a clear visualisation of how a country is doing not only compared to other countries but relative to the best-performing country too.

A radar chart consists of several axes radiating from a centre, each of which represents a separate indicator of policy performance. To present data on a radar chart requires it to be standardised. Each indicator is scaled so that the highest score (the best performance) is 1 and the lowest score (the worst performance) is 0. Therefore, a score of 0.5 indicates a middling performance on that particular indicator. By comparing a country's actual score with the highest score, it is possible to calculate its relative score (or relative performance). But the radar-chart approach has 'much more to offer than just smart graphical presentations of certain performance results' (Schutz et al, 1998, p 38). To summarise each country's overall situation for comparison, the SMOP approach is adopted. This calculates the total surface area of the radar diagram. The better a country is performing, the larger its total surface area. The actual values for each indicator are used to define the area. This is done using the following formula for calculating the area of a polygon:

$$\text{SMOP} = ((I1 \star I2) + (I2 \star I3) + (I3 \star I4) + (I4 \star I5)$$
$$+ \ldots + (In \star I1) \star \text{SIN}(((360/n) \star \text{PI}()/180))/2$$

(I = the indicator score and n = the number of sides)

The score can then be presented as a proportion of the best possible score – that is, the area of the polygon if a country scored the best score (1) on each indicator. We have six indicators and therefore the best score that can be achieved is 2.60. So, if a country was the best-performing on all of the indicators and scored the best score possible it would achieve 100% of the best possible score. The closer the SMOP proportion is to 100%, the better the country is performing in respect of social investment. The SMOP score or SMOP proportion can be used to rank the performance of countries.

There are, however, a number of weaknesses for this method. An important weakness specific to SMOP is that the calculated surface area differs according to the order in which the indicators are placed. It is possible to account for this with a low number of indicators by finding the average of the combinations of orders, although this is more difficult to do for larger numbers of indicators. Mosley and Mayer (1998) demonstrated, however, that the difference between the various combinations is minimal. Also, that the order of the indicators is important in the SMOP approach and can be utilised as a strength, by placing interacting indicators next to each other.

Using the SMOP approach, we examine which states do well in terms of social investment outcomes and which do not. We then relate this back to the expenditure typology outlined above to understand whether states with higher spending on social investment also have better outcomes. There is, of course, always a trade-off between country choice and indicator, but we wanted a spread of countries to represent our expenditure typology captured in Tables 2.1 and 2.2. Unfortunately, however, for some of the chosen indicators certain data is not available for certain countries, leading to the under-representation of Type I, the 'hidden welfare state'.

Overall SMOP

Figure 2.1 summarises the SMOP score for the social investment outcomes as a proportion of the best possible score of 2.60. The two types of welfare states with high social investment spending – the *Social investment with double liability states* (Type IV) and the *Investing in human capital and low protection states* (Type III) are generally the best-performing states, with no obvious differentiation between the two types. The best-performing countries are New Zealand, a state *investing in human capital with low protection* (Type III), reaching the highest proportion (58.8%) and Denmark a *social investment with double liability state* (52.2%). Indeed, these two countries are the only

Figure 2.1: SMOP analysis of social investment outcomes

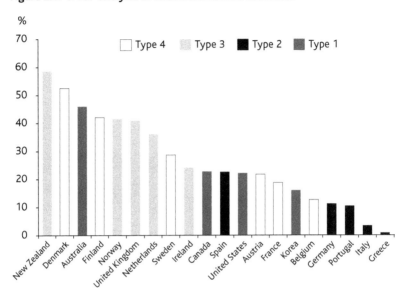

Notes (applicable to Figures 2.1–2.6): Highest possible score SMOP score: 2.60. Indicators, dates and source (applicable to Figures 2.1–2.6): *Female employment:* Female employment rate 15- to 64-year-olds (2011): OECD, 2013a. Employment rate of women, Employment and Labour Markets. *Gender Equality:* Gender gap in mean full-time earnings by tertiary education, 25- to 64-year-olds (2012 or latest year available): OECD, 2014. Education at a glance 2014. *Early childcare education and care:* Enrolment in formal care and pre-school for under-3-year-olds (2010): OECD, 2015: Family Database. *Higher Education:* Adjusted (without international/foreign students) graduation rates of students from first, 'type A,' degrees (2012): OECD, 2014. Education at a glance 2014. *Activation:* Long-term unemployment as a proportion of unemployment (1 year and over) (2011): OECD, 2013a. Employment outlook. *Flexicurity:* Lowest score generated from either: The employment protection legislation score (strictness of employment protection – individual and collective dismissals (regular contracts)) (2011): OECD, 2015. Employment and labour market statistics or the net replacement rate of unemployment benefits (factoring in housing benefit) for a long-term (over 60 months) unemployed married couple with two children (2011): OECD, 2015. Tax and benefit systems.

countries achieving more than half of the best possible score. However, there are three Type IV states, Austria (21.6%), France (18.7%) and Belgium (12.6%), with particularly low SMOP proportions. These scores are on a par with the *Traditional compensatory welfare systems* (Type II), which are generally the countries with the lowest SMOP proportions, with Italy (3.4%) and Greece (1.2%) scoring the lowest, with scores close to 0. The exception is Spain, which scores 23.2% and is placed in the middle of the sample. The *Hidden welfare states* (Type I) in the sample generally fall in the lower half of SMOP proportions, but with Australia as the exception – holding the third-best SMOP proportion (45.5%).

Thus we can see some patterns in outcomes, which broadly reflect the spending types identified above, but there are also differences within the groupings. We will explore the differences within each type by examining radar charts identifying the differences in performance on each indicator.

Type I: Hidden welfare state

We first examine the hidden welfare states, with low spending on social investment as well as low compensatory expenditure. Figure 2.2 shows the radar chart comparing the outcomes for this type.[2] It is apparent that all countries in this type except the US score very well on at least one of the indicators. Australia scores highly on flexicurity and higher education, Korea scores the highest of the sample on activation, and very highly for higher education. Canada scores the highest in the sample for flexicurity. At the same time, the hidden welfare states do poorly on gender equality, with Korea, the US and Canada having the three lowest scores in the entire sample – that is, the widest gender pay gaps for workers with tertiary education. The US scores in the middle for the other indicators. Korea scores the lowest in the sample for flexicurity. Interestingly, despite a relatively high enrolment rate in childcare for under-3s, Korea has the fourth-lowest female employment rate in the sample. In contrast, Canada scores lowest in our sample for childcare enrolment, but relatively highly for female employment – a score of 0.84 and the fifth-highest rate of the sample. Australia does not score very poorly on any the indicators, which explains why it is ranked third of all the countries in the sample in the SMOP.

Type II: Traditional compensatory welfare systems

Figure 2.3 shows how the traditional compensatory systems scored on each indicator. All the countries in Type II had low SMOP proportions, explained by poor performance on most of the indicators. The scores for higher education are mixed, with Portugal having the highest graduation rate of the Type II systems, with a score of 0.69. Whereas Spain, Italy and Greece have the lowest female employment rates in the whole sample, Germany stands out with a relatively high score (0.80). At the same time, Germany, together with Italy and Greece, has a particularly low childcare enrolment rate for under-3s – all in the

Figure 2.2: Radar chart of the scores for Type I: Hidden welfare state

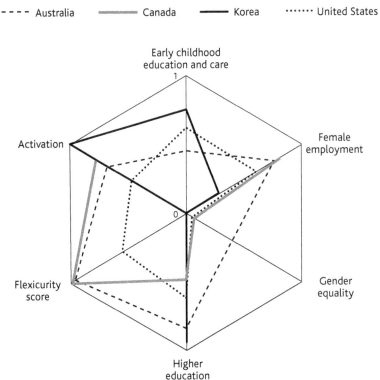

bottom five of the sample. Gender equality scores are generally very low in Type II, with Spain being the noticeable exception, having the best score of the entire sample – and thus the narrowest gender pay gap for those with tertiary education. This explains why Spain ranks more highly on the overall SMOP than the other traditional compensatory welfare systems.

Type III: High social investment states but low protection

Figure 2.4 shows how Type III, high social investment states but low protection welfare states performed. These countries all perform highly on some of the indicators. Only Ireland scores very low on an indicator, being the lowest in our sample on activation – with 59.3% of the labour force unemployed for more than a year. On the other hand, New Zealand achieves a relatively high activation score (0.85), with Netherlands and UK achieving middling scores. All except the Netherlands achieve a high flexicurity score. With the exception of

Figure 2.3: Radar chart of the scores for Type II: Traditional compensatory system

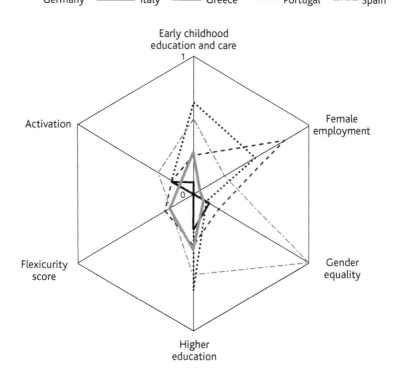

the UK, the countries in this type also score highly on graduation from higher education – although the UK still performs above average. All except Ireland achieve a high female employment rate. But the scoring on early childhood and care is mixed, with only the Netherlands scoring highly in this area. No Type III countries do well in terms of gender equality, with a relatively high tertiary gender pay gap – although better than the overall sample average in the case of UK and New Zealand. Thus, it appears that this group performs exceptionally on some indicators but not so well on others. Ireland's overall SMOP is lower than its group members' due to relatively low scores in all but two of the indicators, especially on activation.

Type IV: Social investment with double liability states

The radar charts for Type IV, social investment with double liability states, are shown in Figures 2.5 and 2.6. Figure 2.5 shows the three states (Denmark, Finland and Sweden) that were the better performers on the overall SMOP, while Figure 2.6 shows the three lower performers

Figure 2.4: Radar chart of the scores for Type III: Investing in human capital and low protection states

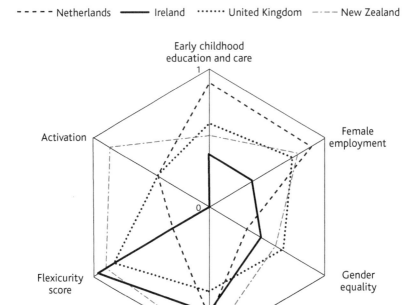

- - - - - Netherlands   ——— Ireland ······· United Kingdom —·—·— New Zealand

of Type IV (Austria, France and Belgium). Denmark is the second-highest overall performer of all the countries in the sample, being the best performer in terms of early education and childcare, but also performing well on female employment (0.89) and higher education (0.83). Nevertheless, its gender equality score (0.37) is on a par with those of Finland (0.43), Sweden (0.32) and Austria (0.44) in Type IV. Finland has a similar profile to Denmark but has a slightly lower female employment score than both Denmark and Sweden, and especially falls short on childcare enrolment (0.36), likely the impact of the longer, at least partially paid, leave in Finland (OECD, 2014), despite availability of childcare. Sweden scores highly on female employment, has a score close to those of Denmark and Finland for both gender equality and activation, and has a childcare enrolment rate that is higher than Finland's. But it has a relatively low graduation rate and scores very low on flexicurity, which explains its lower SMOP score.

The three countries in Type IV with lower SMOP scores are identifiable in that they are not higher scorers on many of the

Figure 2.5: Radar chart of the scores for Type IV: Social investment with double liability: higher SMOP proportion

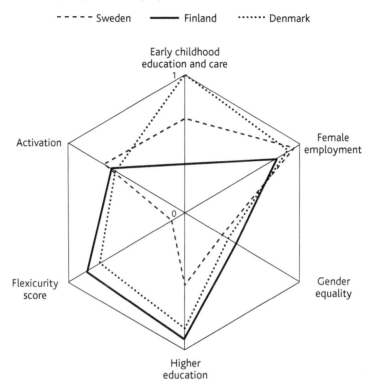

indicators. The exception is that Belgium performs the best of all the countries in our sample on gender equality – having a narrow gender pay gap for people with tertiary education. But Belgium's low SMOP proportion relative to the other countries in Type IV can be explained by its having the worst graduation rate of all the sample, poor flexicurity (0.16) and activation (0.19) scores and relatively poor performance on the other two indicators. France's profile is similar to Denmark's, but with lower scores on all the indicators, albeit with no very low scores. Austria is interesting, since it has a relatively high female employment score (0.76), despite its very low childcare enrolment (0.13), likely relying on grandparents as childcarers (Jappens and Van Bavel, 2012).

Conclusion

The types outlined in Tables 2.1 and 2.2 are somewhat crude and generalised approximations of the social investment model, meaning

Figure 2.6: Radar chart of the scores for Type IV: Social investment with double liability: lower SMOP proportion

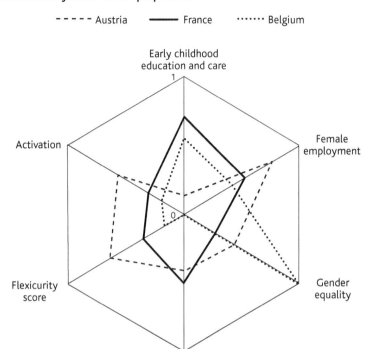

that even if social investment approaches were always effective in boosting social investment outcomes we should not expect to see a perfect link between these types and the outcomes explored in our SMOP analysis. However, it is interesting to note that some patterns can be detected here on the basis of the snapshot data we have analysed.

Firstly, that Type III states (investing in human capital with low social protection) outperform the Type II states (traditional compensatory system) in our SMOP suggests that even the 'light' social investment model may indeed be able to deliver some of the putative outcomes of the social investment approach more effectively than a traditional social protection approach. This, in turn, perhaps provides some support to those advocating the potential of a social investment approach to deliver improved returns in key areas. That New Zealand gained the highest SMOP may show that the 'light' approach can deliver effective outcomes, although we should of course note that our SMOP does not include analysis of any of the traditional social protection that an effective 'modernised' welfare state should address.

It is perhaps surprising that some of the Type IVs do not achieve a higher overall SMOP score; while Denmark, Finland and Sweden rank highly in Figure 2.1, Austria, Belgium and France do not, with Belgium having a rather low score. This mixed performance of the 'heavy' social investment states could be taken as evidence of the social investment model having a weak link overall with putative social investment outcomes. A different take on this may be that the Morel et al/Nikolai classification erroneously places Austria, Belgium and France in the Type IV category. As Morgan (2012) has argued, in Belgium and France strong family policies have long formed part of the welfare state – in contrast to the standard corporatist world of welfare (Esping-Andersen, 1990) – reflecting an early separation of church and state that placed family in the sphere of influence of the latter. Consequently, rather than being an indicator of a social investment approach, their high family policy spending likely reflects their historically rooted pro-family policy variant of the traditional social protection model (that is, Type II). Read this way, the results in Figure 2.1 would provide a clearer link between social investment strategies and social investment outcomes. We might add that the education data for Belgium are distinctive, its low score in our SMOP in part due to its having a very high level of first-degree graduation rates from tertiary-type B (vocationally oriented) programmes not captured in our analysis (which focused on tertiary-type A outcomes). Other 'corporatist' countries such as Germany, France and Austria also have a substantial proportion of graduates from type-B programmes, perhaps underlining that these countries pursue a different approach to social investment that is not easily captured by the Morel et al typology.

As we note above, the overall SMOP scores can mask important variations. One key difference between the Type III and Type IV models (especially if the ambiguous cases are omitted) is their performance in terms of childcare and gender equality. As such, labelling these models as 'light' and 'heavy' social investment approaches may play down key differences between them that stretch beyond their level of spending on social protection. In particular, the cheaper model may well be one where women are asked to pay the price of under-investment by the state. Interestingly, the Netherlands is a key exception here, a 'light' social investment model in terms of spending but producing more equitable outcomes, perhaps because of its comparatively very strong labour market rights (particularly around part-time work) that are simply not detected using expenditure based policy input measures.

We must acknowledge some important limitations arising from the fact that we present only a snapshot analysis in our SMOP. Time lags are a huge issue in an analysis of investment returns; in the case of social investment, for example, participation in social investment may be shaped by levels of education spending almost 20 years earlier, and (in)equalities entrenched in the early years of education could affect gender equity in high-skill segments of the labour market 30 or 40 years later. Our snapshot analysis greatly simplifies the complex reality where slow-moving outcomes are influenced over a time period of decades by long-run-focused social investments. Similarly, there are also limitations arising from our chosen indicators. For example, Sweden's relatively modest overall score may seem surprising. In large part this is a consequence of its weak flexicurity score, which reflects the reality of its rather weak income protection for long-term unemployed couple households with children. In comparative terms this is a genuine weak spot in the Swedish social protection framework: had we chosen to focus on single/single-worker households (with or without children) its flexicurity and overall SMOP scores would have been much higher. Whether our chosen indicator is too fine-grained in focusing on this household type or is accurately pitched in order to reflect the core focus of the social investment model on a dual-earner model is a moot point.

These reservations aside, our snapshot analysis suggests attempts to typologise welfare systems into different (non) social investment types do add analytic value and can help us to understand something about the efficacy of social protection versus social investment approaches and, indeed, of different types of social investment model. However, even the relatively brief discussion offered here has shown that pinning down what a social investment model is, and how both its inputs and outcomes might be measured, is far from easy. Clearly this ambiguity in part has political roots, many of its proponents using the term in a deliberately loose rhetorical manner. Given that the social investment model has been at the heart of debates about how to adapt the welfare state in order to square the circle of social protection and economic competiveness, still more detailed and fine-grained analysis of the best available data will tell us much about how welfare can function in an era of global competition.

Notes

[1] Using mean earnings will capture the full distribution of earnings but at the same time will also be influenced by very high or very low earnings.

[2] Childcare enrolment is for 3-year-olds in Canada, rather than under-3s.

THREE

From social regulation of competition to competition as social regulation: transformations in the socioeconomic governance of the European Union

Antonios Roumpakis and Theo Papadopoulos

Introduction

In this chapter we interrogate the character of contemporary socioeconomic governance in the EU. We explore the extent to which it has transformed into a neoliberal rule of law (May, 2014) that has placed competition at the heart of the European integration process and its related institutions. In this context, we contribute to the growing literature on the euro-crisis and the decline of Social Europe (Busch et al, 2013; Degryse et al, 2013; Hacker, 2013; Hillebrand, 2013; Crespy and Menz, 2015; Papadopoulos and Roumpakis, 2015; Romano and Punziano, 2015) and, more broadly, to the study of the constitutionalisation of neoliberalism (Gill, 1998; Brenner et al, 2014; Gill and Cutler, 2014; May, 2014).

The chapter draws on empirical evidence capturing the type and extent of regulatory changes in the fields of industrial relations, corporate governance and the coordination of macro-economic policy in the EU. These changes were neither mere responses to the eurozone crisis nor did they apply only to the crisis-hit member states. Many of them began prior to the eruption of the sovereign crisis but it is their pace and breadth that have accelerated since 2008. We argue that the effects of these changes are long term, cumulative and mutually reinforcing and should be seen as integral elements of a relatively coherent project to establish a form of transnational polity in Europe that privileges competition as its regulatory rationale.

The chapter analyses two distinct but related (and mutually reinforcing) transformations in EU socioeconomic governance. The first part reviews key *judicial rulings* in the fields of industrial relations and corporate governance. It shows how the European Court of Justice (ECJ) has been institutionally prioritising market freedoms and competition over labour rights, and especially the right to collective action in an emerging transnational regulatory field in the EU. This has led to a fundamental transformation of the regulatory landscape of industrial relations across Europe in terms that are very unfavourable to organised labour and the many nationally embedded arrangements that promote public rather than market-related objectives. The second part explores how recent institutional innovations have transformed the field of *European macro-economic governance* along a similar rationale. The new procedures of European macro-economic coordination construe national wage setting, collective bargaining institutions and, more generally, social policy as adjustment variables serving primarily the purpose of promoting or restoring member states' economic competitiveness. This is to be achieved by means of a very strict, legally binding, transnational regulatory framework, full of depoliticised disciplinary mechanisms that aim to enforce the logic of competition and the primacy of the market. The chapter concludes by reflecting on the implications of institutionalising the predominance of 'competitiveness' over hard-won labour rights and democratic accountability for the political legitimacy of the European integration process.

Social regulation of competition in the process of European integration

The Treaty of Rome (formally the Treaty establishing the European Economic Community) was signed on 25 March 1957. Its preamble[1] confirmed the determination of the signatory states 'to lay the foundations of an ever closer union among the peoples of Europe'. Welfare and employment-related policies were dealt in articles 117–128 of the Treaty, and especially in Article 117, which highlighted the clear commitment of the signatory states to 'promote improved working conditions and an improved standard of living for workers'. These articles articulated a recognition of the social dimension of Europe's politico-economic integration that was meant to have both procedural and normative aspects. Procedurally, provisions such as the monitoring of – and reporting on – social and employment conditions (Article 118) and the creation of the European Social Fund (Articles 123–128) were meant to facilitate the process of integrating towards an 'ever closer union', while recognising that any possible negative effects on employment or welfare required coordinated positive action. The latter included measures such as 'a) ensuring productive re-employment of workers by means of vocational retraining and resettlement allowances' and 'b) granting aid for the benefit of workers whose employment is reduced or temporarily suspended' (Article 125). Normatively, these articles constituted an endorsement of the principles of social justice and the rule of law while recognising the importance of respecting and enhancing socioeconomic rights during the integration process. The values they endorsed echoed those that inspired the International Labour Organisation's 'Philadelphia Declaration' in 1944 (see Supiot, 2012a) and those behind the establishment of the inter-governmental Council of Europe in 1949 that was driven by the firm commitment of signatory states to uphold fundamental human rights. By 1965, a few years after the signing of the Treaty of Rome, the Council of Europe's European Social Charter came into force. Ratified by core member states of the European Economic Community, like Italy and Germany, it became the first international treaty to recognise the right to strike and incorporated fundamental rights in the fields of employment and industrial relations, which included the rights to organise and bargain collectively.

Still, aside from the firm endorsement of gender equality in terms of pay (Article 119) and a commitment to assign the European Commission tasks related to 'the implementation of common measures, particularly as regards social security for the migrant workers' (Article 121), the recognition of the social dimension of European integration envisaged in the Treaty of Rome was not accompanied by a commitment to a specific or even uniform set of policies. Jurisdiction over social policy, public provisions, taxation and especially collective bargaining remained the prerogative of member states – subject to the principle of subsidiarity and, to a large extent, subject to domestic politics between social actors in each state. The principle of subsidiarity continued to underpin the development of more explicit commitments to social provision in the decades to come, as was evident in the 1974 Council Resolution concerning a Social Action Program (OJ C 13/1 12.2.1974).

However, in the same Resolution, the Council of Ministers also agreed that economic prosperity must be mediated through full employment, the improvement of living and working conditions and democracy in the workplace (Hantrais, 2007 [1995]). Indeed, until the early 1980s there was evidently an expectation that convergence towards these common objectives would result in the harmonisation of what were very diverse national welfare systems. 'Social dumping' was meant to be prevented, while the socially and economically disruptive effects of economic competition were to be avoided by means of coordinated actions.

The first fears of an 'unbalanced competition playing field' surfaced with the accession of southern European states that began with Greece in 1981 and was followed by Spain and Portugal in 1986. Their residual welfare states and low wages were seen as potential threats to the social models and economies of the original member states. Consequently, the use of Structural Funds became central in the double effort to support the expansion of social provisions in South Europe while facilitating the lifting of economic protection measures from the southern states' domestic industries and markets. It also contributed to the increase of labour costs in southern European states, thus reducing the potential threat that the 'comparative advantage' of their low wages would have posed for the other members states.

The first phase of EU enlargement took place parallel to the deepening of European integration. As Hay and Wincott argue (2012), the 1980s were pivotal for what Scharpf (1999) called 'positive integration', as a new European legal set of institutions and norms prescribed the power of the ECJ to challenge and override member states' laws if they obstructed market integration (see also Conant, 2002). In 1989, the European Community introduced the Community Charter of the Fundamental Social Rights, comprising a series of directives for the social protection of workers, which followed the principle of 'soft-law' measures (therefore not legally binding for member states). A decade later, the 'Social Europe' agenda, as it came to be known, began to be pursued primarily through the European Employment Strategy (EES), established through the Amsterdam Treaty (1997). The latter stated the aim of increasing employment and productivity at work through 'more and better' quality jobs. As one of the key architects of the EES highlighted, 'this goal underline[d] that neither monetary dumping (currency devaluation) and fiscal dumping (state subsidies) nor social dumping (degradation of social security) can be accepted in the Union and its single market' (Allan Larsson, in Barbier, 2012, p 398).

By the 1990s the impetus for the harmonisation of social protection systems had weakened. On the one hand, the political economies of south European member states could not afford the rapid catch-up with the older member states, while newcomers Sweden and Finland (along with Austria) expressed their concerns for the implications of an effective downgrading of their social protection systems. The British government expressed its opposition to any additional increase in spending on social objectives, while the German government regarded such a harmonisation as a threat to German exports. Essentially, during the 1990s it became apparent that member states were not on a convergence course in social policy: not only did socioeconomic asymmetries remain but there was also little consensus upon the desirability of harmonisation in terms of welfare systems and employment policies. Nevertheless, some consensus was achieved with respect to macro-economic policy, as exemplified by the signing in 1992 of the Maastricht Treaty, and a few years later the Stability and Growth Pact (1996). The Treaty launched a process of economic convergence setting a number of precise fiscal rules and targets (for example, limiting budget deficits to less than 3% of GDP) that member states had to achieve in order to join the monetary union. At the same time, the Treaty also reaffirmed member states' responsibility over social policy, with harmonisation applying only to the freedom of movement of workers, residence within the EU, as well as health and safety conditions.

In 2000, the launching of the Lisbon Strategy had the aim of 'mak[ing] Europe the most competitive and dynamic knowledge-driven economy by 2010'. It conveyed for the first time the effective subordination of social policy to economic goals (Wincott, 2003) and also positioned the European economy in clear competition with other national and regional economies and markets. Substantial changes were initiated in terms of both the content and role of social policy and in terms of the procedures of its transnational governance and coordination. With respect to the former, the normative content and role of social policy was discursively rearticulated to serve as a means to manage labour and the economy via both the removal of policies that impeded market competition and the adoption of policies that enhanced it (Carmel, 2005). Among the key priorities of the EU were to encourage member states to revisit social and labour costs and the sustainability of public pension and health systems. In many member states the reforms that followed were in parallel with attempts to weaken trade unions (Busch et al, 2013). while wealth and income inequality were increasing (Hall and Lamont, 2013). At the same time, the EU promoted what it perceived to be competition-enhancing policies aiming to advance its knowledge-driven economy via investment in human capital (for example, skills, training and so on), encouraging women's entry in the labour market and shifting public spending away from unemployment compensation and into 'active' labour market policies. The European Commission (EC, 2008, p 3) called for 'a balance between the rights and responsibilities of employers, workers and jobseekers and the authorities' and effectively endorsed 'flexicurity' as an attempt to legitimise cutbacks in unemployment compensation in exchange for activation policies. As Barbier (2012, p 387) argued, flexicurity 'was more often than not, a euphemism for promoting stricter eligibility criteria for benefit recipients'.

The accession of the Central and Eastern European (CEE) states vividly illustrated how far away the political consensus was from the goal of 'promo[ting] improved working conditions and an improved standard of living for workers' (Article 117, Treaty of Rome). Such a goal was evidently irrelevant in the case of their membership, marked by the lack of any serious reference to the social dimension of European integration during their accession. Instead, as Busch et al (2013) argue, in an attempt to enhance their competitive advantages, countries like Estonia, Latvia, Lithuania and Slovakia opted to reduce their welfare spending, despite their significant rates of economic growth (see also Supiot, 2012b). In a sense, the accession process of CEE states facilitated the creation of an 'unbalanced playing field' across the EU when it came to welfare and employment policies. Not only would it allow CEE states to attract investment but also, in some cases, it would allow the undercutting of wages and working conditions in the original European member states (Lindstrom, 2010). In this context, the strategy of seeking competitive advantages as pursed by the CEE states (see Woolfson and Sommers, 2006) should not be seen as merely opportunistic. It was fully compatible with the new institutional framework and the new approach to the social dimension that no longer perceived 'social dumping' as a challenge but instead, by design, as a facilitator in setting competition at the heart of the socioeconomic governance of European integration.

Competition as social regulation in the process of European integration

Like others (Anderson, 2011; Supiot, 2012a; 2012b; Crespy and Menz, 2015; Romano and Punziano, 2015), we argue that the foundational premises of 'Social Europe' are being transformed into a market-centred institutional order where democratic institutions are subjugated to market imperatives. In turn, these transformations undermine the very political and democratic institutions that originally underpinned and legitimised the process of European integration (Busch et al, 2013; Papadopoulos and Roumpakis, 2015). There are at least three important dimensions in this process that impact directly of the social dimension of European integration. First, convergence is no longer achieved by means of continuous improvement of working conditions, social protection and workers' living standards but, rather, through reductions in social welfare and by rendering wages as an adjustment variable for restoring competitiveness (Armingeon and Baccaro, 2012; Busch et al, 2013; Degryse et al, 2013). Second, the heterogeneity of welfare and production systems in the EU no longer represents an 'unlevelled playing field' that is undesirable, and is not perceived as a potential threat to the integration process; instead, it is now viewed as integral to the process of European integration because it fosters competition between asymmetrical national political economies (Höpner and Schäfer, 2010; Papadopoulos and Roumpakis, 2013a; Bonefeld, 2015). Third, the legal apparatus of the EU now serves this transformation by *judicialising* what are, effectively, political decisions. Thus, the ECJ is now called upon to adjudicate on the hierarchy of norms and institutions that will govern the emergent transnational regulatory field.

In the following subsections we critically reflect on how a diverse set of mechanisms are now in place to drive these changes.

Competition and the European Court of Justice

Conant (2002) convincingly argued that ECJ decisions reflect sectors of the emerging common market where powerful domestic actors aim to challenge or demarcate the boundaries between national and European law. Echoing this view, we argue that a number of important ECJ rulings during the last decade clearly demonstrate how firms, employers' associations and the European Commission sought through the ECJ to resolve the clash of two fundamental sets of freedoms and corollary rights within the EU: those of labour and those of employers. We further argue that the way in which the ECJ resolved this clash was by legally sanctioning competition as the driving principle in managing the diversity of national regulations pertaining to labour law and social protection within the EU.

Five cases are of key importance to our argument: the ECJ rulings in the cases of *Laval* (C-341/05), *Viking* (C-438/05), *Dirk Rüffert* (C-346/06), *Commission v Germany* (C-271/08) and *Commission v Luxemburg* (C-319/06). The so-called 'Laval quartet' rulings prioritised the freedom of enterprises to post workers with lower wages than those agreed via collective bargaining agreements in the host member state when the latter have not defined minimum wages and public provisions. Thus, any collective action on behalf of trade unions both in private (*Laval*) and public undertakings (*Rüffert*), or in solidarity (*Viking*), were deemed to hamper the freedoms to provide services and of establishment (Directive 2006/123/EC). More than this, the ECJ[2] challenged member states' right to define public policy provision (*Luxemburg*) and procurement law (*Rüffert*). As a result, Germany removed the obligation for tenders to commit to the wages specified by local collective agreements that do not apply universally, while Luxemburg exempted foreign undertakings from a number of requirements that could not be justified any longer by public policy provisions (for details see Papadopoulos and Roumpakis, 2013a).

In making such decisions the ECJ set the hierarchy of norms (by proxy) that were to govern the transnational European socioeconomic 'space'. The ECJ rulings' prioritisation of pan-European market freedoms over nationally defined labour rights had at least three interrelated implications. First, it sanctioned the re-articulation and re-territorialisation of power asymmetries (Brenner et al, 2003) between labour and capital, in favour of the latter, especially as the latter is increasingly becoming more mobile and able to take advantage such a strategic position. Second, the ECJ resolved the clash between market freedoms and labour rights not through the harmonisation of domestic labour markets but through what we have in previous work defined as 'meta-regulation':[3] by rendering competition not only between (posted) workers but, essentially, between the member states' labour laws as the regulatory norm that is to guide their integration. Third, by creating what effectively will become a market of state regulations where capital is empowered to exercise 'consumer sovereignty', the ECJ redefined the role of politics in the process of European integration, while fundamentally transforming key aspects of the institutional terrain within which varieties of national welfare capitalism operate.

The ECJ's approach was hardly new but, rather, complemented similar decisions pertaining to the regulation of corporate governance and company law within the EU that preceded the 'Laval quartet' rulings. For example, as Höpner and Schäfer (2007) demonstrated, the ECJ challenged the decision of the German Federal Court that all firms operating within Germany should apply German company law. Instead, the ECJ deemed that this legal expectation was disproportional,[4] as it impeded the right of establishment of private actors within the EU. The implication was that if a company was established under a different legal system (that is, outside of Germany), then it could not be obliged to follow the co-determination laws that apply in Germany, a key power-resource for German labour unions that is revered internationally as good practice in workplace democracy. Interestingly, in the majority of the cases seeking to exploit the establishment of foreign-letterbox firms, owners established their companies[5] in Britain in order to exploit laxer requirements and, essentially, weakening codetermination institutions and democracy in the workplace. In a similar vein, the ECJ had ruled in favour of companies' and taxpayers' right to 'shop' among competing national tax regulations within the EU, thus establishing their right to seek their preferred tax environment over the revenue requirements of the national public interest (see Genschel et al, 2011).

In the aftermath of the 'Laval quartet' rulings, various firms began exploiting the loopholes on so-called foreign-letterbox companies and posted workers by establishing subsidiaries in neighbouring, predominantly CEE, countries and then 'posting' the very workers that the parent company originally employed back to their place of work, but under weaker labour law and wage agreements (Cremers, 2014). Similarly, other firms established subsidiaries in remote tax havens (such as Cyprus) that would then offer 'hiring services' to the parent company but also benefit through lower social contributions and low corporate tax. The rulings have also been used strategically to oppose collective actions by labour unions. In a now infamous example, the British Airways (BA) management successfully exploited the 'Viking' and 'Laval' rulings to stop the BA pilots' association calling for a strike when the company announced its plans to set up subsidiaries in other EU states (Szyszczak, 2009). Following this case, the International Labour Organization (ILO) Committee of Experts announced their '*serious* concern over the practical limitations on the effective exercise of the right to strike in the UK' (ILO, 2010, p 209, emphasis in the original). Regardless of whether these practices were 'genuine undertakings' aiming to promote competition or adopted with the intent to 'circumvent national regulations, labour standards and social security obligations' (Cremers, 2014, p 4), the fact remains that these practices became possible – and are now legally sanctioned – under these judicial rulings. They constitute part of a body of case law in Europe that operates as the legal framework of the new pan-European institutional order, offering unprecedented power resources to firms and capital vis-à-vis labour unions and workers.

In stark contrast to the ECJ rulings, the landmark ruling of the European Court of Human Rights (ECHR) in the case of *Demir and Baykara* v *Turkey* (ECHR 1345) interpreted the 'right to strike' as beyond the domain of national collective bargaining arrangements (and therefore subject only to national labour laws), but, rather, as a 'human right', following the ILO's conception of this right (Ewing and Hendy, 2010). Thus, the ECHR ruled that the right of workers to engage in collective bargaining and pursue collective action (such as strike) was a fundamental human right under Article 11 of the European Convention on Human Rights (on freedom of assembly and association). Therefore, despite the many similarities between the Viking and Laval cases, the ECHR challenged the ECJ rulings and did not recognise any limitation on the right to strike.

The ECHR ruling is of key importance, as it reinstates the hierarchy of the right to strike over market freedoms. However, the EU (and consequently the ECJ) is not answerable to the Council of Europe and the ECHR as such. Nevertheless, the ECHR contested the ECJ rulings on the grounds that they breached the ILO conventions that are included in the European Social Charter. Drawing on the stipulations of the European Social Charter, the European Trade Union Confederation (ETUC) attempted to review the provisions of the new European economic governance (that was agreed amid the sovereign debt crisis) and requested the wider review of labour market reforms enacted in recent years, including those under the pretext of dealing with the sovereign debt crisis. The European Committee of Social Rights (ESCR, an ECHR committee of experts) declared that the 'Laval' and 'Viking' rulings are in violation of the right to collective action, including the right to strike, although these represented only 2 of a total of 180 violations of the Charter within the EU (ECSR, 2013).

The clash of the ECHR and the ECJ aside, it is now a widely held perception that the rulings of the latter represent a significant attempt to drive European market 'integration through law' (Höpner and Schäfer, 2010, p 20) The ECJ rulings prioritised European market freedoms over national labour law, public and welfare provisions, corporate tax and company laws. We add that in doing so, they also institutionalised a regulatory field where the national labour laws, collective bargaining agreements, public provisions, corporate governance and tax laws of the heterogeneous member states are effectively in direct competition with each other. However, while competition in the domain of social and employment policy is sanctioned, competition in the domain of macro-economic policy between alternative economic strategies is severely limited. As we will show next, the new European economic governance precludes such competition on economic policy and instead opts to use the labour market as an adjustment variable in restoring economic competitiveness.

Competition and EU macro-economic governance

The emergence of the sovereign debt crisis signalled a major overhaul of how the EU reframed economic, employment and social policy. Originally, the lack of a clear and coherent response on behalf of the EC not only led to individual member states adopting their own set of policies and responses but also paved the way for individual member states within the European Council to assume leadership positions. In this way, the responses to the sovereign debt crisis deepened the asymmetric relationships of power and dependence that had been developing between national political economies, and particularly between core and peripheral political economies within the process of Economic and Monetary Union (see Scharpf, 2013; on southern Europe see Papadopoulos and Roumpakis, 2015).

The 'bailout' agreements for Greece, Portugal and Ireland as well as the 'stand-by' agreements for Italy and Spain were accompanied by the demand on behalf of the surplus countries (predominantly Germany, Finland and the Netherlands) to implement far-reaching austerity reforms and drastically reduce social protection (Papadopoulos and Roumpakis, 2013b). New agencies like the so called 'troika' (EC, European Central Bank, International Monetary Fund) were formed to enforce the implementation of these market-enhancing measures as imperatives for boosting the competitiveness of troubled economies, but also to downplay the fears and pressures stemming from the international financial markets while allowing the eurozone countries to recover their economic stability.

However, the most striking institutional change took place over the governance of social security, as for the first time the EU would be involved in policy areas previously under the jurisdiction of national governments (Barbier, 2012). In order to effectively monitor, if not enforce, the austerity measures, the European Council introduced a series of institutional innovations that ascribe to the European Council and EC powers to further limit the ability of member states to decide on their own wage-setting and budget-making policy. In particular, under the rhetorical guise of improving the quality of economic coordination in the EU, and using the 'Competitiveness Pact' (March 2011) as a legal framework, wage policy is now explicitly considered as part of European economic governance and, in fact, 'the most important adjustment variable for promoting competitiveness' (Busch et al, 2013, p 8). Not only does this go against the fundamental principle of the 'voluntary' nature of the contract between labour and capital in a labour market but it violates the EU Treaty (TFEU) itself, which explicitly rules out any EU competence in respect to wage policies (Article 153, et al). The so-called 'Six-Pack' (December 2011) places wage and collective bargaining agreements under an explicit system of monitoring of wage cost developments in both public and private sectors. Wages in the public sector have to be revised in order not to hamper competition with the private sector, while wage increases in the private sector cannot exceed rates of productivity increases. Failure to comply with the rules incurs a financial sanctions penalty equal to 0.1% of GDP. Interestingly, similar mechanisms of surveillance for poverty reduction are not present in the Europe 2020 Strategy (June 2010) that replaced the Lisbon Strategy (de la Porte and Heins, 2015).

More importantly, the signing of the Fiscal Compact Treaty (March 2012) prescribes that states' budgets shall be balanced or in surplus, with the rules having a binding force and permanent character (EC, 2012). The rules have to be enshrined in national law, preferably through constitutional amendments, thus asserting competences to the EC and the ECJ (see Bird and Mandilaras, 2013) while constitutionalising the particular type of (neoliberal) fiscal policy. As Streeck (2013) has argued, nation-state governments, especially in the eurozone, have now effectively surrendered a substantial part of their budget-making power to European institutional organisations.

The new European Economic governance framework (2016) stipulates that all EU member states should aim to regain their competitiveness primarily by restoring their exports in order to achieve a surplus in trade accounts. Given that a substantial part of the economic transactions of the eurozone take place within the eurozone itself it is inevitable that such an approach will apply downward pressures to existing models of social and employment protection. The EC (2014) admits that it is likely that some member states within the eurozone are more likely to experience a trade deficit when other member states experience trade surpluses. However, as we discuss below, it is excessive deficits (and not surpluses) that trigger the corrective and punitive arm of the Macroeconomic Imbalance Procedure (MIP) that entered into force on 13 December 2011 as part of the so-called 'Six-Pack' agreement.

The institutionalisation of this surveillance mechanism sets 'competitiveness alert thresholds' on selected macro-economic indicators. It is therefore of particular interest to consider the key indicators adopted: internal balances and then external imbalances and competitiveness (see EC, 2014). As seen in Table 3.1, the key indicators for measuring member states' competitiveness are Nominal Unit Labour

Table 3.1: External imbalances and competitiveness

	Thresholds
Indicators for external imbalances and competitiveness	
Net International Investment Position (NIIP as % of GDP)	−35%
Current Account Surplus and Deficit (3 year average)	−4% and +6%
Real Effective Exchange Rate (REER % of change, 3 years)	±5% and ±11%
Export Market Shares (EMS % of change, 5 years) and	−6%
Nominal Unit Labour Cost (ULC % of change, 3 years)	±9% and ±11%
Indicators for internal imbalances	
% year-on-year change in Deflated House Prices	+6%
Private Sector Credit Flow as % of GDP, consolidated	14&
Private Sector Debt as % of GDP, consolidated	133%
General Government Sector Debt as % of GDP	60%
% year-on-year change in Total Financial Sector Liabilities	16.5%
Unemployment rates (3 year average)	10%

Source: EC, 2014.

Cost (NULC) and Real Effective Exchange Rates (REER) measured as a percentage of change over three years. The former calculates the remuneration (compensation per employee) and productivity (GDP per employment) to show how the remuneration of employees is related to the productivity of labour, while REER computes the deviation of one country's export prices relative to the prices of its competitors or trading partners (EU and China, Brazil, Russia, South Korea and Hong Kong). While significant current account surpluses are recognised to trigger imbalances within the eurozone, the 'competitiveness alert thresholds' are more sensitive to member states with current account and trade deficits, which, following a process of qualitative assessments and interviews with national experts, are then subsequently requested to 'correct' their performance. Interestingly, social policy measurements (unemployment, poverty risk), along with other financial indicators, are included in the auxiliary set of indicators, not being enough on their own to trigger the alert mechanism.

The mechanism itself has triggered an interesting debate as far as how mechanical these readings are and how member state involvement will be applied (Bobeva, 2013). With evidence already suggesting that the there is room for negotiation, the MIP brings forward many tensions (for an extensive review see Moschella, 2014). In our opinion the most significant is that the mechanism regards member states as solely responsible for their macro-economic imbalances, especially for those in current account and trade deficits, rather than attributing these to the dynamics of the EU itself. EU governance neglects to realise that member states do not operate 'in vacuum' but are in continuous politico-economic interaction which each other, while often asymmetric relationships of dependence develop between them that directly affect their economic trajectories. This approach ignores the origins of the imbalances and suggests that crisis-hit countries adopt austerity rather than expansionary policies that, so far, have exacerbated the downward spiral in economic performance (on Greece see Papadopoulos and Roumpakis, 2012; 2013b) and increased government debt ratios (De Grauwe and Ji, 2013). The MIP thus continues to ignore the structural asymmetries of peripheral welfare capitalisms, placing the latter within a process of internal devaluation.

The response of the new European Economic governance continues to exacerbate these institutional dynamics as it continues to apply a narrow focus on supply-side measures rather than taking into consideration the institutional features of peripheral political economies (De Grauwe and Ji, 2014). In particular, South European as well as CEE member states lack the necessary capital investment to boost their productivity and so are essentially bound to be in competition over corporate taxation, wage and labour costs. This comes at the cost not only of downward pressures on wages, working and living conditions but also intensified labour mobility within the EU, with peripheral political economies struggling to retain their human resources and, effectively, the ability to rebuild their futures (on South Europe see Papadopoulos and Roumpakis, 2015; on the Baltics see Woolfson and Sommers, 2016).

Conclusion

In this chapter we have demonstrated how competition has become a key instituting principle of socioeconomic governance within the EU and we have highlighted the diverse set of mechanisms in place that drive this process. We have particularly interrogated the political role of the ECJ rulings and their importance for enhancing 'market integration through law'. Whether intentionally or not, ECJ's generation of case law in fields of labour law, collective bargaining, public provision, corporate governance and tax law creates transnational markets of national regulations in Europe where capital can (and does) act as the 'sovereign consumer'. Additionally, trade agreements like the Comprehensive Economic and Trade Agreement (CETA) between EU and Canada are more likely to accelerate the drive towards competition-centred regional integration and enhance even further the power of corporate actors.

The second transformation that we have focused on relates to institutional innovations in European macro-economic governance. We have reviewed how for the first time, the European Council has introduced a specific rule-based fiscal pact that prescribes that states' budgets shall be balanced or in surplus, with the rules having a binding force and permanent character. In the absence of any control over monetary policy, and therefore the lack of exchange-rate devaluation, competitiveness is to be achieved through the 'adjustment' of wage-setting and collective bargaining institutions; in other words via 'internal devaluation'.

So far, the attempts to constitutionalise competition and the market rationale as the key organising principles of European socioeconomic governance have not met a great resistance at the level of European political elites. Still, at the level of European publics, the political legitimacy of the European integration process has been placed under serious question. Can this new institutional order be compatible with national democratic politics? Indeed, the future of a united Europe has never been more uncertain.

Notes

[1] The Treaty of Rome, http://ec.europa.eu/archives/emu_history/documents/treaties/rometreaty2.pdf

[2] The ECJ does not have any political authority over the enforcement of the rulings. It is for member states and national courts to respond and respect its rulings. Failure to respond can lead to financial sanctions (Conant, 2002).

[3] Meta-regulation concerns the governing of transnational interactions between (a) the collective rights inscribed in member states' labour laws and (b) the principles and norms embodied in these laws vs the principles and norms regarding the regulation of the free movement of services in all EU member states (see Papadopoulos and Roumpakis, 2013a).

[4] On the 'principle of proportionality' see Martinsen (2011, p 947). Essentially it reaffirms the role of the ECJ as the judge of what is reasonable and where the balance strikes.

[5] The cases refer to the rulings on *Centros Ltd* and *Inspire Art Ltd* (see Höpner and Schäfer, 2007).

FOUR

Housing and mortgage markets in the everyday: how globalisation came home

Stuart Lowe

One of the most persistent lacunae in the comparative and international welfare state literature has been the almost complete absence, over many decades, of housing. In the wave of studies that emerged in the 1990s and beyond housing continued to be at best a marginal analytical variable. Heidenheimer et al (1990), Pierson (1994, 2001), Castles (1998) and Swank (2002), for example, all down-played the role of housing in their otherwise path-breaking accounts of welfare state change. Esping-Andersen famously excluded housing from his seminal 'Three Worlds' study (1990). This situation is changing rapidly. One reason for this is that it has become widely acknowledged that housing and its associated mortgage markets in the US were complicit in triggering the banking crisis following the collapse of Lehman Brothers in 2007 (see, for example, Muellbauer and Murphy, 2008). Before the 1990s, however, the research field exploring the connection between housing and welfare states was limited to a very few scholars, most notably the pioneering work of Kemeny (1981).

Using 'finance' as the analytical lens changes the focus towards what has become known as the 'everyday', the micro-level sphere of individual households. Part of this approach leads to a partial abandonment of the universalistic assumptions implicit in the varieties of capitalism ideas built around corporations, 'productivism' and the industrial firm. It draws from the emerging recognition in the disciplines of the way in which finance capital has become an increasingly autonomous realm separated from the industrial economy (André and DeWilde, 2016).

This is a key reason for the absence of housing in comparative welfare state research, because its realm is embedded in finance capital. Wilensky openly made the point in his 1975 landmark comparative study that housing was too complicated to include because of 'the bewildering array of fiscal, monetary and other policies that affect housing directly' (Wilensky, 1975, p 7). Complexity is no excuse. In particular the creation of global markets through Mortgage Backed Securities (MBS) has had enormous ramifications for housing's connection to a new nexus of institutions that have played out in the financialisation of the 'everyday'. Secondary mortgage markets have fuelled the rise and rise of homeownership in almost all advanced economies, with an accompanying story of personal asset accumulation, debt and risk. Even the social market economies in the Germanic sphere came under this influence.

The focus of this chapter is what this means for homeowners' access to private and insurance-based forms of welfare in the UK, in essence underpinning the competition state. Mortgage markets for three decades before the banking crisis helped to fuel a reconfiguration of the old-fashioned Beveridge welfare state. Individual households' interactions with the financial markets implied new ways of thinking about their homes and an agenda of 'responsibilisation', which trickles down even into social housing through the 'bedroom tax' and associated issues of Discretionary Housing Payments (Lowe and Meers, 2015). In short, housing is not marginal in welfare state research but is widely recognised in the disciplinary journals as a central institutional system that lies at the heart of modern capitalism; and, for our purpose, the competition state can indeed be regarded as its financial fuel. This chapter is an outline of the key elements of this story. It is a theory-driven contribution. It touches on the debates about the nature of finance capital, gives a brief account of the mechanism through which homeownership became financialised in ways that were previously unthinkable, indeed impossible, and explains briefly how mortgages became the conduit between global finance and individual households, leading to an extraordinary re-evaluation in how people think about their homes, not only regarding them as a financial buffer and thus feeding into how they cope with their well-being and welfare, but also shaping attitudes to government redistribution. Herein is the meaning of the title of the chapter.

Financialisation of the everyday

Theorists of modern capitalism have for a long time pointed to the problems of the classical view of capitalism as an accumulation regime based solely on industrial production. In his influential book *A theory of capitalist regulation* (1979), Aglietta argued that a nascent form of finance-driven capital was rapidly overtaking the Keynesian mixed economies. In similar vein, more recently French regulationist theorists argued that the regime of accumulation based on industrial production was flawed because the institutional structures of modern capitalism were in fact substantially finance-led (Froud et al, 2000; Jurgens et al, 2000). This is not the place to discuss in detail this discourse, which is widely debated in the disciplines, but most people would accept that the post-Lehman Brothers banking crisis of 2007/08 was clearly a case of finance capital almost in meltdown and verged on destroying the worldwide political economy. One of the sources of this crisis was the massive scale of bad debts in the US sub-prime mortgage market (Muellbauer and Murphy, 2008), which will be touched on later in the chapter.

A key point arising from this general position is that the orthodox way of thinking about welfare states in the mode of Esping-Andersen contains at least one critical mistake, namely that global finance capital created a new source of commodification on a scale that was almost unimaginable. There was another reality storming the world when Esping-Andersen's study was *looking back* by nearly a decade (his 1990 book was mainly based on data from a single year, 1980) rather than *forwards*, after the liberalisation of the banking system and the emergence of 'weightless trading' through the internet (Ohmae, 1990). As historical institutionalists have persistently shown, issues of timing matter a great deal (Skocpol, 1992; Pierson, 2004). Accuracy in defining beginnings and the sequencing of events is crucial to explaining what happens. Esping-Andersen missed the moment, and by missing out housing too was unable to incorporate the powerful nexus of institutional connections between housing and mortgage markets. As Kemeny explained, housing resolved into *two* regimes, not three, based around the homeowning societies with separate social rental and private sector rental tenures, and unitary rental markets typified at the time by Germany and Sweden, in which home-owning was downplayed (Kemeny, 1995).[1] Kemeny was also thinking about housing and the welfare state connection in his pioneering work showing the kind of processes that might shape outcomes at the broadest level. His key observation here was that owner-occupiers came to have a specific outlook towards taxation and spending on public services because of life-cycle patterns, particularly that mortgage payments are heavily front loaded, expensive at the start but typically paid off after 20–25 years. This was the basis of his debate with Frank Castles on the 'big trade-off' between homeownership and pensions in later life. But Kemeny too failed to see the impact of global mortgage markets, as will be shown in the chapter, for there was a *really, really big* 'trade-off' impact (Lowe, Smith and Searle, 2011).

The exclusion of housing from the Esping-Andersen study thus takes on a new significance because it is in the institutional arena of homeownership and associated mortgage markets that asset-based welfare was born. As Aalbers points out, global finance capital came to view mortgage markets not only as providing access to homeownership but increasingly as a source of financial growth (Aalbers, 2008). Markets become critical to what Crouch refers to as 'privatized Keynesianism' based around an Anglo-American policy regime (Crouch, 2009; 2011). The point that Esping-Andersen missed was that markets were not only embedded in welfare states, as he suggested, but in fact were increasingly *creating* markets (Schelke, 2012).

The era in which the everyday became increasingly financialised points to a new reality that created the conditions for the super-commodification of households living in countries with open, liberal mortgage markets. The growth of mortgage debt in such places and the degree of mortgage securitisation were built on key institutional structures: building societies and banks, estate agents, mortgage brokers (Schwartz and Seabrooke, 2008). For Esping-Andersen to miss out housing because it did not fit was to miss a crucial connection to welfare state change as the 21st century approached, because *this was how homeowners were hooked into global financial flows*, with enormous implications for the provision of well-being and welfare.

One of the principal mechanisms for this was the invention of MBS, leading to a global trade in mortgage debt. The next section explains what happened and how. It involves an explanation of how the US housing market drove the world economy into near melt down but, in the long game, was a key part of the financial engine that caused the massive expansion of global GDP for very nearly half a century. The breath-taking scale of this was captured by the Bank of England, which showed that global GDP – the total value of goods and services – grew from $10 trillion in 1980 to $48.2 trillion in 2006, with a very large part of this growth accounted for by financial assets mostly owned in high-income countries (Bank of England, 2007).

The globalisation of mortgage markets

The story originates in the US housing market and its unique institutional structures established during the New Deal in order to facilitate the expansion of homeownership to low-income families. The Federal National Mortgage Association (Fannie Mae) underwrote mortgages in order to reduce risk if borrowers defaulted on their loans. Fannie Mae was privatised in 1968 but still played the role of overseeing the mortgage market, and especially the expansion of the secondary mortgage market in the 1970s through the securitisation of debt. Securitisation in this case is a process of bundling up individual mortgages into bonds that are then sold on to investors, allowing banks and building societies to offload the long-term risk of these debts to others, to shelter themselves from the unpredictability of interest rate changes and to move debt off their balance sheets, allowing them to refresh their capital (Renaud and Kim, 2007). In essence the process of originating the loans is separated from their long-term investment potential. MBS were a key financial instrument through which mortgage debt began to circulate around the global financial markets. For more than three decades before the banking crisis in 2007/08 international banks, pension funds and insurance companies clamoured for their share of these highly tradable bonds. Pension funds and life insurers, for example, require long-term investments, and MBS are a perfect vehicle for this.[2] Deep inside this story there is therefore a synergy between housing and pensions (Schwartz and Seabrooke, 2008).

The sheer scale of the US housing market played a key role in the recycling of global capital, facilitated through the invention of the idea of securitisation and the development of the secondary mortgage market. This circuit of securitised debt fuelled the creation during the 1980s and, especially, in the period during the 1990s and up to 2006 of the massive indebtedness of owner-occupiers in almost all the OECD countries and was a key reason for the surge in house prices across much of the developed world. A very dark aspect of this was that a huge number of loans were made in the US sub-prime market. These were loans at the riskier end of the business, mostly sold to low-income households and crucially outside the regulatory framework of Fannie Mae's underwriting guidelines (for example, checks on the creditworthiness of the borrower, loan to value of the property and so on). The fraudulent mis-selling of sub-prime loans was on a massive scale. For several decades the private market labels grew dramatically as US house prices surged, rising from $586 million in 2003 to a staggering $1.2 trillion in only two years, mostly loans in the sub-prime market (England, 2006).

The ill-fated commercial bank Lehman Brothers held a very large portfolio of mortgage-backed bonds in the lower end and sub-prime sector of the US market. It had borrowed heavily to make these investments. As an investment bank it was outside the regulatory framework for deposit banks and had made massive profits from very tight gearing of its debts and assets. The problem was that quite small changes in the value of the assets could potentially destroy the book value of the equity. In a pre-emptive move Lehmans closed its sub-prime lender, BMC Mortgages, in 2007 but held on to a huge value of MBS. It is not clear why it did this; perhaps it was simply unable to sell them on. Needless to say, the bubble burst and the rest is history. Lehmans announced a loss of $3.9 billion in September 2008 and filed for bankruptcy shortly afterwards. The US government was not willing to support this commercial bank and the collapse of Lehman Brothers sent waves of panic round the global financial markets and banking sectors. When the crash came its impact was dramatic. US house prices fell by 20% on average and millions of loan defaults and repossessions followed the unwinding of the sub-prime market (Green and Wachter, 2010).

Trillions of dollars of MBS had already entered the global financial circuit of capital and were one of the main reasons for the financial crisis, because a large proportion of these bonds were uninsured, leaving investors in possession of 'toxic' assets. The global economy had come to depend on risk sharing, with trade in bonds based on the highly dubious notion that other investors down the line would take on the debt package. The further from the source, so the risk seemed to dissipate. But bad debts began to fund bad debts on a staggeringly large scale.

While it lasted, for over three decades MBS were a large part of the engine that drove the global economy. The industrialised world economy was held stable by the central banks' focus on low inflation strategies, which created a low interest-rate environment, ideal for homeowners with mortgages. This provided a long period of much cheaper mortgages and, as many (but not all) governments deregulated their finance systems, these policies connected homeowners to the massive flows of global capital. The major consequence of this combination of cheap debt and access to global capital was a surge in house prices almost everywhere, lasting for nearly three decades, rising sharply after 1995 and peaking in the period 2000–05. (Green and Wachter, 2010).

For the first time there was a truly global rather than national house-price boom and it was synchronised with and closely tied to the expansion of global credit (Kim and Renaud, 2009; Girouard, 2010). As Girouard observed, what came into play uniquely at this time was the globalisation of the financial circuit of credit (Girouard, 2010). Mirroring these price increases was, of course, a massive growth in mortgage debt, amounting in many countries to over 50% of GDP (Renaud and Kim, 2007). The sharp rise in mortgage debt in all but a few OECD countries enabled owner-occupiers to gear up their finances on the assumption of an upward trajectory in house prices. The housing wealth effect was strongest in the countries with the most open and liberal mortgage markets. It was very largely this wealth and debt synergy that fuelled the consumption of goods and services over this period (Schwartz and Seabrooke, 2008). Muellbauer preferred to think of this not as housing wealth but 'housing collateral' (Muellbauer, 2008). But it is not in dispute that housing equity could be unlocked through new borrowing, taking on bigger mortgages as house prices grew. This indebtedness is the source of super-commodification through housing because the cost is paid out of private household income. In countries such as Germany, Austria and Italy where mortgage markets were more regulated, the degree of exposure to global capital was much less. In effect the two measures, the proportion of homeowners in a society and the type of mortgage market (open or controlled), created what Schwartz and Seabrooke referred to as 'varieties of residential capitalism' (Schwartz and Seabrooke, 2008). Here is not the place to pursue this argument, but some of the institutional fabric of the integrated rental market countries was impacted on quite considerably by the new wave of global finance. Both Denmark and the Netherlands, for example, have shifted towards the home-owning regime as a result, although the EU's competition regulations were also complicit in this (Lowe, 2011).

Figure 4.1: Changes in house prices in OECD countries 1995–2006

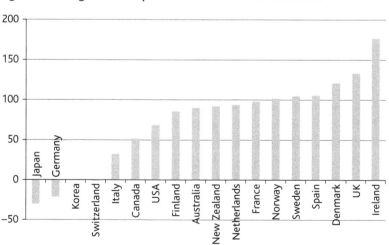

Source: Girouard, 2010

The rise of equity withdrawal

New products were invented on the back of the securitised credit boom. In the UK the Treasury-commissioned Miles Review of the mortgage market identified over 4,000 different products in the prime market place (Miles, 2004). In short, after the creation of securitised bonds – mostly originating in the US housing market – there was an entirely new system for funding home purchasing and in situ re-mortgaging. Banks and building societies could simply buy money in the wholesale market, and so largely dispensed with the traditional 'over the counter' savers. New technologies, notably the internet trade in weightless commodities, the elimination of government-funded regulation and low and declining interest rates created a worldwide circuit of housing finance. In essence the mortgage market became the conduit between this global tsunami of capital and individual household budgets. Financial equity stored in property became fungible in ways previously unimaginable, indeed impossible. This is the process that is the true core of the competition state's impact on the everyday – underpinning and sponsoring the emergence of asset-based welfare (Lowe, 2004).

Alongside the invention of the secondary mortgage market, the process of withdrawing equity from housing is the second key innovation in the financial markets that connects to welfare state change. The extent to which equity can be withdrawn depended on the degree of regulation in national financial markets. It is easiest and on a bigger scale in the open, liberal cases such as the US and the UK, much less available in more tightly regulated economies such as Germany or Italy. In situ re-mortgaging became very large scale in the UK from the early 1980s. Net withdrawals rose from £407 million in 1980 to £16 billion in 1988 (Lowe, 1990), equivalent to 7% of consumer spending (Wilcox, 2010). The surge in house prices in the early 2000s put this figure up to £63 billion in 2003, approaching 10% of consumer spending. In the US case Alan Greenspan, the former Chairman of the Federal Reserve, was so concerned about equity withdrawal that he undertook private research and discovered that in 2005 net equity withdrawal on housing transactions (that is, people taking out more than they needed to buy a new house), *excluding* re-mortgages, amounted to a staggering $180 billion (Greenspan and Kennedy, 2005).

There are, of course, many questions about this process, the scale of debt people took on and what happened when house prices were stagnant or fell, but for well over three decades this was the story, and it was long enough for significant impacts on the Beveridge welfare state as it morphed towards a competition state. Facing a scaling back of public services, the sphere of the everyday became the place where families found new solutions to welfare and well-being in asset-based solutions, for the evidence is that millions of homeowners in the UK, realising the value stored in their property, began to behave and think very differently from the pre-1980s era and this was the case for all ages and stages in the life cycle. The implications for the welfare state of this process of financialisation are the subject of the next section.

Towards asset-based welfare

Evidence of the impact that housing equity was having on social policy in the UK emerged very early from studies of capital accumulation in housing. Hamnett focused on the implications of the trickle down of housing inheritance in flows of inter-generational wealth (Hamnett, 1991). Lowe argued that equity 'leakage' from housing opened up new choices for access to welfare provision for owner-occupiers. Using housing equity enabled homeowners to shift/choose between public and private service provision (Lowe, 1992). Lowe and Watson estimated that in 1984 alone 51,000 elderly owner-occupiers sold up and released £1.8 billion that was used to buy into private sheltered housing or residential care (Lowe and Watson, 1989). Most of the research in the UK at this time focused on the issue of elderly owner-occupiers providing for their care needs by unlocking housing wealth. Later on in a famous debate Jim Kemeny and Frank Castles came to the conclusion that housing costs for owner-occupiers are significantly reduced in later life once mortgages are paid off. Kemeny argued that this reduced pressure on pensions, but Castles argued that low pensions provision might simply be due to weakening welfare states, which provides an incentive towards owner-occupation (Castles, 2005).

This so-called 'really big trade-off' debate was added to and superseded in the UK by a series of studies by Smith and Searle, who investigated what they called the 'increasing fungibility of housing wealth', focusing on housing equity withdrawal. Using evidence from the British Household Panel Survey they discovered that nearly a third of homeowners with mortgages had withdrawn equity from the property by re-mortgaging and that the mean amount taken out peaked in 2007 at £22,600 and that most of this was spent on non-housing-related expenditures. A follow-up study showed that this resource was not blown on 'high days and holiday' expenditure but was triggered as a result of redundancy, changing jobs, as a result of a divorce and particularly after the birth of a child. Their conclusion was mirrored in a parallel study in Australia that concluded that equity withdrawal had to do not only with consumerism but with 'repositioning housing wealth as an asset base for welfare' (Smith and Searle, 2010, p 349).

In their qualitative research they found interviewees talking about housing equity as a 'blanket' or a 'comfort zone', suggesting that housing had become part of how people thought about their responsibilities and how to use this new-found resource. This safety-net idea 'suggests that home occupiers as much as governments recognize that housing wealth has acquired a *de facto* role as an asset base for welfare' (Smith and Searle, 2010, p 351). Lowe pushed the argument further, arguing that a whole series of private services were being accessed by financial resources derived from housing equity. He pointed to Wilcox's study of first-time buyers showing that 80% of new entrants to the housing market sourced their deposits from their parents or relatives, often as a result of the latter re-mortgaging their own property (Wilcox, 2010). In the same way school students are commonly switched to fee-paying schools at the sixth form stage (nearly 20% of sixth-formers attend fee-paying schools). Private, uninsured operations and medical treatments, expensive drugs, dental care, private transport, home renovations and so on all fall within the 'failsafe buffer' of housing equity (Lowe, 2011). Here is the asset-based welfare system, which for decades has opened up choices to millions of homeowners as they re-mortgaged and re-mortgaged again to defend their welfare needs and sustain their well-being. It is also producing key ballot-box behaviours and attitudes towards government redistribution, which is a litmus test for competition state behaviour.

Financialisation and government redistribution

Research on the financialisation of the everyday points very strongly to attitudinal shifts regarding individual responsibility and particularly how people have been led to embrace risk as a necessary feature of engagement with financial products. The democratisation of finance has enabled access to financial products on a previously unimaginable scale and extent, as compared to the privileged access of rentier capitalists and elites of earlier generations (Erturk et al, 2007). The contract implicit in the 'cradle to grave' welfare state is no longer certain, and to an extent is superseded by a form of citizenship that instead guarantees equal opportunity to build up private assets. Citizenship carries no automatic right to support and, as the Myners

Report showed, the current trajectory of state pensions is unsustainable in the long run (HM Treasury, 2001).

Watson argued that the UK Treasury under the direction of Gordon Brown sought to sustain house prices as a key part of a responsible citizen's asset base. New Labour was behind 'the Treasury's preference for using the housing market as a means of social reform' (Watson, 2009, p 49). Households are compelled to live in an individualised world of financial transactions, often ill-equipped to know truly what they are doing and disciplined by their creditworthiness (Aitken, 2007). Structural causes of social problems are very much downplayed in favour of behavioural explanations (Barker and Lamble, 2009, p 323). As van der Zwan argues, this process of internalising the rules of access to financial markets creates a neo-Foucauldian agenda that stresses the exercise of power over the self by the self (van der Zwan, 2014, p 114). Gurney identified a range of what he called normalising discourses around homeownership, self-esteem and responsibility (Gurney, 1999). Homeownership, with its requirement, for most people, of involvement in complex mortgage–market transactions leads also to the internalisation of discourses on risk, responsibility and self-provisioning. Evidence in recent studies suggests that increasing financialisation through engagement with mortgage markets and homeownership generates and then embeds shifts in key political attitudes towards welfare states and government redistribution.

A recent study by André and DeWilde (2016) investigated this in detail in a Europe-wide analysis. They took as a starting point the Kemeny thesis that, broadly speaking, homeowners will tend to support low-tax/low-spend welfare solutions. This arises from the fact that mortgage payments are heavily front-loaded. The compression of housing costs at the beginning of the life of a long loan makes support for higher tax and high-spending welfare unaffordable. Homeowners cannot afford both high taxes and high mortgages. Social market housing regimes such as in Germany and Sweden do not face this problem because the rental market is supported by the state; the mortgage market is much more tightly regulated and homeownership is less attractive, or at least less accessible.

André and DeWilde show that housing regimes have clearly quantifiable impacts on homeowners' and tenants' attitudes to welfare and support for government redistribution. In essence, the degree to which homeownership has become financialised provides a context in which housing assets crowd out traditional support for collective forms of risk pooling. André and DeWilde's interrogation of the 2004 European Social Survey came to the conclusion that across a broad range of indices (age, gender, income, education, household type) in countries with a high mortgage debt ratio – suggesting housing markets that are in the higher spectrum of financialisation – homeowners were significantly resistant to government redistribution, even in those countries with higher risks of boom and bust in house prices. According to further work by Ansell, this was still the case after the 2007/08 banking crisis (Ansell, 2013).

> housing market financialization [renders] home owners even less sympathetic of redistribution as housing markets become more financialized. Our findings show that housing regimes are formative for individual welfare attitudes. (André and DeWilde, 2016)

André and DeWilde thus support the Kemeny hypothesis that housing regime characteristics are formative for attitudes to the welfare state.

Conclusion

Research from across the disciplines has shown that global finance has become an autonomous realm in the advanced superstructure of 21st-century capitalism. The implications of this for comparative welfare state research are highly significant because of the way in which global finance has fuelled the realm of the everyday and breaks out from the dominant, productivist orientation of the traditional canon of the comparative welfare state literature. A second key feature of the financialisation agenda concerns the drawing away from the macro-level focus on the corporation. Instead we zoom in on behaviours and attitudes in the day-to-day well-being and welfare at the level of the household. What has happened is that the mortgage market has become (and remains) a conduit between global finance and the everyday. The home has become financialised in ways that were impossible before banking deregulation. For homeowners the ability to unlock housing equity has been a widely used practice almost since the start of the deregulated mortgage market in the 1980s. This has created a super-commodified realm at the heart of the competition state. The democratisation of access to capital also required a new citizenship contract based around norms of risk taking and self-provisioning. Remarkable evidence of this is continuing to emerge in the literature. More than this, however, is proof of what Kemeny argued many years ago, that homeowners are predisposed to support low-tax public policy because of the front-loading of housing costs. In the process of the life cycle of owner-occupation, attitudes to welfare state spending and government redistribution are embedded that are distinct from those associated with high-tax/high-spend social market approaches. Comparative research by André and DeWilde provides clear evidence of this in Europe and of how it works through in the housing regimes. Inter alia, we should note their findings that owners and tenants have different welfare attitudes. In the UK context the small minority of social housing tenants are the most decommodifed sector of society and the least financialised, although even here the welfare reform agenda bleeds in a 'responsibilisation' agenda in the form of the bedroom tax and discretionary housing payments (DHPs). Families from all domains are caught in a decision process that is not of their own making but that is the stark reality they face. There is no little amount of moral hazard tied up in this story, starting with the irresponsibility of an out-of-control financial system and ending in household budgets.

Welfare state change in the early part of the 21st century needs to be read in the context of the impact of finance capital as it swept across the globe. The competition state entailed the unwinding of the old-fashioned Beveridge model and the emergence of a newly constituted welfare regime based around private and insurance-based services. Social policy's share of this unravelling was shaped by a 'housing' agenda, in particular through mortgage markets that were the conduit through which international finance capital filtered into household budgets, creating a super-commodified domain with enormous resonance for how families began to think about their well-being, welfare needs and protection against the withdrawal of state provision in the everyday. Globalisation literally came home.

Notes

[1] Kemeny argued that the social democratic and the conservative regimes were in reality variants of corporatism.

[2] The attraction is because these debts are amortised, gradually paid off over 20–25 years, and are secured against the value of the properties.

Part Two
The impact of intensifed competition on local governance

FIVE

Delivering fuel poverty objectives within the context of globalised energy markets

Carolyn Snell

Introduction

Fuel poverty, driven by the interaction of low incomes, poor energy efficiency and high energy prices, has been an explicit policy concern since the 1990s (DECC, 2012a). However, fuel poverty policy sits within the wider context of energy, much of this dependent on global energy markets, regulation of multinational companies and political decisions about how and where to levy social and environmental initiatives.

This chapter explores claims made by policy makers in the UK that, despite having no control over global energy markets, existing policy protects households vulnerable to fuel poverty through the regulation of commercial energy suppliers and specific policies that provide cash transfers and energy-efficiency measures. In so doing, it offers a pertinent case study of the challenges policy makers face when trying to reconcile local social policy objectives with the pro-competition, pro-global market policy frameworks that increasingly characterise the once predominantly state-owned utilities such as water, energy and transport. It is argued that exploring fuel poverty policies in the context of the operation and regulation of (globalised) energy markets can tell us much about how discrete areas of social policy do and might proceed in an era of global competition. Keeping energy prices low is an essential part of the UK government's approach to fuel poverty alleviation, but, as argued below, this task is a complex one in which the steering capacity of the nation-state often seems weak and its capacity hollowed out (see Cerny and Evans, 1999; 2004). This is exacerbated by a neoliberal policy direction that funds environmental and social policy measures through charges on energy bills rather through tax-funded programmes.

The chapter argues that existing policy has been somewhat contradictory in its view of the government's power to steer energy markets: while the Department for Energy and Climate Change[1] suggested that the UK has no control over the global energy market, this does not match political rhetoric, which has emphasised the importance of increasing domestic energy security in order to spread risk and reduce dependence on politically unstable fossil fuel-producing states, and has also seen political pressure placed on the six main energy companies to lower energy charges to consumers. The chapter concludes that while the current approach is likely to have had a detrimental effect on the fuel poor, responsibility does not lie solely with the industry, key policy decisions having had regressive effects and the role and remit of the regulator, Ofgem, also being open to question.

Global energy markets, energy security and privatisation

The development of global energy markets

A variety of events have shaped the development of global energy markets since the Second World War. Reliance on relatively cheap Middle-Eastern oil in the post-war period, the 'oil shocks' of the 1970s and subsequent liberalisation in the 1980s (see Newbery, 1997) led to the development of a vast, complex global energy system, still largely dependent on fossil fuels, with many countries lacking self-sufficiency and instead relying on imports from supplier countries such as the USSR. As a result of this system, there is a vast physical infrastructure of pipelines, refineries and distribution systems that operate on a cross-border basis (Chester, 2010). Competition, liberalisation and privatisation of energy occurred throughout many countries during the 1980s and 1990s (Megginson and Netter, 2001; Pollitt, 2012), and in the case of electricity markets this occurred at a rapid pace. These changes led to the breaking up of state monopoly networks, the restructuring of energy markets and new trading markets (Ward and Samways, 1992). While many changes occurred at the domestic level, these were heavily supported by international bodies such as the OECD, World Bank and International Monetary Fund and were supported through trade agreements such as the General Agreement on Tariffs and Trade and the General Agreement on Trade in Services (Chester, 2010).

The development of UK energy markets and concerns over energy security

While liberalisation and privatisation occurred throughout the 1980s and 1990s, a parallel but connected concern, that of energy security, also began to develop. Discussions of energy security have typically included: the continued availability of certain resources such as coal or oil; geopolitics (for example, international relations, political stability and the distribution of natural resources); trends in energy supply and demand; and broader issues such as affordability and environmental factors (Sovacool and Mukherjee, 2011, p 5346). While Pollitt (2012, p 5) argues that debates about 'energy security' are not new, given that 'concerns about energy security lay behind the initial state ownership in oil, gas, coal and electricity sectors in many countries', the complexity, unpredictability and vulnerability of global energy processes, interdependencies and systems described above have shaped political and policy responses to it. While there is no single definition of the term, many of the concerns identified by Sovacool and Mukherjee above have been present in the direction of post-privatisation policy and regulatory styles in the UK (Chester, 2010; Kern et al, 2014). Indeed, Chester (2010) and Pollitt (2012) argue that the term 'energy security' has become more prominent within the field of energy policy and its influence is observable within UK policy development over the past decade. The remainder of this section outlines how the energy sector has developed since the mid-1980s, describing how policy and regulatory styles have responded to concerns around energy security.

In 1986 the British Gas Corporation was floated in one the major privatisations of the Thatcher era and initially became British Gas plc, a monopoly regulated by the politically neutral, independent Office for Gas and Electricity Markets (Ofgem[2]). In 1990 the Electricity Boards were privatised, again initially retaining their monopoly status with oversight by Ofgem (Ward and Samways, 1992; Newbery, 1997). In 1996 gas markets were opened, allowing customers to choose their supplier, with a similar process occurring for electricity markets in 1998. The New Electricity Trading Arrangement (NETA) was introduced in 2001 in order to weaken suppliers' control over the wholesale market and to create a more competitive market (Ofgem, 2002). As a result, governmental power over price controls was relinquished, and since 2001 prices have been set by the market (Ofgem, 2002). The supplier landscape has shrunk since 2001, with the original electricity boards (for example, Yorkshire Electricity) becoming absorbed into the six large energy companies, often referred to as 'the Big Six'[3] (TheEnergyShop, 2015).

The UK's approach to energy markets in the early 2000s has been described as a 'pro market energy policy paradigm' that aimed to 'create and maintain a level playing field open to competitive forces, by establishing and enforcing fair market rules' (Kern et al, 2014, p 516). The role of the state was substantially reduced, with the Department for Energy being disbanded (with responsibilities for energy policy moving to the Department for Trade and Industry, and regulatory responsibility moving to Ofgem) and the Big Six energy companies moving into a more prominent position in terms of their control over energy supply and level of influence within policy circles (Kern et al, 2014, p 517). During this period, where concerns about energy security existed, the underlying governmental assumption was that appropriate regulations and market rules would support and correct any market imperfections such as security and affordability (Chester, 2010).

However, in the mid-2000s the UK's role within energy began to shift from exporter to importer (Ekins and Lockwood, 2011). As a result, public and political concerns were raised over increased dependency on Russian imports and resulting vulnerability to geopolitical shocks and associated price increases (Kern et al, 2014, p 519). This period also witnessed the first substantial increase in wholesale energy costs and represented (according to David Gray, the chairman of Ofgem) the first test of the evolving privatised market (Gray, 2014). Given this, Kern et al (2014) argue that concerns around energy security became a more prominent feature of policy making. Indeed, by 2006 energy security was referred to as one of the two 'immense' challenges facing the policy area, and as a result greater efforts were focused on diversification and domestic production.[4] In 2008 the Department for Energy and Climate Change (DECC) was created, and while markets were still regarded as a playing a key role in energy supply, there was great willingness for governmental intervention (Kern et al, 2014).

While the Cameron-led Conservative-Liberal Democratic coalition government (2010–15) was described by some as attempting to rapidly advance a 'neoliberal agenda … with the dismantling of the tyrannical state at its heart' (Hall, 2011), and political rhetoric confirms the preference for using 'markets power as much as possible [*sic*]' (Davey, 2014), there was also been a willingness for governmental intervention on the basis of energy security concerns. In 2014 the (then) Secretary of State for Energy and Climate Change, Ed Davey, gave a speech on energy security. He listed global energy consumption [increased demand for energy], access to resources [where dependence of the UK on international imports may be hampered by geopolitical issues such as the Ukraine crisis] and the UK's 'legacy' [the ability to generate and distribute energy on home soil] as key security challenges. He argued that these challenges meant that 'without active government and smart intervention, markets by themselves in the UK and beyond will simply not provide enough capacity, and sufficient low carbon capacity in the years to come' (*Ibid*). This has led to a number of energy policy actions including: developing resilience to energy shocks, ensuring domestic production, improving reliability of international markets (through single energy market with Europe and physical infrastructure improvements), ensuring diversity of supply such as alternative markets (such as those located in Africa and East Asia), ensuring reliable domestic delivery networks, domestic energy efficiency, and 'working to insulate ourselves from international fossil fuel markets in the long term' (Davey, 2014). These concerns have been embodied, in part, in the 2013 Energy Act, which introduces a variety of reforms to both the energy industry and planning system in support of more domestic energy generation (both renewables and nuclear) (DECC, 2013a).

Domestic energy in the UK today

So far this chapter has considered the privatisation of the British energy market in the 1980s and 1990s and has explored the complexities of the global and national physical and regulatory infrastructure. However, what has not been discussed is the impact of this system and associated policy responses at the household level. The chapter now considers the social impacts that may result from this complex system, drawing briefly on evidence from a recently completed research project (see Snell et al, 2014 for full details and methodology). The section first considers how energy costs are passed on to domestic households before considering the implications for vulnerable households.

Energy charges

A domestic energy bill is not simply a reflection of energy prices but is made up of a variety of costs and charges that also include 'transmission and distribution network costs, metering and other supply costs, supplier margins, VAT and social, energy and climate change mitigation-related policies (NEA, 2014, p 20). Table 5.1

Table 5.1: Make-up of an average energy bill

Real 2012 prices	Gas bill	Electricity bill	Energy bill
Wholesale energy cost	£383 (55%)	£215 (37%)	£597 (47%)
Network costs	£124 (18%)	£133 (23%)	£257 (20%)
Other supplier costs and margin	£119 (17%)	£121 (21%)	£240 (19%)
Energy and climate change policies	£33 (5%)	£80 (14%)	£112 (9%)
ECO	*£25 (4%)*	*£22 (4%)*	*£47 (4%)*
RO	–	*£30 (5%)*	*£30 (2%)*
EU ETS	–	*£8 (1%)*	*£8 (1%)*
CPF	–	*£5 (1%)*	*£5 (0%)*
Warm Home Discount	*£6 (1%)*	*£6 (1%)*	*£11 (1%)*
FITs	–	*£7 (1%)*	*£7 (1%)*
Smart Meters & Better Billing	*£2 (0%)*	*£1 (0%)*	*£3 (0%)*
VAT (5%)	£33 (5%)	£27 (5%)	£60 (5%)
Total (no Warm Home Discount rebate)	£691	£576	£1,267
Average rebate (inc VAT)	–	–£13	–£13
Total (with rebate)	£691	£563	£1,255

Note: Figures may not add due to rounding.
Source: DECC, 2013a, cited in NEA, 2014.

provides a summary of the various charges that make up an energy bill based on an average household; it comprises three core elements:

- *Energy costs:* Energy costs make up the largest amount of a domestic bill; however, the UK energy system is split into three: energy generators; suppliers; transmitters and distributors. As such, charges reflect these three distinct commercial interests.

- *Environmental charges:* Environmental charges split into three main groups: carbon trading and investment; generation of alternative forms of energy; and energy efficiency. All the listed schemes relate to national or EU climate-change policies that aim to support the UK's 'transition to a low carbon economy'. Specifically, the EU Emissions Trading Scheme (EU ETS) is an EU-driven policy aimed at reducing greenhouse gas emissions through carbon trading (EC, 2015). Closely related, the Carbon Price Floor (CPF) aims to stabilise a base price for carbon in order to encourage investment in low-carbon projects (Ares, 2014). The Renewables Obligation (RO) requires electricity suppliers to source a certain proportion of renewable energy (Ofgem 2015a) and the Feed in Tariff (FiT) is a financial reward paid to households for generating energy (through a range of activities such as the installation of solar panels) (Ofgem,

2015b). The national rollout of Smart Meters to all domestic homes and small businesses by 2020 aims to provide customers with better information about their energy use and to encourage switching of provider (Ofgem/DECC, 2011) and the Energy Companies Obligation (ECO) provides free or subsidised energy efficiency measures in 'hard to treat' or low-income homes. While these policies partly reflect an attempt to correct market failures relating to climate change (see Stern, 2006), others (such as the RO and FiT) also embody energy-security concerns around diversification and investment in alternative technologies.

• *Social policies:* Two main charges are placed on energy bills in support of vulnerable customers. The ECO is the only energy-efficiency scheme that supports energy-efficiency improvements in households vulnerable to fuel poverty. The Warm Home Discount is one of several income-based schemes that provide an energy rebate to vulnerable households that meet particular eligibility criteria (discussed in more depth below).

Fuel poverty

Fuel poverty as a policy concern

The most significant social concern of energy policy is fuel poverty, a situation where a household cannot afford to heat its home sufficiently or has to make unacceptable trade-offs as a result of high energy bills (DEFRA/DTI, 2001). Health impacts such as respiratory diseases, heart disease and strokes; having to make trade-offs over other household essentials (such as food); and 'withdrawal from the community' as a result of not being able to live a 'normal' life-style were all highlighted by the fuel poverty strategy as reasons to act (DEFRA/DTI, 2001, p 7). Indeed, the severe social costs of fuel poverty have been recognised by policy makers (for example, in 2009 the Chief Medical Officer Report found that for every £1 of investment in keeping homes warm the NHS would see a saving of 42 pence – Marmot Review Team, 2011), and national fuel poverty reduction targets and support mechanisms have been in place since 2001. Table 5.2 shows the extent of fuel poverty according to 2010–11 data. Two measures of poverty are presented, as these reflect current governmental practice[5] (described below). Fuel poverty rates across households with and without someone with a long-term illness or disability are presented, as the former are a group

Table 5.2: The extent of fuel poverty[a]

	10% of full income		Low Income, High Cost	
	Household contains someone with illness or disability	No one in household has illness or disability	Household contains someone with illness or disability	No one in household has illness or disability
Percentage of population in fuel poverty (percentage)	20.4	14.6	13.2	10.5
Number of households in fuel poverty (millions)	1.29	2.21	0.84	1.60

Note: [a] Both measures are used by the government: the first is where a household would need to spend more than 10% of its income to maintain a decent standard of warmth; the second defines households as fuel poor if they have a combination of above-average fuel costs and a low income. The latter is the 'official' measure.

Source: Snell et al, 2014.

considered especially vulnerable to the causes and consequences of fuel poverty.

Policy changed substantially under the Conservative–Liberal Democrat coalition government, which both changed the measurement of fuel poverty and withdrew eradication targets[6] (PSE, 2013). Table 5.2 also shows the impact of the change in measurement of fuel poverty (a reduction of 4.1% of households being defined as fuel poor, and 7.2% among households containing someone with a long term-illness or disability). However, at the political level the rhetoric of tackling fuel poverty remained, with the then Secretary of State, Ed Davey, stating that 'Tackling fuel poverty has been a major priority during this government' (DECC, 2015a). This has translated into the following policy statement by DECC: 'The government can't control unpredictable global energy prices but we can help households keep their energy bills as low as possible, support those most in need and take action to help secure energy supplies in the long term' (DECC, 2015b).

Arguably, pro-market ideas about fiscal austerity and limited state intervention were evident in Conservative–Liberal Democrat coalition energy policy (Kern et al, 2014, p 523; see also Snell and Thomson, 2013). Despite the political and policy statements above, overall policy has moved to substantially reduce state support for fuel-poor households, shifting responsibility to the private sector (see Hills 2012; Snell and Thomson, 2013; Stockton and Campbell, 2011), and fragmenting responsibility for fuel-poverty alleviation across a number of bodies including the energy sector, the Department for Work and Pensions (DWP), Local Authorities and, most recently, Clinical Commissioning Groups. The following sections assess the impact of existing policy on the fuel poor, given the claims made above regarding the government's ability to keep energy prices low through the regulation of competitive markets, and specific fuel-poverty measures aimed at vulnerable households.

Energy costs

As described above, the Conservative–Liberal Democrat coalition government suggested that competition within the energy sector can drive down energy bills, with householders being given a choice over supplier and tariffs (Davey, 2014). However, as demonstrated in Figure 5.1, since 2004 domestic energy costs have increased substantially, and well above inflation (as measured by the Retail Price Index). These increases been attributed by the government to rising wholesale commodity prices[7] (Bolton/House of Commons Library, 2014), in part due to a greater reliance on energy imports. According to Citizens Advice Bureaux (CAB) figures, domestic energy costs have increased by more than three times the amount of inflation since 2010, with all six large energy companies increasing costs (see Figures 5.2 and 5.3 for an analysis of this data). Overall, the current outlook is that

Figure 5.1: Domestic energy costs compared to Retail Price Index

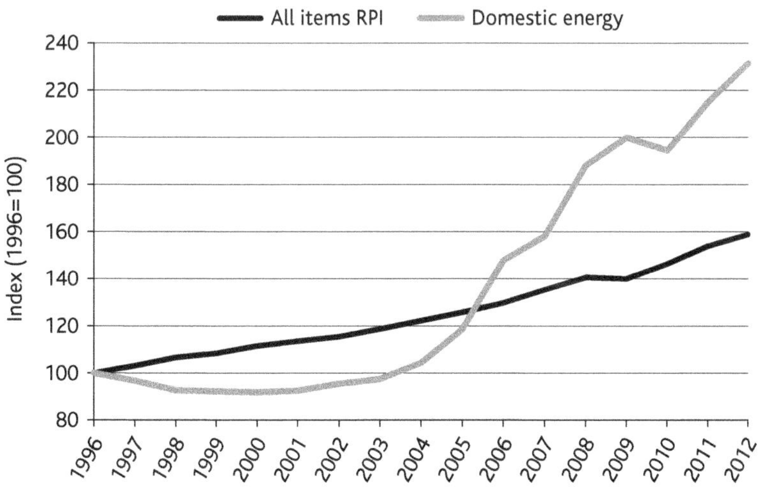

Source: DECC, 2013b, p 29

Figure 5.2: Gas price increases 2010–14 by supplier (%)

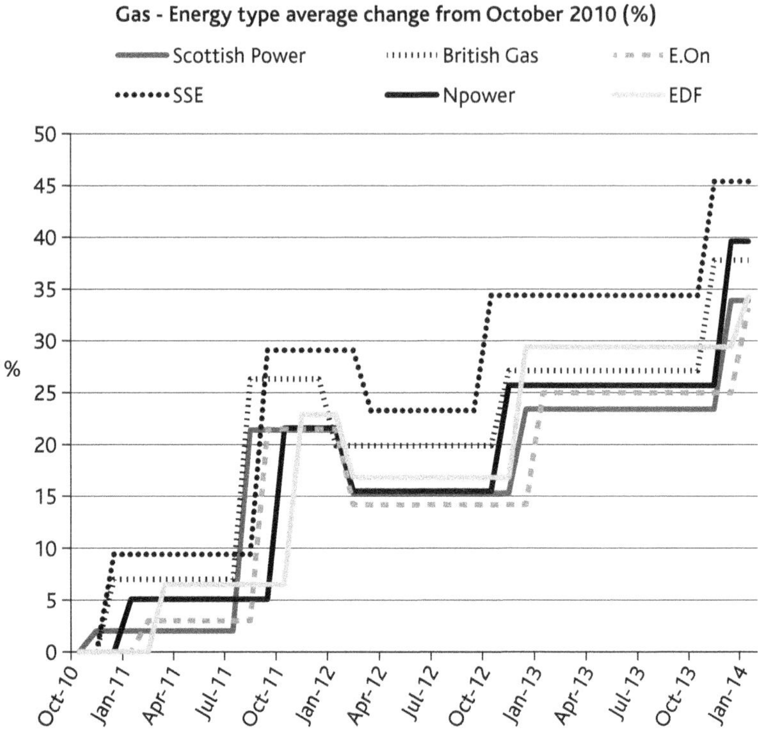

Gas - Energy type average change from October 2010 (%)

Source: Author's presentation of data from Guardian Datablog, 2013

energy prices will remain uncertain, and vulnerable to shocks (Ekins and Lockwood, 2011).

Given these increases, regulation of the energy market has become a focus of controversy. During 2014 and early 2015 wholesale energy prices decreased substantially, with Ofgem finding in June 2014 that gas prices were at their lowest since September 2010 and electricity prices at their lowest since April 2010 (Ofgem 2014a). However, these changes have not been passed on to the consumer.

The Big Six energy companies (which have around 95% of the market – Ofgem/CMA, 2014) have become unpopular among the public and media and a target for politicians. A YouGov survey found in 2014 that '67 per cent [of the public] believed the firms operated a cartel' (Guardian, 2014a); and there was an increase in tabloid news stories such as 'Millions of households being ripped off after wholesale cost halves in six months' (Daily Mail, 2014). The government's 'failure to stand up to the big energy companies' (Guardian, 2013) was denounced by some newspapers, and the controversy led the then

Figure 5.3: Electricity price increases 2010–14 by supplier (%)

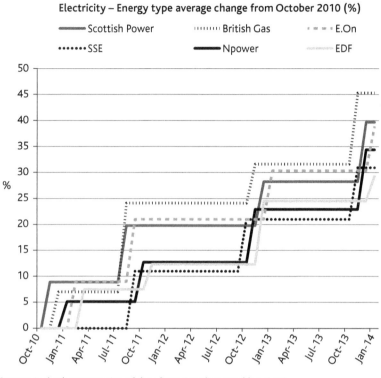

Electricity – Energy type average change from October 2010 (%)

Scottish Power ⋯⋯⋯ British Gas ▪ ▪ ▪ E.On
⋯⋯⋯ SSE Npower EDF

Source: Author's presentation of data from Guardian Datablog, 2013

Labour Party leader, Ed Miliband, to call for reform of energy markets and to announce at the Party conference that, if elected, Labour would freeze gas and energy bills for 20 months (BBC, 2013b).

Reflecting on trends during the post-privatisation period, the chair of Ofgem, David Gray, suggests that as energy companies moved into a 'consumer facing world' they have not managed to keep pace with consumer expectations, citing numerous cases of malpractice associated with doorstep selling in the early days of retail competition (UtilityWeek, 2014). While such practice has ended, Gray highlights current challenges within the market, most notably the complexities of tariffs that make it difficult for customers to compare companies (in some instances leading to Ofgem fines and warnings). Indeed, there is evidence of misconduct within the energy industry, with each of the Big Six companies having been subject to warnings and penalties for a number of reasons, including mis-selling (E.ON: fined £12 million (Ofgem, 2014b); SSE: fined £10.5 (Ofgem, 2013); British Gas: fined £1 million (Guardian, 2014b)); breaching complaint handling rules

(EDF: fined £3 million (Ofgem, 2014c)); and sales processes that have prevented customers from being able to make fair comparisons with other companies (Scottish Power: received a formal warning (Guardian 2014c)).

However, while it has been critical of the energy companies, Ofgem has itself been subject to substantial scrutiny. Criticisms have included a suggestion that Ofgem has failed to regulate the energy market by being too slow to act on investigations, allowing dominance by the Big Six (and thus blocking new entrants to the market) and having a tendency towards new initiatives and schemes without ensuring that existing requirements are being met (see Guardian, 2013; Cityam, 2014). The House of Commons Energy and Climate Change Committee suggested that Ofgem was failing customers by not ensuring openness within the market and not doing enough to force energy companies to demonstrate that they are 'squeaky clean' when making and reporting profits (cited in MindfulMoney, 2013); and in a more politically motivated speech Caroline Flint (Labour's spokesperson on energy[8]) described Ofgem as having 'let the energy companies get away with poor customer service, mis-selling and rip off energy bills' (Guardian, 2013).

At the time of writing, two investigations into the energy industry are underway. In June 2014 Ofgem referred the energy companies to the Competitions and Markets Authority (CMA) for an 18-month investigation. The CMA conducted an initial investigation and concluded that 'there were reasonable grounds for suspecting that features of the energy market were preventing, restricting or distorting competition' (CMA, 2014). The second investigation was announced by the Treasury in January 2015 and set out to investigate whether energy companies were passing savings on to consumers (BBC, 2015). Reports in the media suggested that 'the Chancellor would be watching utilities companies "like a hawk"', with a view to formally calling on them to reduce prices if they did not pass on price falls voluntarily (Telegraph, 2015).

Over and above the effectiveness of the current market, it is important to note that a proportion of customers do not benefit from the liberalised market (by switching either tariffs or suppliers). These customers, typically referred to as 'sticky customers', are most likely to be struggling financially, disabled, without access to the internet (Oftem/CMA, 2014), or may be concerned about the implications of switching, for example, losing access to energy discount schemes (Snell et al, 2014) or be in debt and thus be unable to switch (CAB, 2015). Given the overlap between many of these attributes and the fuel-poor population (Ebico, 2012), whether vulnerable groups are able to take full advantage of competitive energy markets is questionable.

Specific fuel poverty measures

As described above, the majority of support measures are funded through levies and obligations placed on energy companies, and some additional forms of financial support are provided through the social security benefits system. Specific measures that are currently in place to support fuel-poor households include the state-funded financial payments known as Cold Weather Payments (CWPs) and Winter Fuel Payment (WFP), and the energy customer-funded Warm Home Discount (WHD). There are no state-funded energy-efficiency schemes in place (these were abolished in 2013); instead there is the energy customer-funded Energy Companies Obligation (ECO) (Snell and Thomson, 2013). However, there have been substantial criticisms of the ability of these measures to support vulnerable groups. Over and above this, Jansz and Guertler (2012) have calculated that the total budgets contributing to supporting fuel-poor households in England declined by 31% between 2009/10 and 2013, from £3.912 billion to £2.689 billion.

In terms of energy-efficiency measures, the ECO provides energy-efficiency schemes to those on low incomes or in particularly energy-inefficient homes. It replaced the state-funded Warm Front energy-efficiency scheme and two other supplier-funded programmes. The scheme has had substantial problems accessing the fuel poor, and in 2014 the eligibility criteria for households were broadened retrospectively to enable energy companies to meet their ECO targets (DECC, 2014), given the 'complex eligibility criteria' (Energy Saving Trust, 2015) that are sometimes also based on postcode. The ECO has been criticised for a number of reasons. Firstly, as it supports two groups, the fuel poor and those with 'hard to treat homes' (who may be able to afford to make improvements themselves), critics argue that this reduces the proportion of funds available to the fuel poor (Boardman, 2012; Guertler, 2012; Hills, 2012; Tovar, 2012; Snell and Thomson, 2013). Secondly, and closely related, are arguments of regressivity, where the poorest are most affected by increased energy bills associated with the ECO (Stockton and Campbell, 2011; Boardman, 2012; Hills, 2012; Snell and Thomson, 2013). Thirdly, critics question whether energy companies have the capacity or ability to assume responsibility for fuel-poverty alleviation, given that 'cost efficiency will be a greater imperative and accountability likely reduced' (Walker and Day, 2012, p 74). Overall, critics suggest that the scheme (alongside reduced eligibility for the WHD) may have the effect of pushing more households into fuel poverty 'owing to the way in which suppliers add these charges to bill, and the dynamics of who benefits from the subsidy of more expensive measures such as solid wall insulation' (Guertler, 2012, p 97).

A key cash transfer has been the WHD. Eligibility for this is determined partly by governmental regulation and partly at the discretion of the individual energy company making the discount. Eligibility is based on two groups, the core group and broader group. The core group is made up of pensioners who are on low incomes (Ofgem, 2015c). The broader group is more complex, however, as it is up to the individual energy company to set its criteria, households must apply for the discount and there is a limited budget (once this is spent, even if they are in need, households will be ineligible). The definition of the core and broader group for the WHD has proved controversial (see Baker, 2011; Save the Children, 2010), with critics arguing that vulnerable households of working age are most likely to have missed out following policy changes in 2011 (Snell and Thomson, 2013). In addition to the WHD, CWPs and WFP are also important cash transfers. CWPs are typically paid to recipients of key social security benefits/tax credits such as income support, JSA, ESA, or pension credit. Payments are tax funded and are automatically made through the benefits system. The WFP is a universal tax-free payment available to pensioner households, with those aged 80 or over receiving the highest amount (DWP, 2015a). WFPs have been controversial in some quarters (especially in the context of welfare reforms), given that they are not means tested (BBC, 2013a).

Eligibility for schemes and fuel-poverty rates

In addition to criticisms concerning funding sources and budgets, an analysis of fuel-poverty rates among households containing disabled people demonstrates a mismatch between fuel-poverty rates and eligibility for particular schemes. Figure 5.4 presents an analysis of fuel-poverty rates by household composition, and presence or not of a disabled household member. The figures show high levels of fuel poverty among single households, with 21.1% f single disabled people of working age being in fuel poverty, compared to 11.7% of single non-disabled people of working age. Among single disabled people who are aged over 60 years, 8.8% are defined as being in fuel poverty under the Low Income High Cost measure, as compared to

Figure 5.4: Fuel-poverty rates among households with and without one or more disabled members

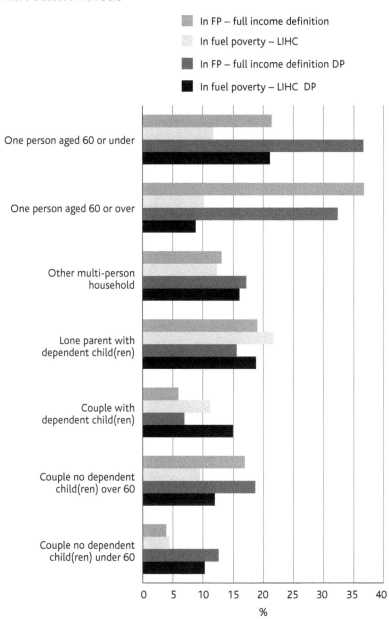

Source: Snell et al, 2014.

10.2% of non-disabled single people. Rates under the 10% measure are substantially higher and reflect the controversial decision of the government to change the definition of fuel poverty (PSE, 2013). The majority of households aged over 60 will be able to access support such as the WFPs and (assuming eligibility) will automatically qualify for the WHD.

However, those aged under 60 will be less likely to be eligible for the WHD, will not receive the WFP, and will qualify for the ECO only if they meet a variety of (often locally determined) criteria. It is also essential to consider that in the wider context of other neoliberal policy reforms those of working age who are least likely to receive fuel-poverty support have also been hardest hit by the welfare reforms, including Housing Benefit, council tax benefit and the cuts to benefits such as Disability Living Allowance (Beatty and Fothergill, 2013).

Conclusion

This chapter set out to explore the government's claims that, despite its having no control over global energy markets, existing policy protects households vulnerable to fuel poverty through the regulation of energy suppliers and specific policies that provide cash transfers and energy-efficiency measures.

There is a tension between the fact that energy markets have clearly been liberalised and internal competition has been encouraged, and the fact that, despite the process of privatisation and the global nature of energy supply, the energy markets are not fully open and competitive. We see state intervention in terms of liberalising and regulating the market only up to a point, and similarly we have demonstrated that government intervention in order to secure social policy outcomes is at best 'patchy'.

Arguably there is a contradiction inherent in UK energy policy discussions. Actions at the international level described at the start of this chapter demonstrate that for a variety of reasons there is both a political desire and an ability to ensure a more secure energy supply and to boost domestic capacity. In fact, then, government *does* have a degree of control over wholesale prices, especially where it chooses to invest in and support the development of low-carbon infrastructure.

On the other hand, despite the regulation of the domestic energy suppliers being explicitly within the government's remit, regulation of energy markets has been weak, with evidence of misconduct across an industry dominated by six large companies. This has resulted in an interesting dialogue, where the rising cost of energy bills has been variously blamed: by the energy companies, on social and environmental levies; by the government and Ofgem, on industry greed, inexperience and misconduct; and by the political opposition, on a weak regulatory system combined with a preference for big business. Given that the market is highlighted as one of the greatest customer benefits of privatisation, far more could be done to manage this market.

Over and above this, there are social needs that cannot be addressed simply through a market-based system. As described previously, fuel-poor households are often the least likely to switch tariff or supplier; and it is also clear that decreased fuel-poverty budgets and an arm's-length policy approach to fuel-poverty alleviation have resulted in a serious social problem in a sector that has limited experience or capacity to deliver support and that may be more inclined to meet targets rather than needs. In addition to this, levying social and environmental charges through domestic energy bills rather than through tax-funded measures is highly regressive, especially given the stricter rationing criteria.

In conclusion, at present the process of alleviating fuel poverty in the UK appears to be a complex one in which the steering capacity of the nation-state often seems weak and hollowed out, which would appear consonant with the work of Cerny and Evans (see Cerny and Evans, 1999; 2003; 2004). However, it is clear that such capacity does exist, even if it has not been exercised, perhaps reflecting the policy priorities of the Conservative-led Coalition government and successive majority government, rather than a structural inability to intervene. At a conceptual level, UK energy policy offers a pertinent case study of the challenges policy makers face when trying to reconcile local social policy objectives with pro-competition, pro-global market policy frameworks.

Notes

[1] The department was abolished in July 2016, with the energy brief separated from climate change and subsumed within the Department for Business, Energy and Industrial Strategy.

[2] As of 2015, the British energy market is regulated Ofgem, whose main function is to protect the interests of energy customers. Specifically, it aims to: ensure value for money, promote security of supply and sustainability, promote security and development of markets and competition, and regulate and deliver government schemes (Ofgem, 2015).

[3] The so called 'Big Six' are the main energy companies and are: British Gas, EDF Energy, E.ON UK, Scottish Power, SSE. Since 2009 there are also a number of smaller energy suppliers, including: Ovo Energy, Good Energy, Ecotricity, LoCO2 Energy and The Cooperative Energy.

[4] Kern et al (2014) note that a focus on 'unstable' foreign supplies has provided a convenient narrative in many respects; for government and industry because it has prevented a challenge to existing energy governance structures; and for the climate lobby because it has encouraged diversification and investment in alternative energy sources.

[5] These results replicate the methodology used by DECC and are consistent with official estimates figures.

[6] The shift from the '10 per cent' definition of fuel poverty to the 'Low Income High Cost' measure had the impact of 'reducing the figures from 3.2 million to 2.4 million households [in fuel poverty] overnight'. Additionally, Coalition policy shifted from a target to eliminate fuel poverty to one to 'address' it (PSE, 2013).

[7] Although electricity charges are predicted to increase over the next decade as a result of electricity market reforms (NEA, 2014).

[8] Labour announced an intention to abolish Ofgem.

SIX

Exporting healthcare services: a comparative discussion of the UK, Turkey and South Korea

Neil Lunt

Introduction: exporting public services

Since the early 1990s the *purchaser/provider split* and *marketisation* have encouraged state organisations across many OECD countries to look to private sector and not-for-profit providers as potential sources of service provision, with competition for state funds in a 'mixed economy of welfare' (Mause, 2009). As such, state strategy switches from providing, to purchasing from private and non-public providers. As these markets develop and competition is embedded in public services we are seeing the emergence of a new 'public services industry' that differs from the traditional agenda of the public sector and involves the commodification of public sector work (Huws, 2008; Gash et al, 2013). One example of such marketisation is the role of non-NHS providers in delivering NHS-funded care in England, a direction of travel that, politically, has proved particularly controversial. Previously there was a limited role for non-NHS providers in delivering NHS-funded care; however, from 2008 the ability of non-public providers to compete for public contracts increased, culminating in the Any Qualified Provider policy from 2012, where NHS patients were given the right to choose to have certain routine treatments performed at any hospital, including private sector hospitals (Arora et al, 2013, p 14; BMA, 2013).

The emphasis on such marketisation is the result of wide-ranging and deep-reaching economic, social and political challenges and is leading to new forms of service delivery and governance across a range of public services (including health, social care, education, probation and childcare). Such stimulation of public service markets generates dividends that flow offshore, given that an increasing proportion of shareholders in UK companies are overseas investors. Public services are also provided in the UK by transnational providers: Sodexo, a

French-based company is contracted to deliver probation services; Ingeus, the largest provider within the Work Programme that supports jobseekers back into employment, is owned by a US company; the French company Atos was contracted to deliver Work Capability Tests for disabled welfare beneficiaries – a contract subsequently awarded to Maximus, an American for-profit provider (Social Enterprise UK, 2012; NAO, 2013; Plimmer, 2014a; 2014b; TUC and NEF, 2015).

Alongside greater competition from non-public providers and public service multinationals within public services markets there are parallel attempts to encourage UK public service organisations to be more entrepreneurial and innovative. Within the UK, policy support for public sector entrepreneurship and leadership gained traction under Labour's modernisation agenda, which perceived entrepreneurship as an engine of change (Sadler, 2000). Political support has continued since then (Cahn and Clemence, 2011). An HM Treasury document (2002) sought to encourage government departments, agencies and public bodies to better utilise their physical and non-physical assets by engaging in commercial services based on them, where appropriate. Exploiting commercial potential may take forms that include selling existing goods and services; developing new goods and services from existing assets; licensing and leasing arrangements; and sponsorship activities.

For government-owned service organisations the prevailing wisdom was that they rarely competed globally (Porter, 1990, p 247). However, neoliberal processes of liberalisation, deregulation and privatisation during the 1990s increasingly undermined this orthodoxy, encouraging a number of mainland European public services, including electricity, telecommunications and postal services – traditionally national-bound organisations under state ownership and control – to expand overseas (Clifton and Díaz-Fuentes, 2008). Moving beyond utilities, this chapter explores the growth in states' *promoting* public services overseas, including elements of welfare state services – education, health, social services. While the exports of goods involved in service delivery are well established (such as medical devices, pharmaceuticals and technology), the actual export of services themselves signals new departures in a global era.

The types of public services that are (or could be) exported are best identified using the Global Agreement on Trade in Services framework, which outlines four modes of trade in services (Chanda, 2002; Sauvé, 2002).

1. Mode 1: *Cross-border trade*, is where the trade takes place from one country into the other country, with the service itself crossing the

border. This includes forms of tele-health such as remote diagnosis, consultation and surveillance, and also the export of regulatory processes for healthcare. Examples in education include online teaching, virtual universities and the sale of education software.

2. Mode 2: *Consumption abroad*, where the customer travels to the country where the service is supplied. Patients may pay with their own funds for treatment in a different country, use portable insurance cover or be funded as part of a formal arrangement between healthcare providers in two countries. Similarly, students travel abroad to receive education and training in a range of settings – universities and further education establishments, schools, language providers and private sector trainers.

3. Mode 3: *Commercial presence*, where the supplier establishes a commercial presence abroad. This includes Foreign Direct Investment (FDI), where facilities based in one country and operated wholly in that country have been financed, established or built by organisations based in another country (including language schools, satellite universities and health providers). Variations may include facilities based and owned in one country being managed or overseen by organisations based in another. Skills may also be exported under this mode, with countries offering (health) education and training to groups located within a different country.

4. Mode 4: *Movement of natural persons*, where the provider of the service crosses the border. Consultation abroad involves the temporary export of skills but there is also movement of healthcare professionals and teaching, academic and research staff on a longer-term or permanent basis.

Combined with the export of relevant goods, the contribution of service exports is growing in significance. For example, the Department for Business, Innovation and Skills (BIS) estimated that education sector exports contributed £17.5bn to the UK economy in 2011 (Conlon et al, 2011). A unit within Education UK Unit, jointly funded by UK Trade and Investment (UKTI)/BIS, was established to support export market development, offering education goods and services and targeting countries in the BRIC (Brazil, Russia, India and China) and MINT (Mexico, Indonesia, Nigeria and Turkey) groupings (see, O'Neill, 2001; 2013) and in the Gulf region.

The UK is not alone in pursuing a health services export strategy. This chapter examines the responses of three countries to the encouragement of health systems to engage in global markets, and moves beyond how competition is embedded in the welfare state to consider how the welfare state is embedded in competition. The three countries examined, the UK, Turkey and South Korea, face similar healthcare pressures but have different private/public healthcare mixes and have developed distinct responses to the increasing private treatment of patients and the wider export of health services. There is a contrast between the strategies of the UK, the more established of the three exporters, and those of the two emerging exporters, Korea and Turkey. In implementing health export programmes, all three countries have sought to emphasise specific system characteristics and strategies that reflect their particular historical and institutional differences.

The chapter begins with the UK's health system, where there has been a strong focus on political development and clinical and organisational reform within national boundaries (see Gorsky, 2008; also Klein, 1989; Webster, 2002), but where the outward-facing influence and role of the National Health Service (NHS) has received less attention. The NHS has long-established bilateral relations with former colonies (treating patients, training clinicians and benefiting from the migration of doctors and nurses who come to work in the public health system). More recently, EU integration has involved the mobility of health workers and patients between the UK and Europe. Under the European Cross-Border Directive, patients may use their European citizenship rights to access medical care in EU member states and their national purchaser will reimburse the costs of their treatment abroad. Under the Directive there are a number of restrictions on who can seek treatment, and for what. In many cases patients must receive prior authorisation by their local health purchaser, especially when overnight hospital accommodation is required. Treatment that potentially poses a specific risk to the patient (or population), or where there may be serious concerns about the quality and safety of care, also requires prior approval. Authorisation may be rejected if the healthcare can be provided in the patient's country of residence within a time limit that is medically justifiable, taking into account the current state of the patient's health and the probable course of the illness. These caveats notwithstanding, cross-border mobility entails forms of multi-state governance for the UK. While the domestic health system always decides what healthcare is available to its citizens (regardless of whether they are treated at home or abroad), UK citizens, as EU citizens, can choose where to be treated and have clear rights to information and redress.

Aside from the political and social relationships, there has been less discussion of the economic significance and overseas reach of domestic health systems. Health exports are of growing interest to a range of countries and involve a variable mix of exports, emerging strategies to promote them and diverse governance arrangements. Increasing attention is being paid to healthcare exports in the UK, Turkey and South Korea, and we discuss the developments in each of these countries in turn. The chapter concludes by looking at the wider implications of such national strategies.

UK export strategy and the NHS contribution

There has since the 1970s been a stream of income derived from the treatment of international patients in UK public and private facilities. These patient inflows constitute system exports for the UK because revenue is generated for the domestic system from overseas patients. The 1970s saw an expansion in the numbers of these patients being treated within the NHS, fuelled by growing oil wealth and significant flows from Kuwait and Qatar. The economic downturns of the 1980s and early 1990s, the squeezing of private activity within domestic health markets and retrenchment in the public sector led to intensified competition among Britain, France and Germany for patients from Arab countries (see Roberts, 1991). NHS facilities treat international patients as booked and planned admissions that are pre-paid or financed through an embassy or insurer's 'Letter of Guarantee' (thus, transactions are pre-arranged, rather than constituting 'health tourism'). Types of treatment centre on complex tertiary procedures (including paediatrics and heart surgery) and also include maternity services and ophthalmic surgery. While the NHS is a key provider, given the international reputation and prolific nature of private medicine concentrated around Harley Street in central London, a significant number of inbound medical tourists also access treatment in the private sector.

Data from the UK suggests that international patient inflows to the UK (independent sector and NHS private services) were in the region of 51,000 in 2010. Major source countries included Spain, Greece, Cyprus and the Middle East (specifically, the United Arab Emirates and Kuwait). Income generated by international patients includes tourism revenue, capturing the general expenditure related to patients' and accompanying persons' visits to the UK, and medical expenditure (revenue to hospitals). Patients and their travelling companions are likely to arrive some days before treatment and remain additional days to fully recuperate, or even take advantage of the opportunity for additional recreational activity. Spending on medical treatment, both private and NHS, is estimated to be in the range of £192–£325 million. Overall, including additional 'tourism spending' some £397–£544 million in revenue is generated for the UK economy per year (Hanefeld et al, 2013). Placed alongside the overall NHS budget, the contribution is relatively insignificant, although for a small number of London-based hospitals it income constitutes a significant proportion of their revenue. The large NHS teaching and specialist hospitals undoubtedly have a brand power that plays a part in attracting foreign patients.

The wider context of this treatment of international patients is the emergence of so-called global patient mobility and global competition (Lunt et al, 2013; Lunt et al, 2015). Treatment of overseas patients appears to have become more competitive with the rise of Asian and Middle-Eastern providers, as well as competition within Europe and among UK-based private and public providers. Since the global recession there has also been a growing domestic debate about the extent to which NHS organisations can become more innovative and entrepreneurial and deliver more for less in challenging strategic and operational environments (DoH, 2010). The financial impetus has led to a growing interest in how NHS organisations might better balance the demands on their resources, and in identifying and seeking additional income from other sources (see Gregory et al, 2012; Lyons, 2014). Innovation in the NHS has been identified as one way of supporting 'growth in the life sciences industry' and so contributing towards economic growth (Coalition Government, 2011, p 7).

As of 2002, NHS Foundation Trusts gained additional freedoms to own their land, borrow from public or private sectors, run joint ventures with the independent sector and make surpluses and losses. It is a moot point whether the primary rationale for Foundation Trusts was competition or governance freedom, but some NHS Trusts have developed innovative approaches for delivering services to international patients and developing international partnerships. A small number opened branches overseas or partnered with commercial interests and healthcare developments in the Middle East. Great Ormond Street Hospital established a regional office at Dubai Health Care City in 2006. Imperial College London Diabetes Centre opened its Abu Dhabi facility in 2006 (and later Al Ain), specialising in diabetes treatments, research and training. In 2007 Moorfields opened a facility in Dubai Health Care City (Moorfields Eye Hospital Dubai) that operates as an overseas arm of the hospital. Since 2007, it has treated more than 33,000 patients from across 90 countries at its purpose-built campus, with around 70% coming from the Emirati and expatriate Arab communities.

Surpluses (not profit) that flow from such international patients and activities must benefit NHS patients, who remain the core responsibility of the hospital board, and core NHS facilities cannot be used to cross-subsidise international activities. In 2012 the amount of income that Foundation Trusts could raise from private activities (private-patient income, external business ventures such as commercialisation of R&D, training and consultancy) increased to 49% of turnover. However, their core legal duty remains that of caring for NHS patients and delivering authorised services. Any major increase in private sector income (increases by 5% or more of total income) requires board-level approval.

The NHS 'brand' and Healthcare UK

While previous export activity was localised around individual institutions (including small groups of hospitals producing marketing literature), attempts to support the international activities of NHS Trusts and organisations have become more strategic and operate at a national level. The 2010 White Paper, *Equity and Excellence: Liberating the NHS* (DoH, 2010), highlighted the potential of the NHS to exploit the power of its international reputation and gain financially from the NHS 'brand' when marketing NHS services to overseas patients. In August 2012 Healthcare UK was launched, supported by the Department of Health and UKTI, to promote and encourage overseas investment and activities from within the NHS in order to provide profit streams for reinvestment in core NHS services (Leonard, 2012; Edwards, 2013; Hanefeld et al, 2013; Lunt et al, 2014). It also promotes the interests of the private sector healthcare industry. Its strategy emphasises the national system of healthcare, identifying public policy as a potential asset (particularly the NHS model and brand, paralleling UK Universities for education and research). Healthcare UK advances trade and partnership options with private and public interests overseas, pursuing both hard export opportunities (infrastructure, investment, devices) and softer export opportunities (education and training, advice, regulation). Health and social care services are both within its remit and it explores opportunities within both traditional export markets and newly identified targets.

Priority markets include China, where health restructuring creates opportunities for construction, R&D and primary healthcare. The Gulf region has strong trade and historical links with the UK and is also seeking to grow its domestic healthcare in order to stem the flow abroad of publicly funded treatment for patients who require specialist care and complex surgery. Major healthcare expansion is underway in Saudi Arabia and infrastructure development (including Health Cities) will see a doubling of capacity in four to five years, as well as investment around medical education and improving traditionally low levels of R&D (The Economist Intelligence UNit, 2014). Similarly, in Iraq the expansion of oil output is supporting primary healthcare developments and the building of hospitals, and further demand also exists around drugs and equipment and information and communications technology. Major developments are also underway in Oman, United Arab Emirates, Kuwait and Qatar (Bambridge, 2013). In competing within such markets, reputation is a lubricant of soft power and becomes increasingly important in driving trade relations.

Healthcare UK typically uses government-to-government agreements with countries in order to promote UK health providers. Such national agreements aim to facilitate more local-level business interactions, especially in countries such as China where central control is strong but initiatives are also devolved to cities and provinces. Healthcare UK reported £749 million of business wins from 26 projects achieved during 2014/15; three of these related to NHS and other public sector organisations and secured £70 million (Healthcare UK, 2015).

Turkey's health export initiatives

Turkey, while situated outside the EU, has a long-standing commitment to accession and integration into European markets. It uses its political and cultural location – as a bridge between West and East – to good effect in developing health exports. The Turkish state has prioritised export development, including healthcare, and the Ministry of Development's 'Priority Transformation Program' (10th Development Plan, 2014–2018) focuses on institutional and legal infrastructure, physical and technical infrastructure and service quality and marketing. In targeting international patients the Ministry of Health and Ministry of Culture and Tourism coordinate different institutions working in this area (TC Kalkınma Bakanlığı, 2013). In 2010 a specific unit for the coordination of inward patients was established and became the Department of Health Tourism. State activities include regulating and improving the provision of health services to foreign patients, and promoting Turkey as a major destination for medical tourism. There are research activities focused on the international patient market and care processes, and an international patient portal has been developed for those considering treatment options in Turkey. For medical travellers there are a web-based registration system and telephone consultation and interpreting services for international patients. The Ministry of Economy provides substantive economic incentives to organisations that engage in promotional activities abroad by giving them financial support to cover up to 50% of their expenses. Since 2013, 50% of revenues obtained from medical tourism have been exempt from tax (Republic of Turkey Ministry of Health, 2013a).

The largest flows of international patients to Turkey are from Libya, Germany and Iraq (Republic of Turkey Ministry of Health, 2013b, p 35). International patients also come to Turkey as part of bi-lateral agreements between Turkey and various countries and agreements between social security institutions (Republic of Turkey Ministry of Health, 2013b, p 12).

Aside from national-level developments, there are city-level initiatives, mainly undertaken by Provincial Directorates of Health under the Ministry of Health and city-based Associations of Public Hospitals that have brought together all public secondary and tertiary healthcare facilities under their authority through the recent restructuring of health services. Cities that are already popular tourist destinations seek to promote themselves as major medical tourism destinations as well. A sectoral business council has been established with a view to promoting the Turkish health sector globally, involving representatives of hospital and travel agency associations, ministry representatives and commercial interests from across the travel, tourism and health sectors. Private hospitals and some non-governmental organisations are also active in the area. Private hospitals, and especially major hospital groups, have international patient centres that offer foreign patients a comprehensive range of services, ranging from assistance with visa procedures to airport transports and accommodation arrangements.

Developments in Turkey are not only concerned with the promotion of the country as a major destination for international patients. At the same time, the government and private sector are pursuing a wider export initiative for health services outside of Turkey. These include the building and operation of hospitals as well as the export of know-how and medical technology. For the public sector, a specific unit has been established under the Turkish Public Hospitals Institution for the coordination of activities linked to hospitals abroad. The

Turkish Cooperation and Coordination Agency (TIKA) under the Prime Ministry also plays a key role in the spread of Turkish hospitals to different regions. Although TIKA was initially engaged in developmental collaboration with Turkish-speaking countries in Central Asia, its activities have been expanded to various regions including the Middle East, Pacific, Africa and the Balkans. Turkish private healthcare providers have also been extending their activities to foreign markets in recent years, mostly as profit-oriented investments.

Medical Korea

Health export policy in Korea has been shaped and implemented by public organisations, including the Korea Health Industry Development Institute (KHIDI) and the Korea Tourism Organization. In particular, KHIDI, established in 1999 under the Ministry of Health and Welfare, provides comprehensive support programmes for strengthening the competitiveness of the national health industry (Kim et al, 2013). The Lee Myung-bak administration (2008–13) focused on national marketing to achieve export-led recovery (Choi and Kim, 2014), of which healthcare was a constituent part, with the branding strategies of Bio Korea and Medical Korea forming major strands of public policy. One element was a focus on promoting advanced technology and products and moving away from the traditional 'Korean discount', which had undervalued brands (Dinnie, 2010, pp 97–8). Taking a lead from the reported success of a number of Asian countries in treating foreign patients (primarily Singapore, Thailand and India), the Korean government sought to enter the medical tourism market. In 2009 it announced medical tourism as a new growth engine for economic development, allowing healthcare marketing to attract foreign patients and introducing a medical visa (Yu and Ko, 2012; Kim et al, 2013).

Many Korean medical institutions and leading hospitals and clinics have supported the venture. Korea's national health insurance system, with government controlling the fee schedule, has resulted in total expenditure on health as a percentage of GDP being kept relatively low – 7.8.% in 2013 (OECD, 2014). Even though the public sector finances over half of health expenditure, more than 90% of medical institutions are private and 90% of all beds belong to private institutions (Jeong, 2011; WHO and Ministry of Health and Welfare, 2012). Hence, medical institutions in the private sector face encouragement to actively increase their revenues by developing new medical techniques and increasing service volumes. In particular, they have sought to increase revenue by treating foreign patients, charging them far higher premiums than domestic insurance rates. Providers also hoped that treating foreign patients would bolster their domestic reputation for medical excellence and entail benefits from improving service quality.

Korean law requires any medical institutions that intend to treat foreign patients to be registered with the Ministry of Health and Welfare. A government agency with responsibility for health and welfare training delivers courses for medical interpreters. KHIDI undertakes key functions around analysis and planning for Bio Health and Medical Korea, including capacity building within the industry (overseas licensing, attracting overseas patients and running overseas branches) and R&D support. KHIDI has sought to raise its national medical brand, Medical Korea, through increasing domestic training for foreign medical personnel and medical missions for patients in underdeveloped countries. Wider health export has also seen Mode Three activities, with the establishment of numerous medical institutions into China, Mongolia, Vietnam and the US.

Strategy, governance and system differences

The export and import of health goods and services has a long history – albeit one played out against the backdrop of colonial and political relationships. The last 25 years or so have seen intensification of social and economic processes, and these are helping to shift the underlying perspective from international relations to global trade. Paralleling a more long-standing trade in goods (devices, pharmaceuticals), global economic competition has provided the pressure and domestic context for countries to focus on health services and to use their system characteristics to promote exports. The ways in which the UK, Turkey and South Korea have responded to such challenges and the wider implications therein is the focus of this concluding section.

First, it is apparent that all three countries are offering national support for health service export, including a measure of highest-level political diplomacy. Despite these health systems exhibiting major differences (ranging from a publicly funded health system in the UK to a system with strong private characteristics in Korea) and distinct regional dynamics (Europe, Asia and EU), the export of health services is a common objective. Such export aspiration is shared by countless other countries, including Germany, France, Japan, Malaysia and Thailand, supporting the view that a wider commodification and commercialisation of healthcare is under way. Such healthcare markets are seen to offer growth potential within both established and newly emerging markets and are attractive to a range of health systems – not simply those with strong private characteristics.

Trade in health services is considered a highly desirable export allowing countries to promote the virtues of their health systems – technology, quality and reputation. The perceived benefits for domestic economies are the ability to generate revenue and secure wider trickle-down effects, as well as the growing influence that a nation derives from exporting such services. There is also domestic political currency to be recouped from such activities, albeit with a proviso that expansion into export markets is communicated carefully to potential critics and opponents.

Countries adopt a range of policy instruments to stimulate export activity. These include *regulatory* instruments (the liberalisation of sectors and the issuing of permits) and *economic* instruments (variously taxes, subsidies and incentives). Country choice of instruments reflects distinct state strategy and political culture. South Korea has focused on deregulating previously restricted environments – introducing medical tourism visas and allowing advertising to target international patients. Turkish strategy has focused on tax incentives to organisations that treat foreign patients. By comparison, the UK has opted for less-direct instruments, for example lifting the income cap on public hospitals for private activities, while eschewing explicitly targeting international patients. Such differences are explained by the political sensitivities of marketing publicly funded healthcare abroad and the need to manage carefully the internal and external stakeholder views, including public misunderstanding of the relationship between the NHS's private patient activity and public waiting lists. Public hospitals may themselves develop an internal communications strategy that emphasises the contribution of private income to NHS facilities.

Across all three countries networks of interests are harnessed for export activities and these operate on behalf of public and private stakeholders, and also the interests of specific economic zones. Public-private partnerships incorporate state interests spanning multiple government ministries, departments and specific agencies (health, economic development, tourism, international relations). These networks are strongly state directed and, because perceived quality is central to such exports, the reputation of country system is becoming a valuable commodity. Irrespective of whether the majority of export activity is conducted by or through private companies, the role of international cooperation between countries, through formal trade pacts or slightly less-formal memoranda of understandings is central. States are taking the lead in shaping a national brand and the (health) system – rather than the product or the nation as a state or the people – is the focus of branding activity, seeking to ensure that the image and identity become synonymous (van Ham, 2001; Simonin, 2008, p 22). As Dinnie (2010, p 96) writes:

> The goals commonly associated with nation branding include export promotion, the attraction of foreign investment, tourism promotion, and, more intangibly, an increase in the influence of the nation in world affairs.

In supporting health export through leveraging health system characteristics such goals potentially coalesce. Using system characteristics has become a platform for exporting services across all four Modes (training and education, encouraging patients to travel, FDI and e-provision of services).

Beyond system branding and networks, distinct forms of governance are emerging around service elements, including independent accreditation schemes aiming to assure the care of particular health facilities. Accreditation involves surveying carried out by a third-party assessment body using a combination of self-assessment and external peer review. The process has come to be thought of as a 'stamp of approval' verifying the authenticity and quality of the services provided. Accreditation has most often been used as a marketing tool by provider hospitals, medical groups and the governments of provider countries seeking to grow their share of international patients. Korea and Turkey have significant Joint Commission International accreditation (Turkey with 52 JCI-accredited organisations, South Korea with 27 as of 2015). There is no universal official agency/group engaged in the delivery of accreditation, the coordination of accreditation delivery, or licensing the existing schemes that deliver accreditation. Hence, accreditation may be provided through market or non-market mechanisms and states may make such badging a requirement for healthcare providers competing in health export activities. The UK has not pursued accreditation as a means to signal service quality but has relied predominantly on the NHS as a national, public system of healthcare that is seen as offering unique advantages in accessing a wide range of clinical trials and studies, and a as model of delivery that is of interest to emerging economies (Lees, 2012).

Promoting elements of welfare service delivery (health and education) that leverage national system characteristics marks something of a departure from a prevailing emphasis on establishing greater competition *within* welfare services and towards situating welfare state activities within competitive market environments. Such export activity is presaged on the state supporting and advancing national interests, but actual strategies, instruments and governance networks differ because of history and culture, particular system characteristics and export aspirations. As domestic healthcare becomes something with global potential, then domestic concerns (including budgets, sustainability, access, safety) become interrelated, with wider export benefits (growth, innovation, social development, reputation).

As national interest hardens with respect to healthcare export, what is the impact of these developments domestically? As Massey notes 'Globalisation isn't up in the air, it's always produced in places' (in Kenway and Fahey, 2009, p 18). The strong advocacy of these service exports must be considered alongside the impacts (beneficial or not) on the local health economy, including patients and health professionals, as well as contributions to public revenues and economic growth. Both top-line growth and the distribution of dis/benefits are important. All export narratives contain assumptions of trickle-down to justify forms of marketisation, re-regulation, national promotion and system branding. Future emprical investigation must begin to show whether optimism is warranted and, if so, what forms of health export best support a state's ability to deliver accessible and high-quality services to its own citizens.

SEVEN

Global competitiveness and the rescaling of welfare: rescaling downwards while competing outwards?

Chris Holden and John Hudson

Rescaling welfare in an era of global competition

Scholars have tended to assume that social policies are *national* policies (Kazepov, 2010, p 35), with comparisons of national data dominating comparative analyses of welfare. This seems natural, since the 'welfare state' developed historically and conceptually within the frame of the 'nation–state', with policies 'characterised by a collective management of individual standardised risks' (Kazepov, 2010, p 42). States became the world's 'social containers', each national population being treated as 'a cohesive social grouping that constituted a moral and practical social system' (Taylor, 1994, p 156). As Keating (2009, pp 268–9) observes, T.H. Marshall's (1992) famous account of the development of citizenship, culminating with welfare states rooted in 'social citizenship', takes for granted that the nation–state is synonymous with the political, legal and social community.

Yet globalisation challenges some of these assumptions. The competition state thesis provides a nuanced account of the adaption of the welfare functions of the state in the face of intensified global competition, whereby the state has been reconfigured to sit at the 'crossroads' of global governance, transmitting the market discipline of the global capitalist economy within the borders of the national state (Cerny, 1997; 2010). A number of authors have observed the ways in which nation-states are increasingly enmeshed within more complex governance structures, ceding powers both 'upwards' to supranational institutions and 'downwards' to subnational levels of organisation (Hirst and Thompson, 1999). Pauly and Grande (2005, p 4) have observed the manner in which governance structures at all levels are becoming increasingly complex, leading to 'multiple and overlapping hierarchies'. While states are now routinely enmeshed in a range of international and supranational organisations 'above' them, they may also have various incentives to loosen controls over subnational units of governance or areas of territory within or 'below' the state as a whole.

Keating (2001, p 53) highlights various strategies states that have traditionally used for managing their territories such that the competing claims of different populations and areas could be reconciled and the state's overall territorial integrity maintained. The 'Keynesian welfare state', in particular, involved automatic stabilisers that mitigated asymmetric shocks by decreasing the tax take and increasing benefit payments in those regions within states that were hardest hit (Keating, 2009, p 269). Regional policies allowed the transfer of resources within states from richer to poorer areas that was far greater than anything considered by way of aid to poorer nation-states (Keating, 2009, p 269). However, this process of territorial management is rendered more difficult in a globalised economy, where states have an incentive to promote their most competitive areas and may find it more difficult to secure the resources to redistribute in order to compensate 'losers' (Keating, 2001, p 53). States thus have an incentive to decentralise some degree of power, or at least to manage sections of territory in a differentiated manner.

The search for global competitiveness may lead states to realise that specific component parts of their territory can compete better than others and thus choose to selectively insert specific slices of territory into the global market in a process that Jones (1997) has termed 'spatial selectivity'. SEZs are a key example of this process, although the same logic may also apply to whole cities or regions. This process of 'selling the local to the global' is particularly important in a context where capital is so much more mobile than labour (Peck and Tickell, 1994). Governments have thus 'become flexible in their management of sovereignty', governing various territories and populations in a differentiated manner in an effort to enhance competitiveness, with the result that 'different production sites vary in their mix of legal protections, controls and repressive regimes' (Ong, 2000, p 66). Ong calls this 'graduated sovereignty', a process in which the state utilises a 'flexible' set of strategies that 'are not congruent with the national space itself, but are attuned to the workings of global markets' (Ong, 2000, p 72).

Different slices of a state's territory may thus come to be differentially inserted into the global market. While the search for competiveness is usually at least partly the driving force, welfare outcomes can vary immensely, depending on the approach taken. While some may find new sites and scales for the reconstitution of social solidarity, the impact of such disaggregation on equity between localities can be profound and the risk remains of a 'race to the bottom'. The disaggregating effects of globalisation processes on governance arrangements therefore raise a number of questions about how the welfare of populations can be protected and enhanced, how equity can be sustained and what the optimum levels and scales are for social solidarity. We investigate these questions further below by examining two contrasting processes by which units of national territory have been differentially inserted into the global economy: SEZs and global cities.

Special Economic Zones and social policy

SEZs represent a particular form of the insertion of specific slices of a state's territory into the global economy. They are usually 'top-down' economic strategies imposed by national states on defined areas of territory, although often (and especially where low- or middle-income countries are concerned) the state itself is following a strategy determined for it by international institutions such as the World Bank and the International Monetary Fund (IMF). In some countries, such as India, while the national state may play a crucial role in facilitating the overall process and setting the political and macro-economic context, sub-national authorities compete with each other, varying subsidies and tax concessions in their zones to attract foreign and domestic investment (Levien, 2011, pp 461–4).

The World Bank (2008, p 2) defines SEZs as 'geographically delimited areas administered by a single body, offering certain incentives ... to businesses which physically locate within the zone'. SEZs thus represent the 'deterritorialisation' of areas of a country for economic rather than social reasons. They are the extreme logical end point of a neoliberal strategy in which, in an attempt to enhance competitiveness, attract foreign direct investment and generate jobs and exports, the state removes its own domestic regulations, which may relate to customs procedures, taxes and/or labour regulations, and treats the zone as though it were not part of the same country. Indeed, the key social policy incentive that many SEZs offer to transnational corporations (TNCs) (in practice if not in law) is the *absence* of a protective social policy, including in terms of the regulation of working hours, health and safety and the right to join trade unions.

Different types of SEZ exist, all of which are based on some form of liberalisation within a defined area of a state's territory (Box 7.1).

Box 7.1: Types of Special Economic Zone

The first 'modern zone' was established in Ireland in 1959. Since then, a variety of different types of zone have evolved:

- Free trade zones (FTZs; also known as commercial free zones) are fenced-in, duty-free areas, offering warehousing, storage and distribution facilities for trade, trans-shipment and re-export operations.
- Export-processing zones (EPZs) are industrial estates aimed primarily at foreign markets. Hybrid EPZs are typically sub-divided into a general zone open to all industries and a separate EPZ area reserved for export-oriented, EPZ-registered enterprises.
- Enterprise zones are intended to revitalise distressed urban or rural areas through the provision of tax incentives and financial grants.
- Freeports typically encompass much larger areas. They accommodate all types of activities, including tourism and retail sales, permit on-site residence and provide a broader set of incentives and benefits.
- Single factory EPZ schemes provide incentives to individual enterprises regardless of location; factories do not have to locate within a designated zone to receive incentives and privileges.
- Specialised zones include science/technology parks, petrochemical zones, logistics parks, airport-based zones and so on.

Source: World Bank, 2008, p 3.

Incentives offered by SEZs may be focused principally on streamlined customs procedures and duty-free imports and exports, corporate tax holidays, high-end infrastructure provision, cheap labour exploitation or any combination of these. Privately owned zones and public–private partnerships are becoming increasingly common and are advocated by the World Bank (2008), although government–administered zones remain the majority. The World Bank (2008, p 7) estimates that by 2008 there were approximately 3,000 SEZs in 135 countries, directly providing employment for 68 million people and over $500 billion of 'direct trade-related value added within zones'. China accounted for about 19% of the 2,301 zones present in developing and transition countries (World Bank, 2008, p 23) and for about 40 million employees, although zone employment outside China doubled between 2002 and 2006, from 13 to 26 million (McCallum, 2011, p 2). While the World Bank (2008, pp 2, 25) now advocates zones that focus on high-end infrastructure provision, it concedes that most zones continue to be engaged in labour-intensive, assembly-oriented activities such as clothing and textiles and electronic goods, that is they are export-processing zones (EPZs), premised upon the use of cheap, low-skilled labour for the assembly and re-export of goods.

Concerns have been expressed about social conditions within SEZs, including in relation to wage levels, working conditions and the denial of freedom of association. Further concerns relate to the fiscal impact on governments and to environmental impacts. Excessive and compulsory overtime is widespread in many zones and health and safety conditions can be poor (McCallum, 2011, p 4). In India, although there is some evidence that zones have the potential to generate waged employment (Aggarwal, 2007), this has been achieved by forcibly dispossessing farmers of their land (Levien, 2011). The result has been to deprive key groups of the sources of their subsistence, often with a devastating impact on the poorest (Levien, 2011, p 467–9). Similar processes of land dispossession have been observed in China (Gopalakrishnan, 2007). There are frequent reports by unions, non-governmental organisations (NGOs) and inspectors in various countries that workers in SEZs are consistently denied the right to organise (McCallum, 2011, p 3; Walsh, 2013). Some countries explicitly deny the right to freedom of association within SEZs, while others do not, but whatever the legal regime, the enforcement of labour regulations and accountability tend to be weak (McCallum, 2011, p 4). Unjust dismissal, blacklisting, intimidation and physical violence against union organisers have all been reported (McCallum, 2011, p 4).

Despite such reports, working conditions and wages are sometimes better within zones than in comparable businesses outside them (World Bank, 2008, p 4). These better conditions are sometimes the result of criticism and increased monitoring by NGOs and others. As McCallum (2011, p 17) points out, the profile of the TNCs that invest in SEZs tends to be higher than that of smaller local firms. Indeed, rather than invest within SEZs, it can sometimes be to the advantage of TNCs to subcontract to those in the domestic economy who are less monitored, as in Bangladesh for example, so that poor working conditions can be exploited in a less visible way; subcontracting allows for the plausible denial of responsibility when poor working conditions are exposed or there are industrial accidents. The zones are thus just one aspect of increased global competition and must be seen in that context. While wages are sometimes higher inside the zones, this simply underscores the low-wage settings within which zones are often situated (McCallum, 2011, p 4) – slightly higher wages within the zone, when combined with tax relief and other incentives, are still attractive to TNCs. However, as ICFTU (2004, p 4) notes, 'By its very nature, EPZ investment is precarious, and likely to leave the country at a moment's notice if more favourable conditions for production, including lower wages, are on offer elsewhere.'

There are substantial gender disparities in wages, a crucial factor when it is realised that women usually comprise the majority of the workforce. Female workers account for 60–70% of the SEZ workforce worldwide (World Bank, 2008, p 25), and for a larger proportion in some countries. SEZs are often a conduit for industrialisation, drawing rural, often female, inhabitants into capitalist wage-labour relations for the first time. In the early 2000s, for example, Ngai (2004, p 30) found that in the archetypal Chinese SEZ of Shenzhen, more than 90% of the total labour force in light manufacturing industries was comprised of women under the age of 25. Since these workers had no residency rights under China's household registration system (*hukou*), most lived in dormitories provided by their employers and relied on familial networks for their welfare needs. The dormitory system provided a means of control for employers, with accommodation tied to employment. Workers typically worked a 12-hour day and could be dismissed at any time (Ngai, 2004).

The fiscal impact of SEZs on governments depends on the exact mix of corporate tax holidays, import duty exemptions and subsidies provided by governments in the provision of infrastructure and essential services (World Bank, 2008, p 38). As the World Bank (2008, p 38) observes, a key issue is whether TNCs would have invested in the zone without the incentives. However, given that the package of fiscal incentives offered by SEZs is now fairly uniform globally (World Bank, 2008, p 48), governments promoting SEZs seem locked into an archetypal race to the bottom. Countries are pushed to compete with each other by offering ever more-favourable deals to mobile capital, and fiscal incentives have to become ever more extreme in order to have any effect. The World Bank (2008, p 48) describes how zones in the Middle East and North Africa already add personal income tax exemptions for expatriate workers, and zero corporate income tax in perpetuity, to the usual measures of import duty exemptions, exemptions from indirect and local taxes, unrestricted repatriation of capital and profits and unrestricted management of foreign exchange earnings.

Ultimately, as Schrank (2001) indicates, SEZs may be used as 'islands' of exploitation, where liberalisation takes place within the zone but the rest of the domestic economy does not really change, or as 'pilots' or areas of experimentation where the goal is to extend successful forms of liberalisation to the rest of the economy. The World Bank, which advises low- and middle-income countries on investment strategies and the adoption of zones, favours the latter type (World Bank, 2008). The aims of this type of SEZ can be any combination of: experimentation to find the best model of liberalisation; a 'demonstration' effect approach, where the aim is to show what works before more extensive liberalisation takes place; or a way of outmanoeuvring opposition by incrementally extending reforms to new parts of the country rather than implementing them for the whole country at the same time.

China provides the archetypal example of using SEZs as a precursor to more extensive liberalisation. Its liberalisation process has been accompanied by the dismantling of old types of welfare based on work units, leaving the Chinese government needing to establish new welfare arrangements in the context of the liberalisation of the economy. Building welfare institutions in this new context is made more difficult by the growing unevenness of wealth and regulatory capacity, and differing central–local relationships between different provinces and localities in China (Zheng, 2007). China's size, demonstrable economic growth and increasing influence internationally have also put it in the novel position of spreading this model of 'zoning' to other countries, either through direct relationships, as in Africa (Bräutigam and Xiaoyang, 2011), or through example, as in India (Gopalakrishnan, 2007; Levien, 2011).

Global cities and social policy

Just as SEZs represent a particular form of insertion of specific slices of a state's territory into the global economy, global cities can be viewed as performing a similar function, albeit with critical differences in how this is achieved. Sassen (1991; 2001; 2005) uses the term to refer to a select set of cities through which the processes of globalisation are most strongly articulated. However, in stark contrast to SEZs, where top-down processes use the levers of state planning to rapidly create competitive advantages for particular localities, the major global cities are built on long-term competitive advantages for certain localities that reflect often centuries-old patterns of international trading and imperialist power. Nonetheless, as Sassen (2001,p 3) notes, it is not merely a case of history, for 'Beyond their long history as centers for international trade and banking, these cities now function in [a number of] new ways.' More specifically, she suggests that they act as command points of the world economy, the global headquarters for key service industries such as finance, and as key sites for the production and consumption of goods and services.

Castells (2010) develops this theme further, suggesting that global cities are connected to the development of the global informational network economy in which the 'space of flows' has superseded the 'space of place': where once industry relied on spatially concentrated co-location of complementary production processes, now there is an 'international spatial division of labour' (Castells, 2000, p 418), with 'a new industrial space [that] is organized around flows of information that bring together and separate at the same time – depending upon cycles or firms – their territorial components' (Castells, 2000, p 424). Yet, the apparent paradox that Castells teases out is that while it is often presumed that place matters less in the new informational economy – because new technologies break down spatial barriers – the reality is that major global cities appear to have become more, rather than less, important as the new economy unfolds. For Castells, this is because certain sites act as hubs or nodes in the network economy: they are the spaces where the flows of information (and the money, power and knowledge they transmit) are most intense. The global informational economy is, he argues (2000, p 429), 'ushering in a new urban form, the informational city', which 'is not a form but a process, a process characterized by the structural domination of the space of flows'.

One of the attractions of global cities as a subject of investigation is that their presence – understood in the form defined above – makes clear that globalisation is an 'in here' rather than 'out there' process, driven by key actors and institutions located in specific locations. From a social policy perspective this means that global cities (reflecting Castells' suggestion that they are a process rather than a place) should be inspected as an active and powerful participant in national and global policy-making processes. We should not, therefore, expect the presence of a strong global city in a country to be irrelevant to the shape of its welfare systems (Hudson, 2012). Indeed, we (Hudson, 2012) have suggested four key propositions regarding global cities and social policy. First, the presence of a global city is likely to have an impact on national political debates about globalisation and welfare, for global cities are places where processes of globalisation are strongest and where global economic and political elites are most visible. Second, the context for social policies in global cities differs from the national picture of the territories they reside in, with global cities typically accounting for a disproportionately large percentage of national GDP and having a broad demographic make-up that often differs substantially from the national norm. Third, global cities are sites of heightened social inequality when compared to the nations they are located in, with much higher levels of income inequality, poverty and social exclusion than average. Finally, global cities are 'magnets' for resources and will often have patterns of welfare provision that differ in important ways from those found in the national welfare regime as a whole.

In London, for example, levels of poverty and inequality after housing costs are considerably higher than the national picture; in particular, so for child poverty in Inner London is at almost twice the

Box 7.2: Types of global city

While Sassen and Castells offer the most detailed conceptualisations of global cities, Taylor (2005) offers us arguably the most sophisticated empirically rooted taxonomy of them. Drawing on extensive data capturing the intensity of flows within and between 300 major cities, he distinguishes:

- leading functionally comprehensive global cities (London and New York);
- functionally comprehensive global cities that make a smaller contribution and with a cultural bias (for example Los Angeles, Paris, San Francisco);
- incipient functionally comprehensive global cities (for example Amsterdam, Chicago, Toronto);
- global niche cities, including those with an economic focus (for example Hong Kong, Singapore) and with a political/social focus (for example Brussels, Geneva).

And, below global city level, he points to 'world cities' with different supporting functions:

- world cities that act as sub-net articulators below global city level, in specialised fields such as culture (for example Berlin) or politics (for example Vienna);
- worldwide leading cities, again below global city level, that make a primarily economic contribution (for example Frankfurt, Sydney, Zurich) in global networks and those that make a primarily non-economic contribution (for example Barcelona, Mexico City, Mumbai, Shanghai) in global networks.

level for England as a whole (DWP, 2014, p 51). At the same time, however, public expenditure per head in London is considerably higher than the UK average in most budget areas, particularly for housing and community services, where spending is over 50% higher than the UK average (Hudson, 2012). London may well be an extreme case – predictably so, given that it is the example par excellence of the global city – and Hudson (2012) has suggested that the nature of each global city is a key variable worthy of exploration when considering the impact of global cities on welfare: his macro-level analysis of leading cities found that where a country's leading global city played a key role in global finance networks, its welfare state was almost always less generous than if it played a key role in global political or cultural networks. We should stress, however, that global city–welfare system linkages do not operate in a simple linear fashion, but that outcomes are contingent upon complex iterative interactions between a wide range of economic, social and political forces, with meso-level political institutions playing a particularly significant role in shaping outcomes in any given context. This context likely includes the extensiveness of welfare provision itself, the form of key political institutions (including devolution of power to regions/localities) and, indeed, the level of economic development in a nation. In Mexico City, for example, a mixture of factors that includes increasing devolution of power to the city, the concentration of economic resources in the city and the effective organisation of political networks in the city have resulted in the city developing a set of local social policy provisions that far exceed the scope of those provided by the national welfare system, with many rooted in universalist principles that challenge the targeted and heavily conditional frameworks that operate nationally (Hudson and Medrano, 2013). Indeed, such is the depth of provision there that it is possible to talk of the development of a 'social city-zenship' within Mexico City (Hudson and Medrano, 2013).

A rescaling of welfare?

What might be learned by exploring the impacts of SEZs and global cities on welfare? Both represent knowing attempts to insert a slice of national territory into the global economy in an enhanced way, and so they provide an excellent opportunity for us to explore globalisation as an 'in here' rather than 'out there' process. Both underline the complex ways in which the authority of nation-states is increasingly being reconfigured – although not necessarily weakened – as nations respond to globalisation with new governance arrangements. While this is evidently so with respect to economic policy, our case studies suggest it is also true with respect to social policy, offering thorny challenges to national-level welfare programmes typical of the 'traditional' welfare state in particular.

SEZs and global cities are among the sites where global competition is most intense, and so they might be conceptualised as being at the 'sharp end of globalisation'. With many social policy challenges systematically intensified when they are compared to their 'host' nations, the case for decentralised and differentiated social policy frameworks for these globalised slices of territory can be a powerful counter to the view that welfare interventions are best organised at the national level. As Kazepov (2010, p 37) notes, the concept of subsidiarity 'implies that matters ought to be handled by the smallest (or lowest) competent authority, meaning that a central authority should perform *only* those tasks which cannot be performed effectively at a lower level'. The nation-state has typically been thought of as the optimum level for the provision of social policies because it is usually large enough to ensure significant redistribution between populations and close enough to its citizens (and, in the liberal-democratic tradition, democratic enough) to ensure some level of accountability. What if, however, the nature of social problems is so distinct in these globalised slices of territory that it demands distinct responses? Moreover, what if the strategy underpinning SEZs or global cities demands a local variation to national welfare frameworks or a toleration of heightened social inequalities in the locality because this is integral to the terms on which the territorial 'slice' aims to compete in the global economy?

These are key issues, but beyond the question of whether devolution of social policy responsibility in these areas will allow for 'better' decisions to be made, there are other issues that are significantly more complex. Indeed, how a state responds to the social consequences of injecting a 'slice' of its territory more deeply into the global economy tells us much about how it seeks to square the global competition–welfare circle, not least because how the highly globalised territorial 'slice' is accommodated will normally have significant implications for the less-globalised parts of the nation. To some extent, Castells foretold this, for in theorising the implications of global cities for national economies he surmised that they would play a Janus-faced role, acting to connect a locality to the global network but, at the same time, 'downplaying the linkages with their hinterlands' (Castells, 2010, p 417), and observed that global cities 'are connected externally to global networks and to segments of their own countries [... while at the same time] internally disconnecting local populations that are either functionally unnecessary or socially disruptive' (Castells, 2010, p 436). Castells' arguments were directed towards economic issues but have clear resonance for social policy too as states seek to accommodate SEZs or global cities in their welfare frameworks. Figure 7.1 summarises the possibilities here; while all four types in the figure are possible theoretically, we expect patterns to be observable empirically. SEZs are often super-exploitative, with workers subject to long hours, poor safety conditions and, often, non-payment of social insurance. Although there may be a 'transparency effect' whereby the visibility of TNCs may lead to better working conditions, typically we expect Types I and II to be the most prominent in SEZs, although this is not always so. With respect to the global cities focused on economic globalisation, Types I and III are likely to be most prominent, although again this is not always so.

What are the implications for social solidarity? There has traditionally been an assumption of the coincidence of nation with state, such that there is an ethnic or at least cultural basis for social solidarity, but, as Keating argues (2009, p 279), there is no reason to assume that 'state-level solidarity is praiseworthy, while solidarity at other levels is mere selfishness … the nation state is itself a partial and spatially limited form, which has no intrinsic moral status'. In Mexico City a social city-zenship has recently developed that extends social policy provision within the city well beyond the frameworks in place nationally, but the question of what this means for social solidarity depends on whether this marks a one-off advance in Mexico City or the first of many extensions of social rights across other localities in Mexico that follow the lead of Mexico City (Hudson and Medrano, 2013). Conversely, we have seen how SEZs can involve the 'selling [of] the local to the global' (Peck and Tickell, 1994), with social rights being suppressed for a portion of the population in order to attract global capital,

Figure 7.1: Welfare linkages between highly globalised slice of territory and hinterland

| | | Welfare provision in hinterland | |
		Low	High
Welfare provision in highly globalised slice of territory	Low	I Minimal welfare state	II Deregulated globalised slice
	High	III Janus-faced globalised slice	IV Globalisation-adapted welfare state

which can mean the SEZ territory and its population remaining as an island of exploitation while social rights elsewhere in the country are better protected. However, SEZs sometimes act as a precursor to the liberalisation of the rest of the country, with the potential for welfare retrenchment and/or commodification becoming generalised.

It follows from the above that, rather than having a simple, linear impact on welfare, the influence of SEZs and global cities is contingent on mediating institutional factors. In particular, the way in which political power is facilitated and constrained – locally, nationally and supranationally – will likely be significant. The expansion of welfare in Mexico City was intimately connected with reforms to sub-national political institutions, for instance (Hudson and Medrano, 2013). How, in what ways and to whom power is decentralised is key. But, again, comparing across SEZs and global cities, we expect to see some observable patterns. In particular, global cities are often distinct from SEZs in that they involve some form of democratic representation. As Keating (2009, p 276) notes, 'Where government is elected, depoliticisation is impossible and … the agenda is broadened to include social and other concerns.' We might therefore reasonably expect political pressures to mitigate the impacts of globalisation through social provision to be much more impactful in global cities than in SEZs. That said, this is not always the case; there are examples of global cities without liberal democracy (for example, Hong Kong, Singapore) and SEZs in democratic countries. Moreover, we should not overlook the fact that the most prominent global cities are also the places that are home to the most powerful global elites.

It is important to acknowledge that the form or type of an SEZ or global city (see Boxes 7.1 and 7.2) is also likely to be a factor shaping outcomes. These variations in the nature of SEZs and global cities themselves reflect prior political choices and important historical legacies. With respect to global cities, their central positions in economic, cultural, political and social networks often reflect long-term competitive advantages that date back centuries, for example, building on trading routes established through imperialist activities. For SEZs, their shape and form is typically intertwined with a nation's political system, level of economic development and degree of subjection to IMF and World Bank policy preferences. This hints, too, that time is a crucial variable, and there is likely to be dynamism in the future as some localities rise and others fall in the global networked economy. There may also be fluidity between mass-scale SEZs and global cities, including via mega-regions that feature SEZs as part of their mix. An obvious example here is the SEZ in Shenzen, which has grown to become a city in its own right and is connected with an established global city (Hong Kong) and an emerging mega city (Guangzhou). Indeed, the rise of mega cities (typically viewed as conurbations with populations of at least 10 million) that do not have full global city significance is a major trend across Asia, Africa and Latin America and a process that is still unfolding. More than a decade ago Castells (2000, p 436) predicted that the Hong Kong–Shenzen–Guangzhou megalopolis would drive 'a major realignment in the global geography of advanced services', and we may see a precursor of future trends here; indeed, mega cities represent an economic strategy adopted by policy makers distinct from the development of SEZs and viewed as an attempt to develop future global cities.

The emerging Hong Kong–Shenzen–Guangzhou megalopolis also underlines that studying SEZs and global cities in isolation simplifies the complex reality of globally connected localities, for it may well be that SEZs and global cities represent interconnected parts of global production chains. To take the example of Apple's iPhone and iPad, these devices are commonly assembled by the Taiwanese company Foxconn in locations such as its Shenzen factories (see Duhigg and Barboza, 2012), but only a small amount of the added value is accrued to mainland China through this activity (Gereffi and Lee, 2012, p 27) – perhaps as little as $10 per iPad or iPhone, and mainly in the form of direct wages to factory workers (Kraemer et al, 2011, p 6). Meanwhile, the majority of the highest-value functions are located at or near to Apple's headquarters (Kraemer et al, 2011, p 7), whether in-house at Apple Campus (its headquarters in Cupertino, California) or through specialised contractors such as the long-term holder of Apple's global advertising account, TBWA\Media Arts Lab, which employs around 250 people on Apple business, primarily in its Los Angeles office (Wakabayashi, 2014). Even from this small example it is not difficult to visualise the links between SEZs and global cities in global production chains. Furthermore, SEZs may often be located in lower-income countries and based around the low-paid, low-value, manufacturing end of the chains, with global cities located in higher-income countries and focused on the high-paid, high-value, service end of the chains.

It follows that while an analysis of SEZs and global cities provides us with useful insights into the ways globalisation may be fostering a rescaling of welfare, a satisfactory resolution of competitive forms of scaling downwards with the need for social solidarity must also involve a settlement at the global or at least world-regional level, since these subnational forms of governance are locked into a process of global competition that, while it might in some circumstances facilitate wealth accumulation, leads to huge inequalities and inequities. There is a fruitful research agenda here that offers potential for deeper understanding of the relationships between globalisation, political and economic rescaling, and social solidarity.

Part Three
The reframing of welfare discourses in an era of competition

Rewriting the contract? Conditionality, welfare reform and the rights and responsibilities of disabled people

Peter Dwyer

Introduction

The ongoing shift from the so-called 'passive' welfare state of the past to the 'active' welfare state of today (Walters, 1997) and the conditionality at the heart of welfare state reform within and beyond Europe have generated extensive discussion (for example, Cox, 1998; Dwyer, 1998, 2004; Goul Andersen et al, 2002; Deacon, 2005; Dean et al, 2005; Wright, 2012). Central to this shift has been a requirement that certain groups of disabled citizens who had previously enjoyed access to largely unconditional social security benefits due to sickness and impairment should now become 'responsible' active agents in their own welfare by seeking or preparing for paid work, rather than relying on social security benefits. The rolling-out of a principle of conditionality, which holds that eligibility to certain basic, publicly provided welfare entitlements should be dependent on an individual's first agreeing to meet particular compulsory duties or patterns of behaviour (Deacon, 1994) has been one way in which UK governments of various political persuasions have sought to rewrite 'the terms and conditions of the welfare contract' (Buck et al, 2006, p 1).

Commentators have highlighted the links between contemporary forms of conditionality and the founding principles of the British welfare state, in which the interrelationship between social security and the social contractual obligations of individual citizens were made explicit in the Beveridge Report (1942) (Freud, 2007; DWP, 2008). However, it is apparent that there has been an intensification of conditionality in many Western welfare states in recent decades, with enhanced use of sanctions and realigned relationships between entitlement, conduct and support (Handler, 2004; Betzelt and Bothfeld, 2011). In the UK these new forms of conditionality seek to limit the rights of social citizenship (Marshall, 1950) by increasing the conditional requirements of welfare access in respect of disability-, incapacity- and unemployment-related welfare benefits (Dwyer, 1998; DWP, 2008; Gregg, 2008; Griggs and Evans, 2010; Patrick, 2011; Rolfe, 2012), as well as in the fields of housing, homelessness (King, 2004; Johnsen and Fitzpatrick, 2010; Flint et al, 2011; HM Government, 2011) and migration (Dwyer, 2010). The UK's New Labour governments (1997–2010) advanced welfare conditionality as a core element of their reform agenda, based on 'the principle that aspects of state support, usually financial or practical, are dependent on citizens meeting certain conditions which are invariably behavioural' (DWP, 2008, p 1). Subsequent Coalition and Conservative governments have further intensified this conditionality (Wright, 2011, 2012) through the introduction of Universal Credit (Dwyer and Wright, 2014), increasing the scope of instrumental intervention and promoting the use of behavioural (or 'nudge') economics and social psychology to achieve behavioural change and public policy goals (Thaler and Sunstein, 2009; Osborne and Thaler, 2010). In a period of austerity, changing public behaviour is viewed as a key mechanism for minimising the impacts of public finance retrenchment (Grace and Simpson, 2009).

Welfare states across high-income countries have been subjected to sustained reform agendas in the last 30 years in order to make them more 'competitive'. A significant rewriting of the social contract so as to place increased stress on work and economic participation is a core feature of this process in many countries. As Cerny and Evans (2004) noted, the UK provides a key example here, being among the first to turn towards a 'competition state' style of agenda. An increasingly central part of this agenda has been the increased 'conditionality' attached to social rights.

The particular focus of this chapter is on the rights and responsibilities of disabled people in the UK and the ways in which their rights to work and social security benefits have been subject to contestation and redefinition, particularly since the introduction of Employment and Support Allowance in 2008. In the past, both governments and citizens generally tended to support the claims of long-term sick and disabled people to social security benefits for two reasons. First, because disabled people fitted commonly held views about a legitimate need for provision of financial support and care through the public welfare system. Second, because the cause of their inactivity in the paid labour market was seen by many as being beyond their control. In short, questions about whether disabled people were 'choosing' to be dependent upon welfare were generally perceived to be of limited relevance because of their inability to work being 'obviously' linked to individual impairment. Such views can be problematic and may reflect wider ideas about disabled people being a 'deserving' case for largely unconditional collective support, and have been identified as disabling by many disabled people and their allies. Barnes (1992) recognised how disabled people have long challenged such discriminatory views and demanded the eradication of disabling attitudes and environments, so that they can realise effective rights to paid employment. Similarly, criticisms of the disabling welfare state and the role it has played in the systematic and entrenched social exclusion of disabled people in respect of their rights to work and welfare must be acknowledged (see for example Oliver and Barnes, 1998; Roulstone and Prideaux, 2012).

This chapter is not intended as an uncritical eulogy to the welfare state of the post-Second World War welfare settlement (see Chapter One), which in spite of its universalistic rhetoric has long been shown by many commentators to be limited in respect of gender, ethnicity and disability (see for example Williams, 1989). Rather, a central aim of this chapter is to document the ways in which New Labour governments and the Coalition and Conservative administrations that succeeded them have used conditionality to reframe and reduce the social security rights of disabled people in the UK. As Hudson and Horsfall note in the Introduction to this volume:

> One of the ways in which welfare states have been reconfigured in response to perceived competition pressures is through a rewriting of social contracts in order to de-emphasise social rights and place a stronger emphasis on individual responsibilities. (p xxx)

The reasons why this recent 'rewriting of the contract' between disabled people and the state may have occurred, and the consequences of such policies, are considered. The conclusion notes that such changes are ongoing in many welfare states beyond the UK, and offers some final comments on the relevance of conditionality to this book's two other main themes of 'competition' and 'cognition'.

New Labour's conditional welfare state (1997–2010) and disabled people's rights to work and welfare

Drawing on new communitarian and right-wing critiques of unconditional social rights (Dwyer, 1998), linking welfare rights to responsibilities became a clear and consistent underpinning principle during New Labour's time in office. The pragmatic politics of 'Third Way' welfare was built on the assumption that whenever possible self-reliant citizens should earn access to their social rights through a combination of hard work, responsible behaviour and personal contribution (Blair, 1998). New Labour's reform project aimed to promote an active, preventative welfare state built around the centrality of paid work whenever and wherever possible (Powell, 1999). Branded by some as the 'renewal of social democracy' (Giddens, 1998), the key responsibility of individual citizens was to actively engage in the paid labour market. Simultaneously, the state's welfare responsibilities to citizens were to be redefined around the rubric of 'endowment egalitarianism' (Page, 1997). Whereas in the 'old' welfare state rights to social security benefits (which citizens could expect to draw on in times of need, such as periods of unemployment or incapacity due sickness or impairment) were seen as a key aspect of citizenship, New Labour saw the state's primary responsibility as being to provide citizens with equal access to education and training to equip individuals with the tools to enable them to successfully navigate the insecurities of late-modern labour markets in order to best meet their own and their families' welfare needs. Those who cannot, or will not, embrace these opportunities suffer negative consequences. Reliance on social security is viewed as being the result of either idleness or bad management of personal risks, that is, making the wrong choices and/or lacking the application to assume responsibility for oneself. The mantra 'no rights without responsibilities' (Giddens, 1998, p 65) is unequivocal; ending 'passive' reliance on social security benefits, and the instrumental use of welfare policy to *reward* worthy citizens and *discipline* irresponsible ones was central to New Labour's Third Way welfare state (Dwyer, 2004). Welfare conditionality and the sanctions that it often implies were tools that New Labour was happy to use in order to achieve these aims. How, then, did this agenda play out in relation to disabled people?

As part of its wider welfare reform programme, New Labour was keen to question many of the previously taken-for-granted assumptions about disabled people's rights and responsibilities in respect of paid work and access to disability and incapacity benefits. As early as 1997 (against the backdrop of an almost five-fold increase in social security expenditure for sickness and disability benefits from £5bn in 1979 to £24bn in 1996/97), four key issues were subject to debate by the Social Security Advisory Committee during New Labour's first term. These were, first, the extent to which disability benefits should be set at a higher rate than long-term unemployment benefits; second, whether or not those disabled people who had previously worked should have the right to a higher level of benefit than those who had not; third, whether or not the system could be restructured to make greater use of incentives to move some of those on incapacity benefits into paid work without stigmatising others incapable of work; fourth, whether reforms could be developed to encourage disabled people to work episodically and/or part time without penalising or reducing the benefits of those who, having tried to enter paid employment, were unable to sustain long-term engagement with work (see Hewitt, 1999, p 58 for fuller discussion).

Initially, New Labour stressed a supportive approach that would enable disabled people to explore routes into the paid labour market and enhance their right to work. For example, the New Deal for Disabled People was targeted at recipients of Incapacity Benefit or Severe Disablement Allowance, but participation was voluntary. Those who enrolled attended work-focused interviews but were also given pay top-ups for the first six months of part-time employment and the ongoing support of a personal advisor once they were in work. Importantly, especially for people with recurrent or episodic impairments, those who signed up for the New Deal for Disabled People were given a guarantee that they could return to their previous level of social security benefit any time within 12 months of taking a job if necessary; the programme emphasised support to increase disabled people's activity in the paid labour market rather than sanctions for inactivity (Dwyer, 2010).

Simultaneously, however, the Welfare Reform and Pensions Act 1999 significantly strengthened the link between work and entitlement to disability benefits. New Incapacity Benefit claimants were required to attend a work-focused interview as a condition of entitlement. The introduction of the 'All Work Test' also refocused the medical examination used to determine eligibility for incapacity benefits so as to emphasise claimants' capacity for work rather than impairments that might limit it. The Incapacity Benefit of those in receipt of occupational or private pensions was also subject to means testing for the first time. Interpretations of the intent and approach that underpinned New Labour's early reform of disability benefits vary (see Heenan, 2002 for a positive appraisal of the New Deal for Disabled People), but critics also argued that the changes should be viewed as a concerted first attempt to rewrite the citizenship contract for many disabled people and enforce work incentives as an answer to the assumed perverse incentives of the disability benefit system.

> The new welfare reform strategy for [Disabled People] of working age reflects a fundament shift in the ideology underpinning social security provision in the UK: a shift away from support for the unconditional 'entitlements' to an endorsement of the role of the state in enforcing citizenship 'obligations', particularly the obligation to work. (Hyde, 2000, p 333)

While recognising that the government was keen to use a range of incentives (for example the Disabled Person's Tax Credit) to encourage disabled people into work, Drake (2000) viewed New Labour's approach as indicative of a desire to restructure the system so as to restrict incapacity benefits to disabled children and those over-pensionable-age people with severe impairments. Subsequent policy developments tend to support this view. Three years later, representatives of the government were openly talking of a need to end the 'sick note culture' (Johnson, 2005) and of using benefit sanctions as a legitimate way to potentially reduce by a third the number of people receiving incapacity and sickness benefits in the UK (then 2.7 million) (Garthwaite, 2011). In March 2007 the then Secretary of State for Work and Pensions, John Hutton, re-endorsed the 'fundamental principle of rights and responsibilities; of something for something' and denounced condition-free systems of welfare as exclusive (Hutton, 2007, p 9). Similarly, the Freud Report (Freud, 2007), commissioned by New Labour to review its welfare reform programme and to consider further ways of reducing work inactivity, called for a 'strengthened framework' that 'rebalances the system' away from unconditional welfare. Freud argued that a clear consensus had emerged among the public and politicians alike to endorse the view that those who are supported to return to work must either accept greater responsibility to help themselves or tolerate the possibility of benefit sanctions. He recommended an increase in the frequency of state interventions, the extension of the rights and responsibilities agenda and the future application of the stronger Jobseeker's Allowance (JSA) conditionality regime for all economically inactive benefit recipients, including the majority of disabled people.

Freud's vision informed the Welfare Reform Act 2007. This initiated the phasing out of Incapacity Benefit, Income Support paid on grounds of disability and Severe Disablement Allowance. These were replaced, from October 2008, with Employment and Support Allowance (ESA), to be paid to new claimants[1] unable to work because of illness or disability. During an initial 13-week 'assessment phase' all new ESA claimants are placed on a basic allowance at lower JSA rates (£73.10[2]) and have to undergo a Work Capability Assessment (WCA[3]) undertaken by a private provider. Three possible outcomes ensue, depending on the results of the WCA. First, a minority who are identified as having severe conditions and 'limited capability for work-related activity' are placed in the 'Support Group'. These individuals have unconditional access to an enhanced rate of ESA (£125.05) and are not required to participate in work-related activities. Second, those placed in the Work Related Activity Group receive a lower level of ESA (up to £102.15) and are required to engage in work-related activity such as job search, attending interviews with personal advisors or participation in work-experience schemes (CPAG, 2007; Patrick, 2012). Sanctions that result in a reduction or loss of benefit ensue where someone is, limited in their capability for work because of their own misconduct, because they remain someone who has limited capability for work through failure, without good cause, to follow medical advice, or because they fail, without good cause, to observe specified rules of behaviour (Welfare Reform Act 2007, s 18). Finally, a third group, those found fit for work following the WCA, are disqualified from the right to ESA and transferred to the JSA regime with its stricter conditionality rules and lower benefits (£71.70). New Labour's consolidation and expansion of a highly conditional welfare state may yet prove to be one of the most enduring legacies of its time in office and was central in moving its social policy away from the Keynes/Beveridge model of welfare (Dwyer, 2008; see also Chapter One in this volume). In relation to disability benefits, the approach was certainly enthusiastically endorsed by the Conservative–Liberal Coalition government that succeeded New Labour.

Workers, shirkers and disability: the Coalition's benefit reform programme

The Coalition government's efforts to 'expand the reach of conditionality' (Patrick, 2012, p 309) occurred alongside unprecedented post-Second World War cuts in public spending that were aimed at meeting the government's priority of quickly reducing the national deficit, with £18bn being cut from the welfare budget in 2010 alone (Hoggett et al, 2013). This commitment set 'the UK on a trajectory of permanently lower spending, lower debt and market-led growth' (Taylor-Gooby, 2012, p 62) and sought to further shift responsibility for welfare provision away from the state and onto individual citizens, private providers and/or local communities. The previously unlimited period of entitlement to receipt of contributory ESA for eligible individuals placed in the Work Related Activity Group was reduced to a maximum of 12 months in the 2010 Comprehensive Spending Review. Justified on the grounds of necessary cuts to the welfare budget, it further reduced the social security rights of those disabled people who had previously contributed via a period(s) of paid employment (Patrick, 2012). The Coalition government subsequently embarked on a comprehensive overhaul of the UK's social security system in which extending and intensifying the principle and mechanisms of conditionality and strengthening sanctions were central elements (Dolan et al, 2010). This included an enthusiastic endorsement of ESA and a restated commitment to the WCA as an appropriate mechanism for reclassifying significant numbers of disabled people as fit for work or work-related activity and training (Marsh, 2012). June 2011 saw the introduction of the Work Programme, a single programme of back-to-work support delivered by a range of private and third sector organisations that are allowed a large degree of discretion in the mix of personalised sanction and support that they use to activate individual clients.

At the heart of the Welfare Reform Act 2012, hailed by the Prime Minister as 'the biggest welfare revolution in over 60 years' (Cameron, 2012, p 1), were the introduction of Universal Credit, a new regime of personalised, enhanced conditionality, and Mandatory Work Activity. Mandatory Work Activity allows advisors to require those claimants who that they feel have a poor work record and limited commitment to job seeking to undertake a four-week unpaid work placement of up to 30 hours per week. The government sees this 'extra support' as being applicable for only a small number JSA claimants who would benefit from a short period of experiencing the discipline, 'habits and routines of working life' (DWP, 2011b). However, as Patrick (2012) notes, disabled people in the Work Related Activity Group are mandatorily subject to the Work Programme once they are judged to be fit for a return to work within a three-month period. Failure to complete a Mandatory Work Activity placement without good cause results in the sanction of JSA for three months. This will rise to six months for a second breach, with a three-year fixed sanction for a third violation. A new, more robust and extended sanctions regime for JSA and ESA claimants was also introduced to align with the Universal Credit model that will ultimately prevail for all benefit claimants. Previously, those in the Work Related Activity Group could lose only either 50% or 100% of the work-related activity component of their ESA for specified periods of time if they were sanctioned.

From December 2012 claimants faced sanctions of 100% of the full value of the prescribed ESA amount, with an open-ended period of sanction applicable to repeat offenders who failed to comply with advisors and re-engage with their specified programme of work-related activity (see DWP, 2012; 2013).

The full cumulative impact of the government reforms on those looking to claim disability benefits was starting to become evident by early 2015. The outcomes for ESA claims are already apparent and perhaps unsurprising, given that policy is focused on activating many disabled people and reclassifying them as fit for work. Government figures on both disallowance (that is, those who, following a WCA, are found fit for work and transferred to JSA) and sanctions applied to ESA claimants are significant. Between October 2008 and March 2013, 980,400 people (32% of all new claimants for ESA) were deemed capable of employment and fit for work, while a further one million withdrew their claim before undergoing a face-to-face assessment as part of their WCA (DWP, 2014). In the period October 2008 to December 2014 a total of 124,613 sanctions were applied to ESA claimants (DWP, 2015b, Table 2.1). Independent analysis of Department for Work and Pensions statistics further notes a 'rapid escalation in sanctions since mid-2013', with '21.0% out of a total of 85,292 sanctioned claimants being sanctioned more than once' and 7.6% being subject to three or more sanctions since the introduction of sanctions for ESA claimants in October 2008 and September 2014 (Webster, 2015).

The WCA, which 'is intended to focus on a person's capability rather than their incapacity ... [and] is designed to be a first positive step towards work for most people' (Harrington, 2010, p 7), has been subject to myriad criticisms, but the head of the independent review established by the government to evaluate its operation remains convinced that, in principle, the WCA is sound (Harrington, 2010; 2012). Others (including disabled people's organisations and mainstream charities) are less convinced, both about the way in which the WCA has been applied and the broader principles of activation and conditionality underpinning ESA. The first review of ESA highlighted numerous problems and noted that Jobcentre Plus staff tended to simply rubber-stamp the decision made by those who carry out the WCAs (Morris, 2011). Initial assessments were seen as unfit for purpose, with the tribunal system buckling under the pressure of ESA appeals, 40% of which found in favour of the appellant. The British Medical Association also called for the WCA to be scrapped (Marsh, 2012). In May 2013 a judicial review instigated by two people with mental health issues found their WCA assessments to be unfair; the judges noted that the WCA substantially disadvantaged people with mental health conditions and was an unjust way to decide if people were eligible for sickness and disability benefits (Gentleman, 2013). A doctor who resigned his post with Atos (the private company that carried out the WCAs until 2014) also questioned the clinical soundness of many decisions (Hutchinson, 2013). As Patrick notes,

> There are understandable fears that the WCA is incorrectly finding people fit for work, while also placing people for whom work is not a realistic prospect in the WRAG [Work Related Activity Group] of ESA with concomitant risks that such individuals are wrongly subjected to conditionality and the risk of benefit sanctions. (2012, p 312)

Aside from the deeply problematic issues related to the operation and implementation of ESA and the WCA, critics raised more fundamental concerns about the Coalition government's social security reforms and how sickness and disability are being re-conceptualised and understood. Although ESA was introduced by New Labour and was subsequently defended by the Coalition as 'enabling people into work' rather than 'abandoning them to a lifetime on benefits' (Welfare Reform Bill 2011), it is underpinned by a more insidious rationale that re-categorises disabled people who are claiming social security benefits as 'shirkers' rather than 'workers' (Newton, Dunn and Ashton, 2012).

Both the media and politicians have played important roles in changing how disabled people are represented in public and policy debates. An essentially moral 'vilifying discourse' that classifies disability benefit claimants as fraudulent 'scroungers' who are capable of work now dominates (Garthwaite, 2011). This renders the claiming of disability benefits as inherently problematic and morally wrong. Successive UK governments have been eager to co-opt social models of disability to justify sanctions and conditionality and the implied problematic passivity of disabled people who cannot or will not perform the tasks required under ESA or JSA rules. However, by focusing on personal capabilities to work, current policy reinforces an individual deficit model of disability that deflects attention from socially constructed barriers and the problems beyond personal impairments (for example, disabling environments and discriminatory attitudes) that many disabled people face when looking for work (Marsh, 2012; Patrick, 2012; Grover and Piggott, 2013).

Those reliant on social security benefits are now perceived by many as undeserving of support because of moral concerns and disgust about their worklessness. UK disability benefit reform is inherently exclusive. It is concerned with a 'contemporary redrawing of the disability category' and reconfiguring the rights and responsibilities of disabled people vis-à-vis work and welfare.

> That ESA is concerned with 'inclusion' is a fallacy. It is about ensuring that only those with what is judged at a particular moment to be a 'true' disability receive out of work benefits … it is concerned with re-working the disability category by making the qualifying criteria stricter and therefore defining more people as capable of working and of making efforts to become more capable of working. The aim has been 'inclusion', to make disabled people more like 'respectable' people, 'hardworking', 'independent' and 'responsible'. (Grover and Piggott, 2013, pp 8–9)

In a move that supports Grover and Piggott's assertion, a further reduction in the benefit rights of disabled people occurred with the abolition of the additional payments made to those in receipt of the work-related activity component of ESA or the limited capability for work payment of Universal Credit. From April 2017, under sections 15–16 of the Welfare Reform and Work Act 2016, new claimants will be paid reduced benefit at standard JSA rates (CPAG, 2016). The additional payment was denounced by the Chancellor as a 'perverse incentive', but critics have argued that the loss of this amount will increase hardship among disabled people and could, paradoxically, push many further away from paid work (Kennedy, 2015).

Conclusions: rewriting the social contract for disabled people

The shift towards a more overtly conditional welfare state represents a significant reformulation of the rights and responsibilities of social citizenship that undermines both reciprocal earned entitlements and universalist provision (Dwyer, 2008; Wright, 2012). As this conditional welfare state, with its stress on individual responsibility, becomes embedded and institutionalised there is a danger that the social, economic and political causes of unemployment, poverty and disability will ceased to be recognised (Dwyer and Ellison, 2009; Hoggett et al, 2013). Increased conditionality, an enduring legacy of New Labour's term in office, has been enthusiastically endorsed, extended and intensified by the subsequent Coalition and Conservative governments. Today the rights and responsibilities of disabled people are subject to ongoing dual processes of reconfiguration and diminution. The combined effects of the Coalition government's welfare reform programme and spending cuts will hit vulnerable and disadvantaged groups, including disabled people, the hardest, with increased poverty and inequality the most likely long-term outcomes (Taylor-Gooby, 2012).

Conditionality helps to individualise and 'desocialise' the causes of unemployment, poverty and disability. Where once ideas of social justice and legitimacy were used to endorse claims to public welfare they are now used to deny them (see Bauman, 1998). In an era of global competition, particularly the current period of austerity, the heady mix of 'money and morals' (Dwyer, 2000) that behavioural conditionality brings together serves as a powerful tool to undermine welfare rights and allows politicians, and indeed wider society, to engage in 'the politics of blame avoidance' (Pierson, 1996, p 179) and to point the finger at those accessing social security rights, including disabled people, while asserting the need to discipline and sanction them for their inactivity and 'irresponsible' reliance on benefits.

While the focus of this chapter has been on disability benefit reform in the UK, the issues and debates outlined have wider significance. Lindsay and Houston (2013) note the predominance of a 'behaviourist reading' among many governments' understandings, within and beyond the EU, of why significant numbers of citizens are claiming disability benefits. Such an approach fails to adequately acknowledge both the structural shifts in labour markets and the individual problems of ill-health and impairment as important factors in generating unemployment among disabled people. In Sweden, a new preoccupation with activation that individualises the causes and potential solutions for receipt of disability benefits and breaks with the principles previously associated with Nordic welfare states has been noted (Ulmestig, 2013). Further afield, Lunt and Horsfall (2013) highlight increased conditionality and compulsion as a feature of New Zealand's reform of sickness and incapacity benefits. The commitment of policy makers in the UK to a punitive, sanctions-based approach to enforce labour market activity among recipients of disability benefits may be more extreme than the responses favoured by their counterparts elsewhere (see for example van Berkel, 2013 on the positive potential of individualised support packages and engagement with employers alongside disabled people in the Netherlands). That said, many governments share common ground in looking to activation as a panacea for the 'disability benefits crisis' (Lindsay and Houston, 2013)

What, then, is the relevance of this discussion of conditionality (and how it has been used to reframe the rights and responsibilities of disabled people) to the wider competition state thesis (see Cerny, 1990; Cerny and Evans, 1999) and the other two themes of 'competition' and 'cognition' that are integral to this book? As Hudson and Horsfall note in their opening comments in Chapter Two, social policies that aim to promote a measure of social and economic equality/justice are now routinely jettisoned in order to deliver the economic competitiveness that is the hallmark of the competition state. Social citizenship in these 'challenging times' has seen the return of an overarching economic imperative. This has enabled recent governments to promote a populist 'politics of resentment' that allows them to present public expenditure cuts and systemic welfare retrenchment as necessary, reasonable and fair (Hoggett et al, 2013). The pursuit of 'more effective commodification' has been identified as the 'modus operandi' of the competition state (Cerny, 2010, p 6). Conditionality, with its apparently common-sense mantra that social security rights are contingent on fulfilling work-related responsibilities, and the active labour market policies that it promotes, serve to *re-commodify* the rights of the majority of working-age, disabled benefit recipients. The ongoing extension and intensification of conditionality has eroded the potential, identified by T.H. Marshall (1950), of *de-commodified* social rights, 'granted on the basis of citizenship rather than performance' (Esping-Andersen, 1990, p 21), to deliver substantive welfare for disadvantaged citizens, including many disabled people.

In short, conditionality delivers the commodification that the competition state demands. This consideration of the instrumental use of conditionality to activate and recommodify disabled people, who are increasingly seen as 'passive and irresponsible shirkers' rather than rights-bearing citizens, serves as a case study of how many states have responded to the realities of global competition by asserting work obligations over social rights. Conditionality and competition have combined to negatively reconfigure the ways in which (in)capacity and the welfare rights and work responsibilities of disabled people are conceived and understood. On a mundane level, it is disabled people themselves who have to shoulder the burdens of this shift, as many of those subsequently deemed fit for work have to then compete in local labour markets, which are increasingly characterised by low pay and insecurity, as global economic competition intensifies.

That said, the sickness and impairment that characterise many disabled people's daily lives does not diminish or disappear just because it is reclassified or downgraded by assessors or governments. Whether or not conditionality can deliver meaningful and sustained employment opportunities for disabled people in the future remains to be seen. However, given the current economic situation, it is unlikely to be effective in the short term. Nonetheless, an increasingly conditional welfare state based on sanction rather than support is the most likely future reality for all but a minority of disabled people with severe impairments. Rights to social security on the grounds of sickness and disability are being systematically reduced and removed. In the conditional, cash-strapped and competitive welfare states of the future it is highly likely that increasing numbers of disabled people will have little option but to accept the responsibility to undertake paid work, whether they are capable of it or not.

Notes

[1] The current intention is that all claimants of Incapacity Benefit (IB), Income Support and Severe Disablement Allowance will be phased onto Universal Credit in future. Although it is much delayed, roll-out began in May 2016 and is expected to be complete by September 2018 (DWP, 2016).

[2] Figures cited are the weekly amount for a single person, aged 25-plus on income-related ESA in April 2015 (https://www.gov.uk/employment-support-allowance/what-youll-get).

[3] In the WCA, applicants routinely undergo two tests: the limited capability to work assessment and the limited capability for work-related activity assessment. Initially, claimants fill in an ESA50 form, with many subsequently being called for assessment by a medical professional at Maximus, UK, the private company that took over the contract for conducting WCA in March 2015.

NINE

Global 'vulnerabilities': new configurations of competition in the era of conditionality?

Kate Brown

Introduction

Increased emphasis on personal responsibility and the steady erosion of social rights have been defining features of changing citizenship configurations in what Cerny and Evans (2004) called the 'competition state'. As is evident in policies such as the extension of conditional welfare arrangements (Dwyer, 2004; 2016 and Chapter Eight this volume) and increasingly punitive criminal justice sanctions in recent decades (Garland, 2001; Rodger, 2008; Wacquant, 2009), the behaviours of those who fail to meet standards of 'appropriate' behaviour are now surveilled and disciplined with intensified fervour (Burney, 2005; Flint, 2006; Harrison and Sanders, 2014). At the same time, though, ideas that gesture towards more inclusive approaches such as 'support', 'social inclusion' and 'partnership' have also influenced recalibrations of welfare in 'advanced' liberal democracies (Lister, 1998; Newman, 2001; Muncie, 2006). It is within this context that vulnerability has taken root as an influential and popular concept in policy making and in broader debates about welfare and regulatory provision. This chapter considers the role of ideas about vulnerability in reconfigurations and recalibrations of contemporary welfare, exploring the governance strategies and cultural scripts that these give rise to in an era of global competition.

Vulnerability is most often a 'taken for granted' or normative idea in policy and public spheres, a malleable and opaque concept characterised by plurality of meaning and constructed in relation to a wide range of factors (Appleton, 1999; Fawcett, 2009; Daniel, 2010). Drawing on the notion to frame its *Report on the world social situation*, the United Nations Department of Economic and Social Affairs (2003, p 8) notes that vulnerability is increasingly referenced in social policies but its use is 'quite loose' and tends to lack 'theoretical rigour'. In the context of austerity politics, organising welfare provision on the basis of prioritising the protection of the most vulnerable is often set out as strategy that makes sound financial and ethical sense. Equally, resistance to current welfare retrenchments or cuts to state services is also often couched in terms of unacceptable vulnerabilities that result from such changes. As one example, in 2013 the European Parliament initiated impact assessments of austerity measures on vulnerable groups within EU member states (see Lambert, 2013). Due in part to links with 'deservingness' in a global context dominated by austerity politics, vulnerability rationales are widely drawn on in debates about how best to foster social justice within a context of apparently scarce financial resources.

'Vulnerable people' seem to pose problems for 'advanced' liberal democracies in a number of ways. That some citizens are exposed to morally unacceptable levels of harm, extreme hardship or precariousness seems somehow to represent a tangible failure of market-orientated systems to 'naturally' ensure that people are provided with sufficient opportunities and resources. Those deemed vulnerable are also significant in that they are (in theory at least) members of the increasingly narrowing group of citizens who are deemed legitimately entitled to receive shelter from the harsher edges of capitalist systems via the welfare state. To be seen as vulnerable is in some ways to be exceptional or exempt from some of the expectations or responsibilities accorded to 'non-vulnerable' citizens, raising questions about how far 'the vulnerable' might be entitled to the enjoyment of equal social rights. In addition, it is unclear how far the popularity of vulnerability as a notion for configuring social difficulty extends to those who are configured as 'vulnerable' (Brown, 2015), linking the notion with stigma in a society that some have argued is increasingly divided into (false) 'them' and 'us' dichotomies (Tyler, 2013).

This chapter explores configurations of vulnerability in policy initiatives and practitioner narratives, and the clues that these may offer about governance in an era of global competition. In focusing on narratives and discourses of vulnerability the chapter draws on ideas of language as an important element of the material world (Fairclough, 2001), with social practices being seen as having semiotic elements that feature in the process of change within society (Wood and Kroger, 2000; Fairclough, 2001; 2003).[1] The first section of the chapter considers how the notion of vulnerability appears in academic work and in international, national and local policy. Some of the implications of focusing welfare initiatives on 'vulnerable' populations are then explored. To illuminate a more textured view of overall trends, the chapter then briefly considers findings from qualitative research into how vulnerability was operationalised by practitioners and strategists involved in local services for 'vulnerable' young people in one large English city. Rather than empirical insights being offered as evidence of global trends, the qualitative data enables links to be drawn between broader policy initiatives and the implications of vulnerability narratives on the ground, taking as an example one local area within a highly conditional and selectivist welfare system such as the UK (compare Dwyer, 2016). Taken together, international and local patterns illuminate that while vulnerability-based interventions create impressions of ethical provision, these can serve a legitimation of enhanced rationing and intensification of competition for resources among the least well-off.

Competing configurations of vulnerability

Although popularly drawn upon in the academic literature, the concept of vulnerability has received relatively little attention and lacks accepted indicators and methods of measurement (Hurst, 2008; Fawcett, 2009; Mackenzie et al, 2014). As I have explored in more detail elsewhere (Brown, 2015), how vulnerability is approached and understood varies considerably depending on disciplinary context and authors' theoretical orientations. For Wallbank and Herring (2013) and Misztal (2011), the indistinct boundaries of the concept make it well suited to reflecting the diversity of human experiences of adversity. For others, this imprecision and vagueness is more problematic, perhaps especially when it is drawn upon in 'applied' settings (see Hurst, 2008; Fawcett, 2009). The way in which vulnerability is configured and understood differently has implications for how it might be addressed, with a range of competing perspectives appearing across the vulnerability literature.

Vulnerability can be seen as 'natural' or 'innate', as is often the case in the child development literature (see James and James, 2008) and in certain disability writings (see Wishart, 2003). Others draw on vulnerability to bring into focus particular adverse experiences or circumstances, emphasising the special vulnerabilities of those who are 'in need' or likely to experience particular dangers or harms. In its situational usage, vulnerability has close links with deservingness and victimhood, often drawn upon in efforts to circumvent disadvantaged groups' being 'blamed' for their problems. Such understandings of vulnerability have been critiqued from a range of sociologically inclined standpoints that have variously argued that positioning individuals as inherently vulnerable can be patronising and obscures the role of social factors in the construction of adversity, which Wishart (2003, p 20) argues amounts to 'victim blaming'. Elsewhere, the 'risk society' thesis (Beck, 1992) has been used as a way of providing critical perspectives on vulnerability, with scholars highlighting how concerns with vulnerability are bound up with ontological concerns about insecurity and increased desire to control apparent hazards, threats or individuals (see Beck, 2009, p 178; Misztal, 2011).

Aside from its more normative use in the literature, carefully theorised socially and politically orientated understandings of vulnerability have also been advanced. Vulnerability has been a key concept in global human development literature for decades, where it has been used in analysis of the effects of natural disasters or environmental hazards. This literature tends to take the approach of 'measuring' vulnerability and how it differs between populations, with the notion often considered in relation to: risks of exposure to hazards; the likely seriousness of problems in the event of these; and the capacity of people/populations to cope with such problems (compare Chambers, 1989; Bankoff et al, 2004). This spatially orientated account of vulnerability draws attention not only to the particular problems or 'adversities' that vulnerable people might face, but to the role of social and political systems in shaping how effectively people can respond to these (see Watts and Bohle, 1993). Individual agency is often obscured in the geo-vulnerability literature, but social researchers have built on this work to show how lived experiences of vulnerability are mediated (over time) by social systems as well as by agency and more personal and individual factors (Emmel and Hughes, 2014).

More 'radical' perspectives on vulnerability have also been offered, which have been especially cultivated in the moral philosophy and critical legal theory literatures. A small but burgeoning literature here has argued that embracing vulnerability as a fundamental feature of humanity (Turner, 2006; Butler, 2012) and bringing it to the heart of the relationship between individuals and the state offers a way of disrupting, resisting and subverting traditional 'neo-liberal' narratives that emphasise entrepreneurship, 'active' citizenship (Fineman, 2013; Wallbank and Herring, 2013) and competition (see Carr, 2013). The 'universal vulnerability' scholars have argued that it is only when we see vulnerability as exceptional and 'other' that it supports market-orientated social policies; instead, it should be accepted as fundamental to human existence (Campbell, 1991; Fineman, 2008; Fineman and Grear, 2013; Wallbank and Herring, 2013). While offering an innovative account of interdependency and citizenship, there would seem to be significant challenges in terms of operationalising such an approach (see Peroni and Timmer, 2013). More generally, considering competing theorisations of vulnerability reveals a tension between broader and narrower ways of understanding the concept. Frictions between these perspectives are also mirrored in how vulnerability appears in policy, as the chapter now moves on to consider.

Vulnerability as a global and regional governance mechanism

A range of local, national and international policy initiatives are now concerned with addressing or highlighting the circumstances of 'vulnerable people', often making exceptions and advocating differential treatment on the basis of 'vulnerability'. Vulnerability has been a key concept in international development for decades (see Kirby, 2006), where spatially and scientifically orientated accounts of the notion tend to be drawn on to inform policy. The World Health Organization (Wisner and Adams, 2002) has drawn on the concept in responses to emergencies and disasters, taking poverty, homelessness and destitution as major contributors to vulnerability, stipulating women and children as among the most vulnerable to the effects of disasters (see Bradshaw, 2013). Although the concept's use in global non-governmental organisation initiatives often overlaps with notions of poverty (see Chambers, 1989), its conceptual reach stretches wider than economic deprivation. For example, in 2003 the United Nations Department of Economic and Social Affairs' *Report on the world social situation* used 'vulnerability' to frame new configurations of uncertainty and insecurity and to highlight globalised discriminations and exclusions that were 'not primarily market-related or market-generated but socially generated' (United Nations, 2003, p 9).

More recently, the United Nations Development Programme (UNDP, 2014, p iv) has placed vulnerability at the heart of efforts to address major international development challenges, advancing it as an 'immensely important' concept in securing human development progress and using vulnerability to make a case for a range of social protections, including universal access to social services (especially health and education), stronger employment benefits such as unemployment insurance and pensions, and a commitment to full employment. Similarly, the ILO has used the notion to delineate processes of marginalisation for the most disadvantaged and to draw attention to those who fall outside of the labour market (see Aassve et al, 2013), in some cases stipulating 'vulnerability determinants' like labour market positioning, limited access to social protections, 'stratification' (gender, education, age on so on) and individual biography, with especially vulnerable groups also identified (such as poor women, migrants and Roma people, see Scheil-Adlung and Kuhl, 2011, p 1). The World Bank (2005) has utilised the notion to configure poverty as a dynamic process and one connected with other social risks such as illness, violence and natural disasters. The OECD (2013b, pp 12 and 13) has also used the concept to investigate and address the integration of welfare services for populations with 'multiple disadvantages and complex needs', with the intention of activating 'vulnerable people' out of 'welfare dependency' over time.

In European governance systems, vulnerability has become highly significant in the configuration and operation of migration and asylum processes (Katsapaou, 2013). Vulnerability classifications have come to play an important role in decision making and case law in the ECHR (Peroni and Timmer, 2013), developments described by legal scholars as a 'quiet revolution' (Timmer, 2013), with groups such as Roma people, asylum seekers and people living with HIV now having secured different entitlements and protections due to their grouping as 'vulnerable'. Vulnerability is also important as a policy instrument in European housing policy (see Council of Europe, 2008; Lévy-Vroelant, 2010), where, again, particular groups are designated as vulnerable and deemed to require special support, including: migrants; disabled people; the elderly; Roma/Gypsy people; 'one-head' households; the unemployed; and victims of disasters and wars.

Turning to UK social policy to illustrate national-level vulnerability governance mechanisms in highly conditional welfare systems, the concept has been drawn upon in 'official' responses to certain social problems since the 1950s, but has become especially significant since the New Labour government came to power in 1997 (see Brown, 2015). It plays a crucial role in the governance of welfare for adults who are seen to lack the capacity to protect themselves (see Dunn et al, 2008; Hollomotz, 2011; McLaughlin, 2012), and in English housing policy 'vulnerability' is one of the several predicaments that trigger 'priority need' (see Carr and Hunter, 2008). It is a key notion in child-protection mechanisms for those under the age of 18 (see Daniel, 2010), and in UK criminal justice policy vulnerability rationales have been advanced in order to address 'unjust' treatment of offenders and victims via exemptions to mainstream police provision and judicial processes (Richards, 2011; Roulstone and Sadique, 2013). In migration policy too, initiatives like the Syrian 'vulnerable persons relation scheme' have made exceptions to 'regular' immigration policy, with 143 'vulnerable' Syrians (specified as victims of sexual violence, elderly people, victims of torture and disabled people) being granted five years' Humanitarian Protection under this scheme during 2014 (House of Commons Library, 2015).

The friendly face of narrowing entitlement?

Recent government initiatives often seem to draw on the strong ethical connotations of vulnerability as a way of legitimating prioritisation within a context of limited public spending. For the OECD (2013b), for example, addressing vulnerability is a means of justifying a targeted model of welfare on the basis that current levels of spending are unsustainable. Its report *Integrated service delivery for vulnerable groups* explicitly states an intention to 'help welfare systems across the OECD do more with less' (OECD, 2013b, p 6). While focusing or re-focusing resources on the most vulnerable can be an important trigger for help and support for some, this is often accompanied by narrowing resources. In the UK, the justification for the abolition of the national discretionary social fund for Community Care Grants and Crisis Loans and the introduction of (reduced) locally distributed Local Welfare Assistance was that 'societal needs [had] developed' since the Community Care Grant's introduction, and it had become 'difficult' for the Jobcentre Plus to identify the 'most vulnerable customers' (DWP, 2011a).[2] The impact assessment of the policy stated that the intervention was 'necessary in order to maximise the impact of funds currently allocated [...] on the most vulnerable people in society' (DWP, 2011a, p 1). In English local housing provision too, the Coalition government made claims to have 'prioritised protection for vulnerable people' under the 2010 austerity-led spending review (see Department for Communities and Local Government, 2012).

Initiatives that draw heavily on the prioritisation of the vulnerable could be considered to place those who face severe hardship into a competition for increasingly scarce state resources. This has been noted in relation to European housing policy (see Lévy-Vroelant, 2010), with homelessness developments in England perhaps illustrating this especially vividly. Meers (2014; 2015) notes that vulnerability classifications in English housing policy (sometimes called the Pereira Test or the vulnerability test) have been largely premised on competition for scarce resources, as, until recently, to be legally classified as vulnerable an individual must have been deemed to be in a worse situation that an 'ordinary' homeless person. Meers (2014) argues that in practice this resulted in 'downward drag' of vulnerability classifications, with the numbers of people deemed vulnerable in English homelessness provision having steadily declined in the last decade. The Scottish Government has now phased out the vulnerability test, favouring a more 'entitlement'-based system (see Watts, 2014), and a recent Supreme Court ruling in England has revised the vulnerability test in the light of such problems. The Court's judgment document notes that vulnerability is a 'comparative concept', with its delineation involving verdicts that deem that circumstances such as heroin addiction, acute learning difficulties, severe health problems, suicidal tendencies and psychosis 'would not necessarily be anything unusual' (*Hotak v London Borough of Southwark*, p 8). While the court ruled that the comparator should henceforth be an 'ordinary person if made homeless' (rather than an 'ordinary homeless person'), the principle of relationing endures. Such developments underline how notions of vulnerability can induce surprisingly close points of comparison when drawn on operationally in determining provision.

When particular groups or individuals are singled out for special treatment on the basis of vulnerability, this would often seem to involve a process of inclusion and exclusion, or a policing of the boundaries of entitlement or resources. This is perhaps especially pertinent where policies draw on the notion of particular 'vulnerable groups', which tend to be 'identity based' (related to factors such as gender and ethnicity) and/or 'status based' (related to circumstances) (Fineman, 2013, p 16), although who is deemed to constitute this group varies widely. Where vulnerability lines are drawn has important implications in practice. Peroni and Timmer (2013) argue that while the 'vulnerable-group formulation' has provided the ECHR with a valuable means of addressing the inequalities, discrimination and prejudices that highly disadvantaged groups such as Roma people, people with HIV and asylum seekers have faced, at the same time a 'narrowly defined set of factors' (Peroni and Timmer, 2013, p 1069) mean that other citizens who experience similar discrimination do not enjoy the same justice and protection (national minorities, religious minorities and LGBT people, for example). Group-level vulnerability classifications can obscure difference within social groups, too.

Considering international, national and local vulnerability governance instruments highlights tensions between structurally inclined views of vulnerability and more individually orientated perspectives. Where they appear normatively as a way of designating people for special attention or 'deservingness', vulnerability narratives arguably strip away the political and economic dimensions of disadvantage, implying that vulnerability is 'accidental' or 'personal', triggering 'helping' interventions rather than responses that address underlying social inequalities (Ecclestone and Goodley, 2014; Ecclestone and Lewis, 2014). When applied in policy, vulnerability is often a concept tied to particularism, delineated to include and exclude in some way. While some internationally orientated vulnerability initiatives would seem to bring into focus a view of disadvantage and precariousness linked with the structures and institutions that shape or mediate it, these are perhaps similarly inclined to support a view of 'deservingness' based on moral capital rather than entitlement. Turning now to findings from in-depth qualitative research into how 'vulnerability' operated in services for 'vulnerable' young people in an English city, we can explore how some of these broader themes might play out at the 'front line' of provision in one geographical area within a highly conditional national welfare context such as the UK.

A local view: vulnerability in practice

The empirical data presented here was generated through semi-structured interviews with 15 key informants who were involved in delivering, managing or commissioning services for 'vulnerable' young people, along with other ethnographic insights gathered through informal meetings, interactions and conversations. Throughout the research there was a deliberate focus on processes of exclusion and inclusion in relation to how the concept of vulnerability was operationalised (see Brown, 2013). While findings were particular to one local English context, they provide insights into some of the ways in which the classification of vulnerability operates to reconfigure and recalibrate welfare in the context of an increasingly conditional and selectivist welfare system such as the UK's.

Global and national patterns of prioritisation based on vulnerability were to some extent mirrored in practitioner narratives of their day-to-day deployment of the concept. In the business of local provision, vulnerability functioned as a kind of informal currency or lever by which resources could be triggered. The concept was frequently used as an organising principle by which to prioritise people within the wider operation and delivery of busy services:

> "it might be that from looking at referrals, we identify the children we think are most vulnerable and needed seeing more urgently possibly than others". (Project Worker, young carers' service)

Vulnerability was seen as a "kinder" way of configuring disadvantage than other ideas. For example, as one retired Commissioner phrased it, calling a young person vulnerable was "better than saying the child is stupid or is neglected or deviant". Interestingly, though, the language of vulnerability tended to be drawn upon mainly within professional contexts rather than in direct work with young people and their families (see Brown, 2015).

Identifying and prioritising vulnerability seemed to be core to the effectiveness or 'entrepreneurship' in service provision. Informants commented on how the notion was well suited to processes of 'rationing' support and assistance for young people:

> "it makes people actually focus on those particular groups. And I think it works well because I mean basically because there's less money around they've got to target services ..." (Manager, Youth Counselling Service)

Offering reflections on this rationing process in times of welfare retrenchment, one senior clinical psychologist explained how vulnerability classifications might be reconfigured as wider resources issues became more pressing:

> "in times of economic plenty when government spending is higher, then people are more generous in terms of applying their criteria, and at times where government spending is restricted, people are a bit more clear about drawing lines around their referral criteria. And so the pool of the young people which don't fit into any category becomes bigger." (Senior Clinical Psychologist, Child and Adolescent Mental Health Service)

In these quotations we see evidence of vulnerability functioning at the local level as a type of currency and moral capital, drawn upon in a race for resources, raising important questions about where the lines and demarcations of vulnerability are drawn.

Vulnerability meant different things to different people, and practitioners often noted that defining it was difficult. While a focus on vulnerability offered opportunities for a wide range of young people's difficulties to be taken into account – often leading to dynamic and interrelated rather than static accounts of adversity – this also meant that it was difficult to pin down who might be included and excluded in the classification. As I have argued elsewhere (Brown,

2015), vulnerability judgements were to some extent contingent on personal judgements and dependent on the values and perspectives of practitioners. As one Family Intervention Project practitioner put it, how people assessed vulnerability was dependent on someone's "world view". While practitioners felt that this presented problems in terms of consistency and objective measurement, another reading of this might be that the subjectivity of the concept also offered potential spaces for resistance to increasing tendencies to manage and classify people based on 'objective' risk factors (see Feeley and Simon, 1992; Lupton, 1999).

Qualification for support via vulnerability-based interventions was also contingent to some degree on behaviour, and on 'vulnerable' young people responding 'actively' or 'appropriately' to interventions. Here, in a discussion of interventions for vulnerable young people, we see concerns about vulnerability merging with ideas that young people may not be sufficiently enterprising (compare Kelly, 2006):

> "I think we've really moved from doing it 'to' people to supporting them to do it for themselves in that sense. You can keep throwing services at families for as long as there are hours in the day but if they don't – I'm not saying something unique you know – if they don't actually want to change or want to do something different or want to have a better something or even see that what you're offering them is better, you're on a hiding to nothing you're wasting your time." (Commissioner, Education Services)

There are clear echoes of the responsibilisation agenda here, and, as I have argued elsewhere (Brown, 2015), this means that ideas of vulnerability when drawn on in practice can map onto the operation of a kind of 'agency tightrope', where those on the receiving end of interventions are expected to behave in ways that conform to somewhat contradictory preoccupations about the *lack of agency* associated with deference and passivity and also *active* agency associated with contemporary citizenship arrangements.

Young people who were seen to behave irresponsibly or problematically were less likely to enjoy the benefits of vulnerability classifications (see Brown, 2014 and 2015), but this went beyond simply individual practitioner judgments and moral views. As Lipsky (1980) highlights, such individual practitioner judgements were shaped by wider structures, systems and processes that underpinned the provision of services at 'street level'. In the case of vulnerability mechanisms in the context of a race for resources, some informants implied a tension between their service being able to stick to its agreed performance indicators (most often aimed at reducing specific difficulties) and the significant challenges that 'vulnerable' young people's behaviour could pose in the course of achieving these targets:

> SOCIAL CARE MANAGER: ... vulnerability is a phrase that's used a lot, but I guess I tend to think that a lot of the people who provide the services for vulnerable children, if you like, cherry-pick the easy to engage. I'm not sure they always reach the most needy and the most vulnerable.
> KATE: Why do you think that?
> SOCIAL CARE MANAGER: Well, I guess because if you're being commissioned to provide a service, you want to show that, you know, you've been very successful, so you pick the quick wins [...] I think it can sometimes mean that those who are most vulnerable, most in need, most at risk get less services.

Some informants alluded to a tension between achieving 'outcomes' and managing 'problem' behaviour. One informant from a private sector education service spoke about her efforts in trying to include a young person who had been volatile:

> "it's just the way she talks, 'fucking bastard' and that sort of stuff, I said it's just not [acceptable] ... and it's starting right back at that and how she dealt with people on a day to day basis, but you're trying to do that alongside trying to do five lots of GCSE coursework ..." (Manager, Education Service)

In a context of target-based and outcome-orientated performance measurement systems for organisations that support vulnerable people, vulnerability classifications would often seem to support tacit conditionality when operationalised, with the 'least enterprising' individuals potentially less well served in provision.

Concluding comments: a race to the bottom?

Vulnerability has become an increasingly prevalent and important notion in policy making, internationally and in national and local contexts. Indeed, the concept seems to be something of a zeitgeist or 'spirit of the time' in contemporary social policy; an intellectually fashionable notion that reflects and recalibrates welfare and disciplinary processes in a range of ways (Brown, 2014; 2015). Its popularity might be explained in part by its capacity to reconcile 'supportive' and more punitive approaches, on the surface at least. Although in theory it is a concept that can emphasise interdependence and would seem to offer alternatives to economic liberal citizenship models, normative vulnerability initiatives often serve to support a competition for resources among those who are least well off, averting the gaze from wider questions about the distribution of resources and (dis)advantages in society. In this respect, vulnerability-based interventions might form part of wider moves in the direction of narrowing entitlement, further underlining social divisions of welfare and social control (Harrison and Sanders, 2014).

Vulnerability mechanisms operate to form an additional 'net' for those who might fall through the gaps in a broader 'safety net'. In welfare systems within what Cerny and Evans (2004) might describe as competition states, practices aimed at addressing vulnerability seem simultaneously to function as instruments for insulating people from severe economic and social hardship, and also to serve wider recalibrations away from more universal approaches based on entitlement. Vulnerability represents a focal point that most can agree is important, and its malleability may well add to its appeal, but differentiated and contested understandings of the concept also seem to give rise to fragmented responses to social difficulty. Harvey (2005, p 177) draws attention to how tendencies to disperse and diversify support for those less well off help to accelerate the withdrawal of state provision and a fragmented system of provision where dispossession can advance more rapidly. Although deployed with progressive aims in mind and often in well-meaning ways, vulnerability rationales could perhaps be seen as one of the latest incarnations of such developments.

If, as Tyler (2013) has argued, stigma is an important element of 'advanced' liberal governance, it might be questioned how far vulnerability narratives in policy serve a wider problematisation of the behaviour of particular individuals, implying distinctions between the actions/situations of certain populations and the behaviour/circumstances of supposedly 'ordinary' (or 'non-vulnerable') people. Discretion associated with vulnerability rationales can also support the currency of 'moral capital' being important in the drawing down of state support. This has particular implications for which individuals/groups are likely to be the forerunners and stragglers in a race for resources based on vulnerability. Those popularly imagined as vulnerable and those who conform to norms of 'acceptable' or 'compliant' behaviour would seem to be advantaged. The English context suggests that in highly conditional welfare systems at least, vulnerability rationales are bound up with tacit behavioural conditionalities in welfare provision, facilitating state actors to exert managerial accountability and political control over who gains access to support and resources. While there is nothing new about welfare support being tied to particular behaviours, the rise of vulnerability in policy and practice perhaps represents a reconfiguration of these dynamics, wrapping retrenchment and conditionality in a friendly face.

This is not to say that vulnerability rationales are not helpful in some respects. Tracing global and local vulnerability governance mechanisms highlights that important support is distributed to some groups and individuals via vulnerability initiatives. Entitlements can be safeguarded or enhanced for those who are most in need. Vulnerability policy and practice mechanisms can also help to create spaces in which state actors and schemes can mobilise to mitigate against the severe social difficulties faced by some, perhaps resisting or contesting the narrowing of provision, or expanding entitlement in certain instances. Especially in more international vulnerability initiatives, there are indications of the concept's being deployed to illustrate more structural and multidimensional accounts of disadvantage. At the same time ,though, it is hard to escape that even where structural accounts of vulnerability are evident, such a gaze still avoids relational questions about whose lives and vulnerabilities count more than others in a deeply unequal world (see Butler, 2004; 2012).

Cerny and Evans (2004) argued that the welfare state is founded on a paradox of supporting market-based political systems by insulating people from the dysfunctions of such systems, while also carrying the potential to undermine such systems through offering shelter from the harsher edges of capitalist societies. 'The vulnerable' seem to occupy a social and conceptual space at the very heart of this tension. In capitalist societies, acute vulnerability is in some respects unacceptable and in need of mitigation, a tangible failure of market-orientated political systems. At the same time though, unconditional support for vulnerable people also threatens to expand the welfare state beyond levels of acceptability in 'advanced' liberal democracies. In this context, subtle behavioural regulation and exclusionary processes are infused and extended through the increasing popularity of vulnerability narratives in social policy. The capacity of the vulnerability zeitgeist to induce a direct competition for scarce resources between individuals who face the extremes of hardship should be noted as part of wider recalibrations of welfare and erosions of social rights.

Notes

[1] Understanding of 'discourse' was influenced by definitions provided by Fairclough (2003, pp 123–4), who sees discourse as rules governing groups of statements or 'bodies of texts'. Fairclough's understandings of discourse are heavily influenced by Foucault (1972; 1984), as are more general approaches to critical discourse analysis.

[2] Thanks to Chris Grover for flagging these developments.

TEN

Convergence of government ideology in an era of global competition: an empirical analysis using comparative manifesto data

Stefan Kühner

Introduction

One of the tenets of the competition state and globalisation efficiency theses has been that the end of Keynesian demand-led policies triggered a convergence of partisan and government policy positions in regard to the market economy, government efficiency and the welfare state. For instance, Cerny (1997; 1999, p 3) saw 'the recasting of party ideology' – which they understand as 'accepting the imperatives of international competitiveness and consumer choice as having a higher ideological status than domestic social solidarity' – as a key dimension of the competition state. This key dimension of competition 'stateness' has, however, proved extremely difficult to operationalise. For instance, Horsfall (2010, pp 59–60; see also: Horsfall, 2013a), in the most serious attempt to empirically test the competition state thesis to date, bemoans the complexity of quantifying government ideological shifts and cautions against simplistic dichotomous, unsystematic, naïve or subjective attempts to capture convergence of partisan and government ideology in an era of global competition. As a result, Horsfall (2010; 2013a,b) refrains from including any such indicator in his analysis altogether.

The focus in the competition state literature on political agency mirrors a long-lasting debate on the effect of partisan difference in the comparative welfare state research. Here, the dominant question has become whether 'party ideology actually matters' for the policies and politics of the welfare state (see Häusermann et al, 2013 for a comprehensive summary). Indeed, a number of important quantitatively informed applications have failed to find any partisan effects (for example Huber and Stephens, 2001; Allan and Scruggs, 2004), while the 'new politics' thesis of the welfare state – primarily drawing on comparative historical evidence – forcefully contends that partisan difference has ceased to matter for welfare state change post-1980 (Pierson, 1996; but see also Giger and Nelson, 2011; Bonoli and Natali, 2012 for more recent appraisals). Here, analysts have increasingly made use of data published by the Manifesto Research Group/Comparative Manifesto Project (MRG/CMP/MARPOR) (Budge et al, 2001; Klingemann et al, 2006) to better capture the ideological positions of parties, electors and governments. This project has been in operation since 1979, coding literally thousands of party manifestos issued by hundreds of parties in 57 countries roughly covering the period from 1950 to 2015 (see Volkens et al, 2014). Given the many limitations of alternative attempts to trace government ideology placements across time and space, MRG/CMP/MARPOR offers the most preferable data readily available to date. In 2003 the MRG/CMP/MARPOR received a prize from the American Political Science Association for the best data set in comparative politics, and it now benefits from a long-term grant from the German Science Foundation.

The primary purpose of this chapter is to consolidate discussions within the disjointed competition state and partisan difference literatures outlined above. It will make use of MRG/CMP/MARPOR data to fill an obvious lacuna within the competition state literature and test empirically whether 'the recasting of party ideology' identified by Cerny (1997) and Cerny and Evans (1999) has *actually* occurred in comparative and historical perspective and, if so, whether there are specific processes of government ideology convergence that the proponents of the competition state thesis should be mindful of. To answer these questions, the chapter will employ a series of relatively simple descriptive statistical and graphical tools to test whether the variation of partisan and government policy placements has been reduced and whether the overall policy space of parliamentary parties and governments has shifted across a sample of 12 mature Western welfare regimes. Analysis of the MRG/CMP/MARPOR data suggests that, despite a considerable degree of convergence of party preferences after 1980, the rather broad-brush notion of a general 'race to the right' is overstated, as the processes of shifting ideological party positions vary hugely in different countries.

This sample was deliberately chosen to provide a balanced variation across key consociational and corporatist constitutional structures. Three countries were chosen in each of the four corners of Lijphart's

(1999) two-dimensional map of consensus democracy; six of these, namely Australia, Canada, France, New Zealand, the United Kingdom and the United States, are typically classified as pluralist, whereas the other six, Austria, Denmark, Finland, Germany, the Netherlands and Sweden, score high on Siaroff's (1999) integrated corporatism scale. Six countries, namely Australia, Canada, France, New Zealand, the United Kingdom and the United States, feature majoritarian or median voter-dominated electoral systems, with a comparatively small number of effective legislative parties, whereas the others, with exception of Austria, have proportional systems with a relatively high number of effective parties (Iversen and Soskice, 2006). The 12 countries are also distributed evenly around the mean of overall welfare generosity scores (Scruggs and Allan, 2006, p 68) and represent different memberships to the competition state ideal-types identified by Horsfall (2010; 2013b), namely neoliberal (Australia, Canada, United States) and pro-competition (United Kingdom, New Zealand, Finland; weak pro-competition: France) versus active (Denmark, Sweden, Netherlands, Austria) and conservative (Germany).

Tracing party ideology with MRG/CMP/MARPOR data

Inherent in Cerny and Evans' (Cerny, 1997; Cerny and Evans, 1999) competition state thesis is the notion that party ideology is not constant but, rather, subject to considerable shifts in response to the changing global economic context. MRG/CMP/MARPOR data is based on textual analysis of party manifestos made by parties themselves and, unlike similar data based on expert surveys, captures party ideological positions across time and space. The MRG/CMP/MARPOR project codes policy statements using a mixture of trained human coders and computerised counts of certain keywords in party election programmes. Each sentence of each political text under scrutiny is placed into one of 56 policy-issue categories, which are subsequently grouped into seven major policy areas (see Appendix Table A10.1). Each category is a variable that represents the percentage of the total number of policy statements dealing with this specific policy strategy. The sum of policy statements always adds up to 100%, making manifesto information comparable across all party manifesto documents. Importantly, this characteristic of MRG/CMP/MARPOR data enables the construction of encompassing indices of Left–Right party positions. In probably the most common of such indices, Laver and Hunt (1992; see also: Budge et al, 2001) divide 26 of these policy issue-categories into 13 'Left' and 13 'Right-wing' categories (Table 10.1).[1]

Table 10.1: Left–Right index of party position (Laver-Hunt)

Right-wing categories	Left-wing categories
• Free enterprise	• Market regulation
• Incentives	• Economic planning
• Protectionism: negative	• Protectionism: positive
• Economic orthodoxy	• Controlled economy
• Welfare state limitation	• Nationalisation
• Constitutionalism: positive	• Anti-imperialism: positive
• Political authority: positive	• Military: negative
• National way of life: positive	• Peace
• Traditional morality: positive	• Internationalism: positive
• Law and order	• Democracy
• Social harmony	• Welfare state expansion
• Freedom and human rights	• Education expansion
• Military: positive	• Labour groups: positive

Note: Positive = favourable mentions or support; negative = hostile or unfavourable mentions or opposition.

Broadly defined Left–Right ideological positions scores are, however, too wide in scope to be of much value to test Cerny's (1997) and Cerny and Evans' (1999, p 3) specific focus on shifting party preferences in regard to 'deregulation, liberalisation, and flexibilisation', as well as the subordination of the welfare state 'to economic policies supporting, maintaining and even promoting transnational and international market processes and governance structures'. Although not a perfect fit, Cusack and Engelhardt (2002) developed an alternative Left–Right index that is more useful for the purposes of this chapter. Their approach considers party manifestos' commitment to the 'market economy' and 'governmental and administrative efficiency' (identifying Right party preferences) versus commitment to the 'welfare state' and the 'planned economy' (identifying Left party preferences). Thereby, the commitment to the 'market economy' is computed as the average of the individual scores for the variables 'free enterprise' and 'economic orthodoxy'; the 'welfare state' measure combines positive mentions of 'social justice' and 'welfare state expansion', while the 'planned economy' looks at the variables 'market regulation', 'economic planning', 'Keynesian demand management', 'controlled economy' and 'nationalisation'. The Cusack-Engelhardt (2002) index is calculated using the equation provided in Table 10.2; the party position is indicated by index scores that can vary between -100 (pure Left) and +100 (pure Right). In other words, a positive score represents a bias towards Right, a negative score a bias towards Left policy preferences.

Comparing shifts within the four Left/Right concepts comprising the Cusack-Engelhardt (2002) index helps to shed light on Cerny

Table 10.2: Left–Right index of party position (Cusack and Engelhardt, 2002)

Concept	Variables
Market economy	Free enterprise + economic orthodoxy
Governmental and administrative efficiency	Governmental and administrative efficiency
Planned economy	Market regulation + economic planning + Keynesian demand management + controlled economy + nationalisation
Welfare state	Social justice + welfare state expansion

$$= ((\text{Market economy} + \text{Governmental and administrative efficiency})$$
$$- (\text{Planned economy} + \text{Welfare state}))/\text{BASE}$$

Note: The 'base' combines all categories in the nominator.

and Evans' claims about shifts in party ideology. To minimise complexity, the discussion will initially focus on the major parties in the four countries that have featured most frequently in comparative welfare research in recent years: the United Kingdom, Germany, the Netherlands and Denmark (see for example Vis, 2010).

Unsurprisingly, there are important differences in the respective parties' preferences according to the MRG/CMP/MARPOR data (Table 10.3). First, considering the mean scores for the periods between 1950 and the early 2010s, an emphasis of the 'market economy' has been a key feature of the Conservative People's Party in Denmark, while the Christian Democratic Appeal in the Netherlands lags behind both the Conservative Party in the United Kingdom and the Christian Democratic Union/Social Union in Germany. Rather than a commitment to the 'market economy', the data suggests that the Christian Democratic Appeal in the Netherlands has historically had a comparatively strong emphasis on 'governmental and administrative efficiency' and the 'welfare state' (the latter being roughly similar to the German Christian Democratic Union/Social Union).[2] This is not to say that the Conservatives in the United Kingdom and Denmark are necessarily hostile to the welfare state per se. Indeed, the sum of positive mentions of 'social justice' and 'welfare state expansion' in party manifestos is not too dissimilar to the commitment to 'governmental and administrative efficiency' in all four countries – at least, prior to the very early 2010s, where, in response to the financial crisis, we see a general surge in emphasis of 'governmental and administrative efficiency' by the Conservative Party in the United Kingdom and to slightly lesser extent by the Christian Democratic Appeal in the Netherlands. Compared to this, the Conservative and

Table 10.3: Tracing party ideology with MRG/CMP/MARPOR data

United Kingdom	Conservative Party				Labour Party				Liberal Party			
	ME	EF	WS	PE	ME	EF	WS	PE	ME	EF	WS	PE
1950s	1.44	1.3	2.9	1.8	0.3	0.0	6.1	3.2	3.8	2.7	2.1	0.7
1960s	3.7	3.2	4.3	0.4	0.5	1.8	6.6	1.2	0.4	3.7	6.0	1.0
1970s	2.6	3.9	5.2	0.8	0.8	1.4	5.4	2.6	0.6	1.9	4.9	2.1
1980s	6.4	6.6	2.4	0.3	0.9	0.7	7.0	2.6	1.5	2.7	5.0	1.3
1990s	3.4	4.6	3.6	0.9	1.0	3.7	7.4	1.0	1.1	1.6	6.3	0.9
2000s	1.2	2.8	3.8	0.4	0.6	1.9	5.9	0.4	0.7	3.6	4.2	0.7
2010s	2.3	8.7	3.1	0.4	2.4	1.8	5.8	0.6	2.8	5.5	3.4	0.9
Mean	3.3	4.4	3.6	0.7	0.9	1.6	6.3	1.7	1.6	3.1	4.5	1.1

Netherlands	Christian Democratic Appeal				Labour Party				People's Party for Freedom and Democracy			
	ME	EF	WS	PE	ME	EF	WS	PE	ME	EF	WS	PE
1950s	–	–	–	–	1.1	2.0	8.6	1.5	10.8	1.9	4.3	1.2
1960s	–	–	–	–	0.8	1.8	9.2	1.8	6.9	1.7	4.2	1.2
1970s	1.5	2.6	4.8	1.5	0.2	1.5	11.0	1.7	7.5	4.5	4.2	0.6
1980s	2.1	6.3	5.3	0.7	1.7	5.8	7.4	1.3	5.7	9.0	3.8	0.5
1990s	1.0	6.1	4.0	0.8	0.5	4.0	5.5	0.5	2.2	8.6	2.0	0.4
2000s	1.7	5.6	5.5	0.4	1.1	4.5	6.0	0.4	3.5	7.3	3.4	0.3
2010s	2.6	6.5	4.8	0.5	1.4	4.7	7.4	1.2	4.7	11.5	3.0	0.6
Mean	1.8	5.4	4.9	0.8	0.9	3.4	7.9	1.2	5.9	6.3	3.6	0.7

(continued)

Germany	Christian Democratic Union/Social Union				Social Democratic Party				Free Democrats			
	ME	EF	WS	PE	ME	EF	WS	PE	ME	EF	WS	PE
1950s	6.6	2.9	3.3	1.1	1.3	1.9	4.3	1.5	5.3	4.8	3.1	0.6
1960s	3.3	4.5	3.8	0.5	2.5	4.9	4.5	0.8	3.6	7.4	4.1	0.8
1970s	3.4	4.6	6.1	0.9	0.7	3.2	9.1	0.8	3.8	4.1	3.3	0.9
1980s	5.1	2.6	5.7	0.2	1.2	2.6	7.8	0.4	2.7	5.3	3.2	0.6
1990s	1.4	2.8	2.9	0.7	0.6	3.7	6.9	0.9	3.9	7.5	3.2	0.4
2000s	3.3	9.0	2.7	1.0	1.1	5.6	6.4	1.4	4.5	10.5	2.8	1.0
2010s	1.9	3.0	3.8	1.2	0.9	1.0	9.7	2.0	4.7	8.0	2.7	1.1
Mean	3.6	4.2	4.0	0.8	1.2	3.3	7.0	1.1	4.1	6.8	3.2	0.8

Denmark	Conservative People's Party				Social Democratic Party				Venstre – Liberals			
	ME	EF	WS	PE	ME	EF	WS	PE	ME	EF	WS	PE
1950s	8.3	1.2	2.1	0.2	0.3	0.0	7.2	0.9	6.4	0.6	1.1	0.3
1960s	11.4	2.9	2.7	0.2	0.2	0.7	7.5	0.4	6.2	3.6	3.7	0.1
1970s	8.5	2.3	1.4	1.3	0.7	0.8	10.0	1.0	6.7	0.9	2.4	1.0
1980s	5.5	4.3	2.0	0.2	1.3	1.4	3.3	1.1	7.9	2.9	2.0	0.4
1990s	5.0	5.8	3.1	0.3	1.3	2.2	7.4	0.4	6.5	2.9	2.0	0.4
2000s	5.7	2.3	8.2	0.2	0.7	0.9	10.9	0.5	5.5	3.5	6.6	0.4
2010s	7.4	0.0	6.3	0.0	2.1	8.3	8.0	2.1	6.8	0.0	12.6	1.2
Mean	7.4	2.7	3.7	0.3	0.9	2.0	7.7	0.9	6.6	2.0	4.3	0.5

Note: ME = market economy; EF = governmental and administrative efficiency; WS = welfare state; PE = planned economy. Figures refer to averages scores for all variables in each concept (see Table 10.4).

Christian Democratic parties' commitment to the 'planned economy' – maybe unsurprisingly – has been much lower historically.

As for the Labour/Social Democratic parties, the overall emphasis on the 'planned economy' is also relatively low, certainly considerably lower than commitments to the 'welfare state'. Here, the Labour Party in the Netherlands and the Social Democratic Party in Denmark are slightly ahead of the MRG/CMP/MARPOR scores of the Labour Party in the United Kingdom and the Social Democrats in Germany. The German Social Democratic Party stands out – together with the Dutch Labour Party – for its relatively strong emphasis of 'government and administrative efficiency'. The key dividing line between the Conservative/Christian Democratic and Labour/Social Democratic parties, then, is the commitment to the 'market economy', which remains relatively low in the latter cases across time. Finally, the findings for the main Liberal parties in the four countries also show some interesting differences: again somewhat unsurprisingly, the scores for the 'planned economy' are low throughout. At the same time, the Danish Liberal Party and the Liberal Democrats in the United Kingdom score relatively high in regard to their commitment to the 'welfare state', while the key feature of the Free Democrats in Germany has been their long-lasting commitment to 'government and administrative efficiency'. The Dutch People's Party for Freedom and Democracy scores high on the two Right categories, namely, its commitment to the 'market economy' and 'governmental and administrative efficiency'.

There are, of course, important changes over time that are not captured simply by looking at overall mean scores, and considering the dynamics of MRG/CMP/MARPOR data over time provides a much better test for the alleged 'recasting of party ideology' identified by Cerny (1997) and Cerny and Evans (1999). Indeed, there are some clear indications supporting the notion of party ideology convergence. There is relatively little movement in the scores for the different Conservative/Christian Democratic parties and the key differences in the characteristics discussed above largely remained intact across time (with the possible exception of the German Christian Democratic/Social Union, which saw a reduction in its commitment to the 'welfare state' during the 1990s and 2000s). Developments within the Labour/Social Democratic movements are maybe more instructive. In the United Kingdom, there has been a clear increase in the emphasis of the 'market economy' and 'governmental and administrative efficiency', especially since the 1990s; simultaneously the commitment to the 'planned economy' dropped considerably, while emphasis of the 'welfare state' remained fairly stable despite some small reductions during the 1970s and 2000s. In the Netherlands, we can see a similar development. There is a marked increase in emphasis of the 'market economy' and 'governmental and administrative efficiency' during the 1980s and since the 2000s, with a similar reduction of the commitment to a 'planned economy' during the same time. What is more, the MRG/CMP/MARPOR data suggests that the Dutch Labour Party's commitment to the 'welfare state' about halved between the 1970s and 1990s/2000s. The German and Danish Social Democratic parties also show reductions in commitment to the 'welfare state' during the 1980s and 1990, but the party manifestos show a reversal of this trend since the 2000s.

Adding to the general impression of a Right shift of the party ideological space is the fact that Liberal parties in the four countries have also emphasised more clearly the Right categories in the Cusack-Engelhardt (2002) index. There is a considerable increase in the commitment to 'efficient governmental and administrative practices' in the Dutch People's Party for Freedom and Democracy (the scores for the 1980s–2010s are more than double those prior to the 1980s), the German Free Democrats (particularly in the 1990s, 2000s and 2010s) and – with some distance – the Danish Venstre Party (scores increase after the 1970s in particular). Here, the changes are slightly different for the United Kingdom's Liberal Democrats, where the commitment to 'governmental and administrative efficiency' increased relatively late (not before the 2000s).

Tracing Left–Right party positions with MRG/CMP/ MARPOR data

Examining only three parties within four countries provides a limited perspective, so this section extends the analysis to consider all major parliamentary parties covered in the MRG/CMP/MARPOR data to test for *sigma convergence* of ideological preferences (see Appendix Table A10.2 for a full list of the parties included). Two possible mechanisms of sigma convergence are typically distinguished in the literature: one simply being concerned with reductions of variation across time and space (sometimes referred to as 'growing together') and one additionally considering shifts in the overall policy space of parliamentary parties to indicate the general direction of travel (sometimes referred to as 'race to the top/bottom', or here 'race to the Left/Right') (see Heichel et al, 2005). In order to capture these different processes, standard deviations of partisan ideology are computed over ten-yearly intervals; I also consider changes in the mean scores of partisan preferences according to MRG/CMP/MARPOR data. For reasons of simplicity, these summary statistics are not weighted by the number of parliamentary seats for each party. To make the vast amount of available data manageable, I move beyond the consideration of individual policy-issue categories from above and focus the discussion on the Cusack-Engelhardt (2002) index of Left/Right party positions introduced above (Table 10.4).

This confirms the picture of party ideology convergence identified above, but again suggests that the empirical picture is slightly more intricate than is typically appreciated. We can see a fairly common trend of Labour/Social Democratic (and Socialist) parties moving towards the centre ground after the 1980s, a development that is particularly pronounced in Australia, Austria (until 1999), Finland, France, New Zealand (during the late 1970s and 1980s) and Sweden (from the mid-1970s until the early 2000s). Indeed, the standard deviation of Left–Right party positions decreased in no fewer than 10 out of the 12 observed countries between the 1980s and 2000s, with particularly pronounced changes in Austria (a reduction of the standard deviation from 60.3 during the 1980s to 34.1 in the 2000s), Finland (47.1 to 19.2), France (68.8 to 45.1), the United Kingdom (53.2 to 35.2) and the United States (59.3 to 39.4). There are only few cases in which the overall reduction of the standard deviation coincides with a general shift of party preferences to the Right according to the overall mean scores of all parties; here it is again the 1980s that present a clear dividing line in countries such as Austria (a change in the mean Left–Right party position from -30.6 during the 1970s to +15.5 during the 1980s), the Netherlands (from -24.2 to +7.1), New Zealand (from -43.5 to -1.1), Sweden (from -52.9 to -21.8) and the United Kingdom (from -37.9 to -10.6).

However, these Right shifts have been sustained only in the Netherlands and (to a lesser extent) the United Kingdom and there has been an apparent general Left shift of party preferences during the 2000s elsewhere. This trend is somewhat surprising, but there are three developments that help to explain this finding. First, it was not only Labour/Social Democratic countries, but also some Liberal/Conservative/Christian Democratic parties that noticeably moved towards the centre ground. Second, many party systems have experienced the introduction of new parties, particularly Green parties (but also new Left alliances, often disappointed with the Labour/Social Democratic/Socialist movements, and even, at times, new nationalistic/radical right parties increasingly opposed to the impact of

Table 10.4: Tracing Left–Right party positions with MRG/CMP/MARPOR data

	1950s	1960s	1970s	1980s	1990s	2000s	2010s
Australia							
SDEV	47.7	71.9	71.3	63.8	55.5	49.6	62.1
Mean	34.1	−2.6	30.5	35.0	−19.4	−40.6	−6.6
Austria							
SDEV	56.4	36.8	41.1	60.3	46.5	34.1	–
Mean	−10.2	−34.4	−30.6	15.5	23.8	−54.7	–
Canada							
SDEV	57.1	42.2	72.5	44.5	75.4	27.8	32.6
Mean	−12.7	−31.8	−15.5	−38.0	−9.8	−51.3	−19.2
Denmark							
SDEV	73.8	67.6	68.5	66.6	68.4	48.5	53.6
Mean	11.7	−6.8	−23.7	−7.3	−13.2	−45.9	−30.0
Finland							
SDEV	47.9	32.3	25.9	47.1	40.8	19.3	39.7
Mean	−42.8	−66.0	−74.9	−66.0	−54.2	−77.4	−21.4
France							
SDEV	53.8	55.4	53.5	68.8	66.2	45.1	40.9
Mean	−28.8	−50.7	−31.6	−6.9	−25.2	−30.6	−44.7
Germany							
SDEV	51.5	32.1	51.5	51.2	53.7	50.4	54.5
Mean	−11.7	15.7	−6.9	−14.1	−23.7	1.3	−16.0
Netherlands							
SDEV	36.2	38.3	44.2	42.2	48.3	37.2	37.0
Mean	−2.8	−17.4	−24.2	7.1	0.2	3.0	4.4
New Zealand							
SDEV	41.2	33.7	18.6	33.8	40.0	56.4	61.3
Mean	−30.7	−21.1	−43.5	−1.1	−33.0	−18.7	−39.3
Sweden							
SDEV	59.3	69.9	38.6	58.4	57.4	46.2	27.8
Mean	−17.1	−37.0	−52.9	−21.8	−19.6	−53.2	−76.9
United Kingdom							
SDEV	59.2	49.7	45.0	53.2	35.3	35.2	37.5
Mean	−32.2	−18.5	−37.9	−10.6	−21.2	−14.8	20.7
United States							
SDEV	39.4	27.4	29.4	59.3	36.7	39.4	59.6
Mean	16.6	43.4	45.0	6.1	17.3	−12.5	4.8

globalisation[3]), that appear far-Left according to Cusack-Engelhardt's index, especially due to their commitment to the 'welfare state' (for example, this is the case in Australia, Canada, Denmark, Germany and New Zealand). There are legitimate questions as to whether these new

Left and Right parties can be adequately described with the policy-issue categories in the Cusack-Engelhardt index (see for example Bobbio, 1996; Jahn, 2010). Third, we see a general shift to the left in manifestos directly following the 2008 financial crisis; yet, by the very early 2010s the centre of gravity of policy placements had generally shifted much more firmly to the right once more, particularly so in Australia, Canada, Finland and the United Kingdom. This goes hand in hand with common appraisals of immediate crisis reactions emphasising demand-side employment and stabilising protective policies, followed only shortly afterwards by an austerity narrative with the predominating goal of deficit reduction (see for example van Kersbergen et al, 2014). However, there are some noticeable exceptions to this pattern, namely Germany, France, New Zealand and Sweden, which suggest that further analysis of the discourse on government profligacy and social investment in these countries might be a fruitful endeavour.

Even if the 'recasting of party ideology' was a key feature of party competition after 1980, it seems clear that the above findings caution against broad-brush statements on party convergence. It is very interesting, however, that the United Kingdom is the only country that experienced a clear shrinking of the party ideological space, with the range of party positions on the Left decreasing from around −100 prior to the 1980s to merely −64.9 during the 1990s/2000s, while the maximum Right party ideology score remained broadly stable. It is certainly no coincidence that much of the formulation of the competition state thesis – including its focus on the 'recasting of party ideology' – was based on the UK case (Cerny, 1997 and Cerny and Evans, 1999). The United Kingdom has typically featured comparatively small numbers of partisan and institutional veto players (Tsebelis, 2002), which raises questions about the extent to which the United Kingdom's experience can sensibly be taken as instructive for other countries that rely much more frequently on coalition governments. This question will be discussed in the next section.

Tracing government centres of political gravity with MRG/CMP/MARPOR data

The discussion so far has concentrated on the ideological positions and shifts of individual parties. However, the comparative welfare state literature has been more concerned with conceptualising and measuring the policy preferences of (coalition) governments as a determinant of policy outputs and outcomes. In the following,

I therefore consider the centres of political gravity of the cabinet (CPGC) (Gross and Sigelmann, 1984) – which are computed as the sum of each cabinet party's ideological position weighted by its relative strength in terms of cabinet posts – for the analysis of government ideological preferences. Rather than presenting our findings with more data tables, the two types of sigma convergence from above are presented graphically (Figure 10.1).[4]

Here, model (A) describes a type of convergence of CPGC where both Left and Right governments' preferences over time meet in the centre of the Left–Right policy space (that is, combining 'modernisation' of both Left and Right parties). To facilitate interpretations, black bars represent CPGG scores for governments in which a majority of cabinet seats is occupied by Left parties, grey bars for governments in which a majority of cabinet seats is occupied by Centre parties and light grey bars for governments in which a majority of cabinet seats is occupied by Conservative parties. The black dotted lines are meant to indicate roughly the overall shifts of government ideology for subsequent cabinets over time. A second model (B) of government ideology convergence is conceivable that is more closely related to discussions in the competition state literature. Here, the model suggests a 'race to the Right', where it is mainly Left governments that adjust their policy preferences in favour of enhancing competition-stateness at the cost of traditional Left commitments, whereas Right parties and Right governments are under less pressure to move towards the middle. The remainder of this chapter explores whether these models bear a resemblance to the empirical picture provided by the MRG/CMP/MARPOR data.

It comes as no surprise that sequences of CPGC differ considerably across countries (Figure 10.2). This, of course, is to be expected, not least because of the variation of constitutional structures, electoral and

Figure 10.1: Theoretical types of government ideology convergence

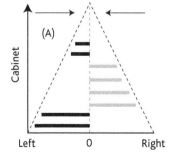
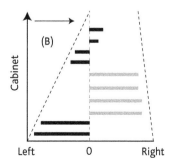

party systems and – as a consequence – the dominant characteristics of party competition in the observed countries. Still, it is possible to identify empirical patterns in the data that are not too dissimilar to the theoretical ideal scenarios of government ideology convergence outlined above. It is interesting that of the four countries discussed in Table 10.1, two appear to have witnessed a type (A) and two a type (B) convergence. We see quite clearly that first New Labour under Blair I–III and then the Conservative–Liberal Democrat coalition (Cameron I) moved closer to the ideological centre ground with their respective party manifestos. Obviously, Labour and Conservative cabinets did not end up being identical (which would result in CPGCs of zero), but there is evidence of a narrowing of government positions post Wilson IV and Thatcher I–III, thus confirming our previous analysis. A similar picture emerges for Denmark in the post Schlüter V/P.N. Rasmussen I era in the early 1990s. Government positions of the P.N. Rasmussen II–IV as well as the A.F. Rasmussen I–III and Thorning-Schmidt I administrations since the late 1990s have been much closer to the centre of the ideological space, as compared to previous decades.

The development of CPGGs in Germany and the Netherlands also suggest a degree of government ideology convergence, but here the empirical picture is closer to model (B) above. In Germany, the CPGG of the Kohl I–VI and Merkel I–II cabinets remained remarkably stable (with the exception of Kohl IV, which was directly affected by German reunification). At the same time, German Social Democrats under Schröder I–II made a noticeable turn to the Right and, despite being in coalition with a much more Left Green party, showed CPGC scores much closer to zero than the previous Social Democratic governments under Brandt III and Schmidt III. The impression of significant party convergence is further strengthened when we consider that Merkel I and III are grand coalitions between the Christian Democratic/Social Union and the Social Democratic Party, suggesting that the shift of party preferences was sustained after the departure of Schröder as German chancellor. In the Netherlands, again, we see relatively little difference between coalition cabinets between the Christian Democratic Appeal and the conservative liberal People's Party for Freedom and Democracy (Lubbers I–II), the Christian Democratic Appeal and the Labour Party (Lubbers III) and the various Christian Democratic-led multi-party coalitions (Balkenende I–V) during the 2000s. Instead, it is again the Labour Party-led coalition with the conservative liberal People's Party for Freedom and Democracy (VVD) and the social liberal Democrats 66 (D66) during the 1990s (Kok I–II) that shifted considerably to the Right, as compared to previous Labour Party-led coalition governments during the 1970s (Den Uyl I).

As for the other countries in Figure 10.2, Australia and France show some evidence of type (A) convergence similar to that in the United Kingdom and Denmark, but the findings are less clear cut. In the case of Australia, this interpretation is mainly based on scores relatively close to zero for Howard I–IV and Rudd I following great variation in CPGC of the Fraser II–IV and Hawke I–IV/Keating II administrations in the 1970s–1990s. In France, Raffarin II–III, Villepin I and Fillon II were situated on the Left side of the political spectrum rather than the Right, which makes them very different to the previous non-Socialist Juppé II, Balladur I, Chirac II and Barre III cabinets. Finland and Sweden, again, are slightly more similar to type (B) convergence, although, again, this classification can be made only with some reservations. In Finland, Social Democracy-led governments under Lipponen I–II have moved towards the centre ground and were much more similar in terms of their CPGC to the previous centre-right coalition under Aho I than the various Social Democracy-led Sorsa I and Koivisto II governments of the 1970s. However, the starting point of CPGC in the 1970s is such that it does otherwise not fit the model very well, as CPGCs are generally classified as Left according to the Cusack-Engelhardt (2002) index. Sweden is similar to Finland in this sense, but again we see a significant shift to the Right of Bildt I as well as, maybe more importantly, Social Democratic governments Carlsson IV and Persson II–III (at least when compared to the Palme III–IV cabinets of the 1970s and early 1980s).

There are also countries where the changing nature of party competition and convergence is more difficult to explain with reference to CPGC. Canada and the United States do not have Social Democratic movements of a similar fashion to the other countries in the sample, and New Zealand has experienced a shift from a first-past-the-post to a proportional election system, with profound impacts on party competition (it is interesting to note here that it is the only case in our sample to have experienced a widening of CPGC). Austria is commonly characterised as a strong concordance/consensus democracy (Lijphart, 1999) that has seen grand coalitions of the Austrian Social Democrats and the conservative liberal People's Party much more consistently in its history. Although these coalitions were typically led by Social Democratic Chancellors (Vranitzky II–V and Klima I), broadly equal cabinet shares can explain the somewhat exceptional CPGC for this country.

Figure 10.2: Tracing government centres of political gravity with MRG/CMP/MARPOR data

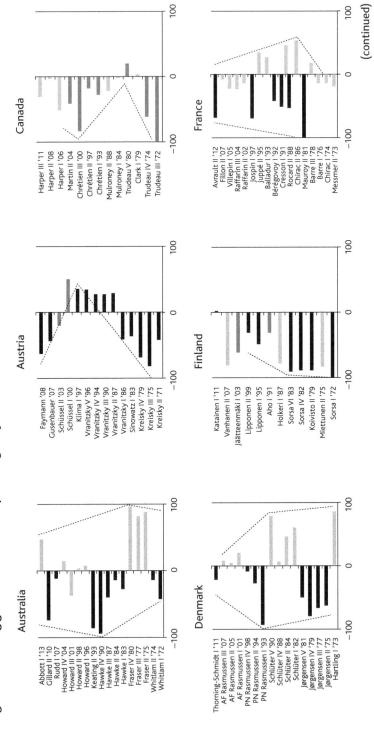

(continued)

Figure 10.2: Tracing government centres of political gravity with MRG/CMP/MARPOR data (continued)

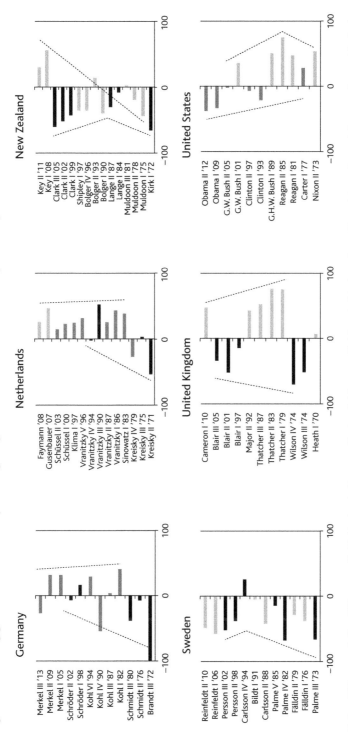

Note: -100 = pure Left; +100 = pure Right; black = Left; grey = Centre; light grey = Right party ideology; investiture dates, prime ministers and party ideologies from Armingeon et al, 2015

Conclusion

The primary purpose of this chapter was to address the lack of systematic attempts to map 'the recasting of party ideology' empirically within the competition state literature. Using MRG/CMP/MARPOR and different summary measures of the Left–Right positions of parliamentary parties and governments, a considerable degree of convergence of party preferences has become apparent, especially if taking the 1980s as a dividing line and comparing empirical data before and after this point in time. Rather than a broad-brush 'race to the Right', however, the different analyses have shown that the processes of shifting ideological party positions vary hugely in different countries. More importantly, some of the identified processes of convergence seem to at least qualify key assumptions/statements within the competition state literature. Three key findings should be stressed in particular.

First, while there are clear indications for overall party ideological convergence, this seems to be caused primarily by increased commitments on the part of Labour/Social Democratic/Socialist movements to 'governmental and administrative efficiency'. The issue categories of 'social justice' and 'welfare state expansion' were also de-emphasised after the 1980s, albeit to varying degrees. This finding broadly confirms the common notion that Left parties adopted a more Right orientation that embraced recommodification policies and thus weakened social rights, especially during the 1990s and 2000s (see for example Vis, 2010).

Second, although there is evidence for sigma convergence, with the variation of Left–Right party positions being reduced in most cases since 1980s, there is little evidence of a general shift of party systems to the Right. Instead, many, if not most, observed countries have seen a decrease in the standard deviations of party political positions that has been accompanied by a general shift of the party system to the Left. To what extent the apparent diversification of party systems is determined by convergence of the mass parties to the ideological centre ground would be an interesting question for further study. Equally, to what extent the current emphasis on austerity (see Schäfer and Streeck, 2013; Farnsworth and Irving, 2015) will continue to limit the policy space for more progressive investive alternatives will be possible to explore only once new waves of MRG/CMP/MARPOR data is available.

Third, although sigma convergence can also be identified once we move beyond single party ideological positions and consider government ideological positions, there are at least two types of policy convergence than can be characterised as 'growing together' versus 'racing to the Right'. Further exploration of precise reasons behind these different processes of government ideology convergence in the observed countries cannot be addressed here; further exploration and clarification are clearly warranted. Focusing on the cases that have 'bucked' more general trends, according to MRG/CMP/MARPOR data, may present a useful starting point for such further analysis.

In conclusion, MRG/CMP/MARPOR data is not uncontested[5] and there are important questions about the use of party manifestos as an explanatory variable for policy outputs and outcomes.[6] There is a strong argument in the literature suggesting that the distinction between socialism on the Left and liberalism/conservatism on the Right is not fully captured by Left–Right dichotomies (see Bobbio, 1996; Jahn, 2010). There is also increasing reason to believe that the ideological battlegrounds between Left and Right parties have at least to some extent shifted away from the different MRG/CMP/MARPOR policy-issue categories employed in the Cusack-Engelhardt index. In an era of global economic competition Left politics has increasingly been concerned with post-modern notions of self-realisation, resilience, societal openness and gender inequality – all of which arguably led to a different understanding of 'progressiveness' and 'cosmopolitanism', specifically promoting human capital investment, life-long learning and the dual-earner/carer model (Morel et al, 2012b,c). While these discussions are beyond what this chapter has been able to deliver, they further underline that the 'recasting of party ideology' in the context of ever-changing compositions of the electorate hardly ever means the same thing and so warrants much more precise conceptualisation in order to be meaningful for future research on competition state*ness* in historical and comparative perspective. Not least, this investment is key for attempts to go beyond empirical descriptions of competition state*ness* and may go some way in helping to explain the shifts within and across the neoliberal, active and pro-competition ideal-types previously identified (see Horsfall, 2013b).

Table A10.1: The MRG/CMP/MARPOR coding scheme

Domain	Variables
External relations	Foreign special relationships: positive or negative; Anti-imperialism: positive or negative; Military: positive or negative; Peace; Internationalism: positive or negative; European Community/Union: positive or negative
Freedom and democracy	Freedom and human rights; Democracy; Constitutionalism: positive or negative
Political system	Decentralisation; Centralisation; Governmental and administrative efficiency; Political corruption; Political authority
Economy	Free enterprise; Incentives; Market regulation; Economic planning; Corporatism; Protectionism: positive or negative; Economic goals; Keynesian demand management; Productivity; Technology and infrastructure; Controlled economy; Nationalisation; Economic orthodoxy; Marxist analysis; Anti-growth economy
Welfare and quality of life	Environmental protection; Culture; Social justice; Welfare state expansion; Welfare state limitation; Education expansion; Education limitation
Fabric of society	National way of life: positive or negative; Traditional morality: positive or negative; Law and order; Social harmony; Multiculturalism: positive or negative
Social groups	Labour groups: positive or negative; Farmers; Middle class and professional groups; Underprivileged minority groups; Non-economic demographic groups

Note: positive = favourable mentions or support; negative = hostile or unfavourable mentions

Table A10.2: Party manifestos covered

Australia	AD Australian Democrats (1990–2001); ALP Labour Party (1951–2013); Australian Greens (2004–13); CLP Country Liberal Party (2013); CP Country Party (1951–74); DLP Democratic Labour Party (1955–77); Katter's Australian Party (2013); LNP Liberal National Party of Queensland (2010–13); LPA Liberal Party (1951–2013); NCP National Country Party (1975–80); NPA National Party (1983–2013); PUB Palmer United Party (2013).
Austria	ÖVP People's Party (1953–2008); BZÖ Alliance for the Future of Austria (2006–08); FPÖ Freedom Party (1956–2008); Freedom Movement (1995–2002); Green Alternative/Green Party (1986–2008); KPÖ Communist Party of Austria (2002–08); Liberal Forum (1994–95); SPÖ Social Democratic Party (1953–2008).
Canada	Bloq Quebecois (1993–2006); Reform Conservative Alliance (2000); CCF Cooperative Commonwealth Federation (1953–58; 2008); Conservative Party of Canada (2004–08); Green Party of Canada (2008); Liberal Party (1953–2008); NDP New Democratic Party (1962–2006); PCP Progressive Conservative Party (1953–2000); Reform Party (1993–97); Social Credit (1953–74).

(continued)

Denmark	CD Centre Democrats (1973–2005); Danish People's Party (1998–2011); DKP Danish Communist Party (1950–84); DU Independents' Party (1953–68); Red-Green Unite List (1994–2011); FK Common Course (1987); FP Progress Party (1973–98); KF Conservative People's Party (1950–2011); KrF Christian People's Party (1971–2011); LC Liberal Centre (1966–68); Ny Alliance (2007); RF Justice Party (1950–84); RV Radical Party (1950–2011); SD Social Democratic Party (1950–2011); SF Socialist People's Party (1960–2011); V Liberals (1950–2011); VS Left Socialist Party (1968–84).
Finland	Agrarian Union (1951–62); Centre Party (1966–87); Christian Democrats (2003–11); KK National Coalition (1951–2011); LKP Liberal People's Party (1951–91); NSP Progressive Party Young Finns (1995); PS True Finns (1999–2011); RKP/SFP Swedish People's Party (1951–2011); SK Finnish Centre (1991–2011); SKDL People's Democratic Union (1951–87); SKL Christian Union (1970–99); SMP Finnish Rural Party (1970–95); SSDP Social Democrats (1951–2011); TPSL Social Democratic League (1958–66); VL Green Union (1983–2011); VL Left Wing Alliance (1991–2011).
France	AC Centrist Alliance (2012); CD Democratic Centre (1967–68); CDP Centre Democracy and Progress (1973); CNIP National Centre of Independents and Peasants (1951–78); FDG Left Front (2012); FN National Front (1986–2012); Ecology Generation (1997); Greens (1993–2012); MoDem Democratic Movement (2007–12); MR Reformers' Movement (1973); MRP Popular Republican Movement (1951–62); NC New Centre (2012); PCF French Communist Party (1951–2007); PDM Progress and Modern Democracy (1968); PR Radical Party (2012); PRG Left Radical Party (2012); PS Socialist Party (1973–2012); RPF Rally for the French People (1951–56); RPR Rally for the Republic (1993–97); RRRS Radical Socialist Party (1951–68); SIFO Socialist Party (1951–68); UDF Union for the French Democracy (1978–2002); UD-VE Democratic Union of the Fifth Republic (1967); UDCA Union for the Defence of Traders and Artisans (1956); UDF Union for French Democracy (1978–2002); UMP Union for the Presidential Majority/Union for a Popular Movement (2002–12); Union for a New Majority (1981–88); UNR Union for the New Republic (1958–62).
Germany	90/Greens Alliance '90/Greens (1983–2013); CDU/CSU Christian Democratic Union/Social Union (1953–2013); DP German Party (1953–57); DZ Centre Party (1953); FDP Free Democratic Party (1953–2013); Refugee Party (1953); PDS Party of Democratic Socialism (1990–2002); Pirates (2013); SPD Social Democratic Party (1953–2009); The Left Party (2005–13).
Netherlands	ARP Anti-Revolutionary Party (1952–72); CDA Christian Democratic Appeal (1977–2012); Christian Union (2002–10); CHU Christian Historical Union (1952–72); D'66 Democrats 66 (1967–2012); DS'70 Democratic Socialists (1971–77); GL Green Left (1989–2012); KVP Catholic People's Party (1952–72); LN Liveable Netherlands (2002–03); LPF List Pim Fortuyn (2002–03); PPR Radical Political Party (1971–86); PvdA Labour Party (1952–2012); PvdD Party for the Animals (2006–12); PVV Party of Freedom (2006–12); SGP Reformed Political Party (2006–12); SP Socialist Party (1994–2012); VVD People's Party for Freedom and Democracy (1952–2012).

(continued)

New Zealand	ACT (1996–2011); Alliance (1993–99); Green Party (2005–11); Jim Anderton's Progressive Coalition (2002); LP Labour Party (1951–2011); Mana Mana Party (2011); Maori Party (2005–08); NP National Party (1951–2011); NZDP New Zealand Democratic Party (1987–90); New Zealand First Party (1993–2002; 2011); Progressive Coalition (2005–08); Social Credit Political League (1954–84); United Future (2002–11).
Sweden	Agrarian Party (1952–56); Communist Party (1952–64); CP Centre Party (1958–2010); FP Liberal People's Party (1952–2010); Green Ecology Party (1988–2010); KdS Christian Democratic Community (1985–2010); MSP Moderate Coalition Party (1970–2010); NyD New Democracy (1991); Right Party (1952–68); SdaP Social Democratic Labour Party (1952–2010); Vk Left Party (1968–2010).
United Kingdom	Conservative Party (1950–2010); DUP Democratic Unionist Party (1992–2001); Labour Party (1950–2010); LDP Liberal Democratic Party (1950–2010); SDP Social Democratic Party (1983–87); SF Sinn Fein (1997–2001); SNP Scottish National Party (1992–2001); UKIP UK Independence Party (2001); UUP Ulster Unionist Party (1992–2001).
United States	Democratic Party (1952–2012); Republican Party (1952–2012).

Notes

[1] Selection of these categories was undertaken mainly on theoretical grounds, albeit the results of this reasoning were cross-checked via factorial analysis. The index itself is calculated as the sum of percentages of statements falling into any of the 13 'Left' minus any of the 13 'Right' categories.

[2] This speaks to studies that have shown that, historically, Christian Democratic parties in Western Europe have often also been responsible for key expansions of the welfare state (see for example van Kersbergen, 1995).

[3] Notably, this was not the case for the National Front in France (1986–2007) and the United Kingdom Independence Party (2001).

[4] The additional data necessary to compute CPGC was accessed through Cusack and Engelhardt's (2002) *Parties – Governments – Legislatures* file collection – with the exception of CPGC for the most recent cabinets, which are based on the author's calculations on the basis of raw ideological positions of parties made available by Volkens et al (2014) and data on cabinet composition published in various issues of the *European Journal of Political Research* Political Data Yearbook.

[5] See https://manifestoproject.wzb.eu/publications/cmp_criticism for a list of general MRG/CMP criticisms and responses.

[6] Discussion of this issue is beyond the reach of this chapter, but see Kühner (2010; 2015).

ELEVEN

Crisis, austerity, competitiveness and growth: new pathologies of the welfare state

Kevin Farnsworth and Zoë Irving

Introduction

Periods of economic crisis inevitably increase the tensions between social policy and the economy. Public expenditure is underpinned by strong economic performance and, in the face of financial crisis, social policies can offer some effective short-term gains by boosting consumer demand and maintaining political legitimacy. However, slowing economic growth and recessions risk precipitating fiscal crises, where revenues fall and public sector debt rises. Thus, economic crises often lead to welfare state crises, and the post-2008 financial crisis was no exception to this.

As governments within the wealthiest economies grappled for solutions to the emerging global financial crisis and the ensuing 'Great Recession', they distanced themselves from dominant neoliberal ideas and, for a short period at least, Keynes was revived. Gordon Brown announced in 2009 that:

> The old Washington consensus is over. Today we have reached a new consensus – that we take global action together to deal with the problems we face; that we will do what is necessary to restore growth and jobs; that we will take essential action to rebuild confidence and trust in our financial system, and to prevent a crisis such as this ever happening again.[1]

The IMF announced in the same year the end of structural adjustment programmes for any (developed) economy that might need its assistance.[2] Five years later, however, it was Keynes that was on the defensive. Although we have argued that 'the' global economic crisis is actually better understood as a distinct number of national crises linked to both the immediate events of 2008 and the subsequent economic fall-out effects, some common patterns emerged across the global economy and in policy responses (Farnsworth and Irving, 2011b; 2012). Social policies have come under increasing attack and there are signs that neoliberal economics has been strengthened, not weakened, in the post-2008 era (Seymour, 2014; Streeck, 2014; Jessop, 2015). Two key questions at the heart of the political economy of welfare have nevertheless remained constant: what is the proper role of the state versus the market; and what is the effect of the welfare state on economic competitiveness? Periods of crisis test these two questions to their limits. The answers vacillate according to ruling party, ruling ideas and the depth of the economic (and political) crisis. What can arise in such periods is a shift in previous ideas and economic models – what Kuhn refers to as a 'paradigm shift'. But comparative analysis demonstrates that crises can, and do, often subside and lead to a reversion to welfare state type over time (Pierson, 2004). What this chapter seeks to do is to shed light on some of the tensions between economic and social policy during the recent period of crisis and to investigate the tensions between social policy as a tool of social protection and social policy as a tool to manage economic performance. By way of historical context, we begin with the last major global economic crisis prior to 2008: the oil crisis of the 1970s.

Perpetrator, victim or Samaritan: post-crisis pathologies of the welfare state

The 1970s provides ample evidence of the way in which economic crisis can lead to major transformations in social policy. The period also led to increases in understanding of how social policies emerge, evolve and perish in the face of crisis. Some of the great advances made in theoretical and empirical studies of the relationship between social policy and the economy occurred as a result of the major challenges to welfare states that arose at the time. The neoliberal political challenges to social policy in the 1980s and 1990s had their roots in the early 1970s, as did the divergent paths subsequently pursued by Sweden and Finland, for example (Esping-Andersen, 1990; Hall and Soskice, 2001).

Although the fundamentals of the 1970s economic crisis (high inflation linked to increases in oil prices, falling economic demand, rising unemployment) were quite different to the post-2008 crises, the debate surrounding the role of the welfare state in its cause and proliferation was similar during both periods. For the radical

Right (and to some extent the radical Left offered a similarly based explanation for the crisis in the 1970s) the cause lay in the fact that the welfare state had grown too large and was denying private producers, especially industry, much-needed private capital. Put more simply, it was argued that too much of the national wealth was being invested in the unproductive state rather than in the productive private sector (Bacon and Eltis, 1976; Gough, 1979). The debate echoes the arguments put forward by some governments in response to the post-2008 crisis, that their economies needed rebalancing, with a greater emphasis placed on the private (wealth creating, industrial) sector. The fact that economies and the size of the public sector have both expanded in most welfare states since the 1970s suggests some key problems with the analysis in the 1970s. In any case, the antidote to economic crisis was very different for the Right and Left, although it was the former that succeeded in reshaping economic and social policy over the subsequent three decades.

What the 'new Right' was successfully able to achieve during this period was the creation of a politically convincing narrative, at least among a majority of the voting public in the US and the UK, that the causes of the 1970s economic strife lay in the economic and moral shortcomings of the welfare state. Thus, for the Right, the welfare state not only 'crowded out' private investment and replaced 'efficient' private providers with 'inefficient' public services, but it undermined the dynamism of markets and ultimately led to lower growth, lower levels of national competitiveness and, ultimately, less national wealth (see Friedman, 2002 [1962] for example). The welfare state was also blamed for the creation of an irresponsible, deviant citizenry: social policies fostered dependence on the state, a lack of individual and social enterprise and a deterioration of virtuous moral values, particularly in family life.

This early pathologisation of the welfare state that took hold in the 1980s came to define the periods of Thatcherism and Reaganomics, enabling a compassionless and punitive social politics of 'welfare' to become entrenched in the already residualised US system of social protection, and allowing the focus of UK social policy to be narrowed to the individual incentives required of social provision: to seek independence from state support, to be flexible in the supply of labour and to conform to the traditional family forms and life-styles that the state deemed appropriate. In the UK in particular, the critique of the operation of the welfare state agencies also opened up a discursive space where solutions located in processes of marketisation, deregulation and more efficient public management could be instituted to develop ambitions such as 'quality' and 'consumer choice' in services – characteristics that were argued to be absent in state monopoly provision. This period of welfare state restructuring was eruditely captured in a range of analyses of the time (see for example Jessop et al, 1991; Keat and Abercrombie, 1991; Abbott and Wallace, 1992; Wilding, 1992; Burrows and Loader, 1994; Gamble, 1994; Cerny and Evans, 1999). The key challenge of the welfare state – to balance competing social, economic and political demands (including fiscal strains, apparent unwillingness to pay higher taxes, insecurity in labour markets, ageing populations, the movement of people and so on) lies at the heart of the 'crisis' that began in the 1970s (Gough, 1979), developed in the 1980s and 1990s (Keman et al, 1987; Pierson, 1998; Huber and Stephens, 2001) and has returned to prominence in studies of political economy post-2008 (Castles, 2010; Crouch, 2011; Farnsworth and Irving, 2011a; Armingeon, 2013; Schäfer and Streeck, 2013).

However, what also seemed apparent by the early 1990s was that even in economies where governmental desire to shrink the size of the (welfare) state was more ideological (such as in the UK) than pragmatic (such as in Germany), the process of social policy reform was constrained. Some constraints that operated are contained in the policy process (the stickiness described by Paul Pierson, 2001), others are linked to the popular expectations created by post-war social settlements – particularly in relation to pensions and healthcare. It has often been noted, for example, that in the UK the only area of the welfare state that was successfully 'shrunk' by the Conservative governments in power from 1979 to 1997 was local authority housing, and even this was ultimately a cost-shifting exercise from capital spending to cash transfers in the form of housing benefits. Nevertheless, although the economics of welfare reform did not achieve the intended aims of spending reductions, the political success of symbolic shifts such as the demunicipalisation of housing in the UK should never be under-estimated. While the institutional shifts are often a more practical challenge to governments (greasing the path of retrenchment through institutional reform requires more obvious solutions), changing expectations requires a much greater attention to hearts than to minds, as these are more significant for the 'immovable objects' that Paul Pierson (1998) identified in his analysis of the period.

The post-2008 crisis in context

As already noted, the 2007–08 economic crisis did a great deal to demonstrate the weaknesses of neoliberalism. It exposed some of its fundamental flaws and, in particular, the 'public bad, private good' assumptions that lay at its heart. It was, after all, the state that had come to the rescue of some of the largest and previously successful capitalists – major financial organisations in a number of economies. Most damningly, the key policy strategies that underpinned neoliberalism – deregulation, low taxation, private property and personal responsibility – had together created the very conditions that led to the crisis, first in the US, and then spreading to Western Europe and Asia. The crisis demonstrated not just the importance of government as a corrective to market failure, but the importance of comprehensive, coordinated macro-economic and social policy interventions. Regarding the latter, even governments that presided over minimalist welfare states acknowledged that social policies can make positive contributions to economic stability and growth as well as offering social protection.

This shift in thinking about social policies was important but relatively short lived. It emphasised the positive contribution of social-protection expenditure as an important tool of macro-economic stability that could contribute positively to competitiveness and growth. Thus, in nations as diverse as the US and China, post-2008 social protection was expanded in order to boost economic demand (see Farnsworth and Irving, 2011a). This was a change in economic strategy. Neoliberalism had previously shifted social policy efforts towards relatively narrow 'productivist' and corporate-centred welfare solutions that boosted those services that made direct and the most obvious economic contributions – education and training, in particular – and arguably transformed other parts of the welfare state as tools to coerce citizens into work (Jessop, 2000). In the early stages of the 2008 crisis at least, the welfare state was viewed as important in that it prevented an even deeper recession than would otherwise have been experienced, and offered some protection to some of those who were hit by the financial crisis and subsequent recession.

The problem is that those very same social and public policies that helped to mitigate the economic and social effects of the financial crisis began to come under increasing pressure from governments as the international banking crisis gave way to the Great Recession that, in turn, led to national fiscal crises (Farnsworth and Irving, 2012). The high costs associated with bailing out national banking systems, the additional burdens placed on social welfare systems, and falling tax revenues led to serious fiscal crises in a number of states (Gough, 2011).

In this sense, it is not surprising that welfare expenditure and public debt have increased exponentially – although in many economies debt remains lower in 2015 than it was in 1950. This is to be expected, given the size of the threat posed by the global financial crisis; 2008 is widely recognised to have been the biggest global crisis since the 1930s' Great Depression. However, opponents of the welfare state have cemented the idea that current levels of debt are unsustainable, despite the historical evidence demonstrating that debt in most countries remains lower than levels experienced in the past. Politicians on the Right have selectively drawn on academic studies (including the much-cited but subsequently derided Reinhart and Rogoff, 2009) and the arguments of sympathetic international governmental organisations (including the European Commission and the IMF) to convince sufficiently large numbers among electorates that social policies helped to cause the rise in debt, and that increasing levels of debt mean that social policy will be unaffordable in future. Thus, from the disorder of political unreadiness and policy incoherence, existing neoliberal orthodoxy has emerged, reinvigorated and with a strengthened mission to shrink the state. Unsustainable debt, fiscal crisis, unsustainable deficits, weak productivity and low growth are recurring themes in national and global policy discourse that pours doubt on the sustainability of the welfare state.

In considering the essence of the contemporary challenges to progressive social policy, the core arguments of scholarship assessing the 'crisis' of the welfare state in the 1970s have thus taken on new relevance as welfare states confront pressures from governments with renewed hopes of cutting their way to growth. The power of austerity as both an economic and an ideological tool is such that without it, recovery and 'the future' are unthinkable. Austerity measures have consequently been widely implemented across advanced economies and beyond, even in those countries where the notion of austerity has been downplayed in political discourse, allowing a degree of optimism regarding welfare state resilience (van Kersbergen et al, 2014; Farnsworth and Irving, 2015).

Within this process of neoliberal reinvention, the counter-arguments to the success of austerity measures in securing economic growth have been routinely ignored, as have been the public and social cost of welfare state reconfiguration. There is ample economic evidence to support the claim that austerity does not beget growth, certainly not the kind of growth that is most desirable and compatible with other goals such as social justice. However, austerity is not concerned with state-induced growth; rather, it seeks to shrink and reconfigure the state in order to build an alternative economic model based on a purer form of neoliberalism than was possible prior to the crisis.

The following sections summarise the ways in which the 2008 crisis challenged, unhinged and subsequently reformatted neoliberalism, and its variable impact on welfare states and social policy development. This is followed by an examination of how, rather than being simply a victim of the post-2008 economic crises, the welfare state came to be positioned as a causal factor, reflecting a deliberate disregard for its historical function and future potential in resolving the economic challenges faced by nation-states. The final section further explores the ways in which austerity has emerged as a political and economic tool that combines neoliberal ideological imperatives with popular economic truths in the contemporary growth strategies preferred by national governments and international policy actors.

Varieties of crises

For many commentators, the global financial crisis of 2008 presented an irrefutable instance of the failings of neoliberalism, the first opportunity since it had begun its ascendance to pause, assess the economic disarray and alter the political course. Not only this, but the fact that the crisis was 'global' indicated a level of internationally coordinated response, previously unachievable in the context of global competition. Financial deregulation had led to loss of control within and across borders, the power of states was in question and their legitimacy was threatened. These elements of the crisis were apparent in the collapse of banks and related financial institutions in the UK (for example Northern Rock and HBOS) and the US (for example Lehman Brothers and Merrill Lynch, among others), the inability of countries to account for domestic financial losses (Iceland and Ireland) and the political fall-out that both governments and international actors anticipated (or confronted, in the case of Iceland).

The 2008 crisis, although global in reach, was not uniform in impact, nor did it begin and end with the banking collapse of that year. As we have argued elsewhere, the unravelling of the sub-prime mortgage market from 2007 initiated a variety of crises that continue to progress in waves as the results of systemic failings of contemporary capitalism are downloaded into nation-states (Farnsworth and Irving, 2011b). Location of the 2008 crisis in history and in the periodisation of capitalism has emphasised the more recent combination of deregulation and financialisation, which while seemingly resolving the crisis of lack of economic growth in the 1970s, were bound to create a future crisis of their own (see Gamble, 2009; Harvey, 2011). The complexity and unequal interdependencies of the global market, however, have determined very different national post-crisis strategies (Farnsworth and Irving 2011a; Bermeo and Pontusson, 2012) and, as Starke et al (2013) argue, some predictable crisis routines.

Because the initial effects of the 2008 crisis were financial, the countries most exposed were those where finance dominated: the US and UK (and, for unique reasons, Iceland), followed by eurozone countries where the delicate threads of housing-linked finance held the rest of the economy together (Ireland, Spain) and countries that were considered by financial markets and other governments to have unsustainable debt-to-GDP levels (Greece, Italy and Portugal). The effects of the 'Great Recession' from 2008–10 also spread rapidly to strongly exporting countries (Germany, Japan and China). Even for each of these countries with shared economic features, however, the variety of crisis experienced immediately following 2008 was further mediated through other political and economic factors at the national and international levels. The key determinants of the type and extent of crisis experienced were shaped by many factors, the most important of which included: control over financial instruments, including interest rates and money supply; the extent to which national debt was funded by other economies and international financiers as opposed to their national citizenry (which explains Japan's exceptionally high but relatively 'manageable' debt levels); the relative importance of the economy within the world financial system; the strength and liquidity of key national financial institutions and/or the capability of governments to underwrite them; the extent to which the economy is balanced between different sectors; and the ability of governments to control expenditure (which in turn depends on the balance between discretionary and non-discretionary forms of expenditure) (see Blyth, 2013; Streeck, 2014).

As a result of the number of risks presented by the initial crisis, further crises emerged from 2008, including a significant global economic slow-down resulting from falling consumer demand in the most developed economies. Thus the waves of crisis continue. In mid-2015, for instance, China, the country that weathered 2008 most successfully, experienced a stock market crisis in the midst of declining GDP growth – an economic combination that was deeply and immediately troubling for other Asian economies and Australia, and ultimately globally destabilising, given the China–US relationship.[3] Thus there is no sense in which 'the crisis' is over, and the probability of further economic volatility continues to present challenges but also possibilities for welfare states.

Several years on from 2008, and despite the early indications that states may need to exercise both collective spirit and Keynesian principles, it is clear that the exposure of the failings of neoliberalism has not fundamentally challenged either the economic orthodoxy underpinning it or political support for this orthodoxy. According to Crouch (2011), this 'strange non-death of neoliberalism' can be explained by a kind of ideational lock-in where it is difficult to imagine and operationalise alternatives to neoliberalism. To do so would mean the wholesale restructuring of the privatised state. For Jessop (2013a; 2013b), the non-death of neoliberalism is not strange at all, given the historical and contemporary global dominance of the US, and the processes that have developed since the 1980s: the systemic competitive demands on states; the dis-organisation of labour; the gains made by the financial super-elite; and the gradual erosion of social-protection rights. In this context, the return of a neoliberalism reinvigorated by the post-2008 strategy of austerity is a more predictable outcome.

With this return of neoliberalism come new pathologies of the welfare state facilitated by the waves of economic instability. The 2008 crisis has enabled a redirection of attention from distributive justice to the 'burden' of public debt; from the role of public investment to the reduction of 'the deficit'; and a political reimagining of the cause of the 2008 crisis: not deregulation in the financial sector, but profligacy in the public sector. These messages regarding the unsustainability of public expectations of what welfare states can or should do, as discussed above, are not new, but the previous era of hostility to the notion that states should be active in the redistribution of resources to promote societal health had provoked vulnerabilities in support for the welfare state, allowing its fundamental premises to be challenged. These premises included its integrative goals (in the Titmussian sense) or solidaristic dimensions – the recognition that all citizens benefit from and contribute to welfare state provisions; and its economic function as an essential mechanism in supporting production (and social reproduction).

Since 2008, the pre-existing erosion of the fundamental socio-political rationale for the welfare state has provided the groundwork that has enabled a further offensive, deepening and widening (in the context of migration for example) the divisions instituted between contributors and recipients. However, what the 2008 crisis has enabled in terms of the economic rationale is a much less sophisticated representation of the welfare state, or, more specifically, pre-crisis levels of public spending (relative to revenue) as the 'cause' of post-2008 levels of national debt (relative to GDP) and austerity as the solution to this 'problem'. The welfare state has thus become a perpetrator, if not of the financial collapse itself, then at least of states' inability to recover from it.

In considering the post-2008 European political economy, Hay and Wincott (2012, p 196) have observed that:

> Above all it is important to consider whether the welfare states might be seen to be implicated directly in the crisis itself or whether it is more accurate to see the welfare state as an indirect (perhaps even an innocent) casualty of the broader political and economic damage the crisis has wreaked.

There are plenty of counter-arguments to the notion that welfare states 'caused' the crisis, and many others to suggest that they are more than an 'innocent casualty', since this implies that they are simply collateral damage in a rational post-crisis economic recovery strategy (see Mirowski, 2014; Seymour, 2014; Farnsworth and Irving, 2015). The welfare state as 'victim' of irresistible pressures on governments to reduce spending, improve productivity and regain competitiveness ignores both the ideological motives driving efforts to shrink the state and, more importantly for the goal of a return to growth, the significance of welfare state activity in promoting and supporting a robust economy.

Following the economic crisis of the 1930s and the conflict of the 1940s, the early development of the welfare state was characterised much more by an understanding of the Samaritan qualities of social intervention. This involved the Keynesian approach to public investment and the assumption that social protection measures would act as an automatic stabiliser in times of economic turbulence. Added to this were the ideas that decommodification was a generally desirable social goal (although nationally differentiated) and that states had a duty to regulate for employment security. It is these features, essential to both economic and social growth, that have become lost in what Joseph Stiglitz, among others, has termed 'deficit fetishism'[4] and the strategy of austerity, discussed further below.

Austerity, competition and growth

If the economic crisis initially placed neoliberalism on the back foot, austerity politics represents its fight-back and revival. Austerity represents a repackaged neoliberalism that has sought to dissociate politics from economics and thus discard pre-existing ideological baggage, but, in essence, it amounts to the same thing. Austerity is offered as the antidote to declining competitiveness.

In this new era of austerity, the public sector is again considered to be a major barrier to national competitiveness and economic growth, although it is not necessarily the size of state but the type of state that is perceived to be the problem. The major assumptions and beliefs underpinning the new politics of austerity can be seen most clearly in the policy prescriptions of the IMF and the European Central Bank. The IMF, for example, has made clear the fact that public expenditure and social policies have been important to staving off global recession, but in its policy prescriptions is the assumption that public policies should be 'corporate-centred' rather than 'citizen-centred'. Thus, social policy is advocated where it makes a clear economic (rather than social) contribution; it is condemned where the economic gains are less clear (for example, IMF, 2012). For the IMF, the privatisation of public services remains a key tool by which governments can both raise revenues and provide opportunities to private companies, but, paradoxically in this age of austerity, other public sector cuts are condemned where they might have a negative impact on the global economy in particular, but advocated where the global economy shows signs of recovery. In this respect, the social benefits of public expenditure have been downplayed and divorced from the economic benefits. If Keynes was given a momentary reprieve by the crisis, the same cannot be said for Beveridge.

The problem is that austerity remains flawed as an economic strategy, regardless of its effects on social cohesion. Growth outside the economic powerhouses of India and China remains relatively low and is likely to continue so for the foreseeable future (IAGS, 2015). This presents a major challenge to welfare states, since, even if another serious crisis is avoided over the next couple of decades, demands on social policy from ageing populations will only increase. Moreover, the propensity for income and wealth inequality to increase across most of the major economies shows no signs of slowing, and austerity politics is increasing the gap between rich and poor (Piketty, 2013; ILO, 2015). Cerny (2010, p 9) suggests that the current 'return of the state' involves an element of 'social neo-liberalism' coupled with 'increased political awareness of the need for compensating losers'. Cerny sees this in productive measures such as education and training, but the move towards productive 'investment states' is by no means inevitable. The tendency for governments to socialise production through active labour market programmes is itself placed under attack by austerity as programmes are reduced or privatised and workers have to either settle for less or contribute more towards social welfare programmes (see Farnsworth and Irving, 2015).

Austerity policies that are aimed at increasing national competitiveness, productivity and growth are undermining the sustainability of the welfare state in various different ways. Firstly, austerity itself arguably undermines economic growth through emphasis on balanced budgets over targeted investment, through the effects of lower wages and the gap between these and prices, and more generally through the deepening of social divisions. The most striking example of this latter effect is inter-generational inequality. One of the groups hardest hit in the aftermath of 2008 has been young people. In Greece and Spain, youth unemployment is well over 50%. This represents a major challenge to policy makers and, given that it signifies a significant under-utilisation of labour power, seriously undermines future productivity and growth. In terms of both public and popular investment in the welfare state, austerity involves a deliberate depletion public sector jobs that tend to be more heavily unionised and, at least for the lower-paid, to be more stable with better terms and conditions of employment. And in contrast to the notion of an 'investment state', in the increasingly desperate competition for capital investment to close gaps left by the withdrawal of public funds, austerity is also encouraging countries to compete by cutting corporate taxes (undermining revenues) and also utilising resources to socialise private sector risks and subsidise wages, thereby diverting resources from 'social' welfare to 'corporate' welfare (see Farnsworth, 2012).

Conclusion

This chapter set out to explore the complex relationship between the welfare state and the economy during a particular period of deep economic crisis. Although the economic trends leading to 2008 were different to those of the 'oil crisis', many of the pathologies of the welfare state that emerged from the early 1970s have been elaborated in the wake of the global financial crisis. The challenges faced by governments subject to variations of the unfolding economic crises since 2007/08 have centred on two key questions: first, how to use social policies in strategies for recovery; second, how to deal with the massive economic costs imposed by the crisis. Since the impact of the crisis varied between states, so the policies employed by governments to deal with the crisis have varied. In some cases they have been driven by national economic and political factors, in others they have been driven by world-regional and international factors. The strategy of austerity plays a central role in the future growth models advocated by both national governments and international financial organisations and it is the economic and political success of this approach that shapes the prospects of the welfare state.

Notes

[1] http://webarchive.nationalarchives.gov.uk/20130109092234/http://number10.gov.uk/news/speeches-and-transcripts/2009/04/g20-press-conference-18934.

[2] http://www.guardian.co.uk/commentisfree/2009/apr/27/editorial-imf-international-financial-crisis.

[3] See for example http://www.democracyjournal.org/36/the-coming-china-crisis.php?page=all.

[4] http://www.huffingtonpost.com/2012/08/09/joseph-stiglitz-inequality_n_1760296.html.

Part Four
Conclusions

TWELVE

Conclusion: social policy in an era of competition

Dan Horsfall and John Hudson

Transcending the competition state/welfare state dichotomy

As we noted at the outset of the book, Cerny's (1990) much-cited competition state thesis – and, specifically, his suggestion (with Evans: see Cerny and Evans, 1999; 2004) that the intensification of global economic competition would sound the death knell of the welfare state – provided the immediate impetus for our text. That was directly so for us as editors of the text, for we have worked for some time on exploring the veracity of their argument. Some of our colleagues included in this collection have been less concerned with directly examining the competition state thesis but have instead been engaged in detailed empirical examination of key processes or trends that Cerny and Evans placed at the core of their thesis.

In bringing together these theoretical and empirical research agendas our aim has been, firstly, to address major theoretical debates in the social sciences about how the intensification of global competition has influenced the direction of welfare state reform processes across the OECD in recent decades and, secondly, to offer empirically rooted alternatives to the 'competition state thesis' that can better account for how welfare states have responded to competition imperatives in reality. In this chapter we synthesise key arguments from across the book in order to set out an integrated agenda for future research and to underline the value added to these debates when they are approached from a perspective that fuses the applied empirical concerns of traditional social policy scholarship with the broader theoretical perspectives found in comparative political economy and macro-sociology.

As we noted in Chapter One, with the benefit of hindsight we can say that Cerny and Evans over-estimated the threat to the welfare state, but few dispute their central argument that welfare states across the OECD have been subjected to reform agendas that have stressed economic competitiveness. Our task here, therefore, is neither to praise nor to bury the competition state thesis, but instead to articulate a new research agenda addressing the implications of intensified global economic competition for social policy that transcends the welfare state and competition state dichotomy.

At the outset we identified three broad umbrella terms that capture key dimensions of change connecting the arguments made across the book as a whole: competition, cognition and conditionality. We begin our task of drawing together key arguments by returning to these three themes in the light of the arguments presented in the earlier chapters.

Competition

Competition obviously represents the starting point of our analysis and it impacts on and permeates welfare states in many ways. While the competition state thesis as developed by Cerny and Evans emphasises the global nature of competition – and this provides our starting point – competition is not simply an economic imperative engaged in by states. Competition exists not only at the global or even other territorial levels, but has pervaded all aspects of social policy. The individual chapters have addressed this from a range of different angles, beginning with a macro-level focus on welfare states in a global economy, through to individuals and vulnerable groups essentially competing for scarcer and more conditional access to resources and support.

To this end one of the chief issues explored in the book is *the impact of intensified global competition on the social wage*. Notably, Chapters Eleven, Seven, One, Four and Three all directly explored the impacts of intensified global competition on the macro-economic environment in which the welfare state operates. Farnsworth and Irving (Chapter Eleven) and Horsfall (Chapter One) addressed the 'new economic realities' supposedly wrought by globalisation, while questioning the veracity of claims that a scaling-back of welfare expenditure has occurred or is inevitable. At the same time, these chapters also pointed to significant changes to the institutional context in which policy making is taking place, be they the often subtle and technically rooted influence of international organisations such as the EU highlighted by Roumpakis and Papadopoulos in Chapter Three, the powerful internationalised mortgage markets discussed by Lowe in Chapter Four or the globalised networks of economic production that span across nation-states that were explored by Holden and Hudson in

Chapter Seven. As these chapters have shown, while claims that global competition has produced a race to the bottom in social expenditure are too simplistic, arguing that these processes have had little impact seems to be an untenable position also. Instead of being caught between these two poles, more nuanced analyses highlight that responses to increased global competition have varied across and within countries, with impacts felt unevenly across different groups in society.

While examining the impact of competition on the social wage has been a key concern, a related angle of *how social policy provision feeds into competition*, particularly how it may boost competitiveness, has also been a focus. In Chapter Eleven Farnsworth and Irving underscored the complex relationship between the welfare state and economic competitiveness, the crisis serving to underlining the various roles that the welfare state plays in boosting economic competitiveness. Lunt's chapter (Six) highlights how health services have increasingly become sources of export growth themselves as governments look to exploit economic opportunities presented by the global demand for healthcare services. This trend is both an outcome of enhanced economic competition *and* a contributor to it; indeed, as Lunt notes, it has led to competition *between* welfare states in the healthcare sector. As Finch et al highlighted in Chapter Two, the hunt for a framework that reconciles equity with economic competiveness has underpinned much of the social investment model debate, particularly within key international organisation such as the OECD and EU. Their examination suggests that there is evidence to support the view that such a strategy can deliver on its promises, but they note that the agenda is nebulous and difficult to evaluate empirically as a consequence. Farnsworth and Irving (Chapter Eleven) showed that, following the shock of the global financial crisis, many countries relied on public services and public spending to reboot economic growth.

A third major angle explored by our contributors is that of *economic competition as a driver of new social policy governance mechanisms*. Many of the chapters make contributions here, teasing out a wide range of new or shifting governance mechanisms that have developed in part as a response to enhanced global economic competition. Holden and Hudson deal with attempts to insert specific 'slices' of national territory into the global economy on a differential basis, but also reflect on how these mechanisms often have important implications for social policy, such as SEZs often featuring a downgrading of key social rights or global cities having more intensive investments in key public services. Roumpakis and Papadopoulos (Chapter Three) demonstrated the complexities of European-level governance, not the least the interplay of nation-states, the EU, the ECJ and the ECHR in determining key labour rights. In Chapter Five Snell underscored how the hollowing-out of the nation-state has weakened its capacity to reconcile environmental and social policy objectives in energy policy; the UK government ceded control of what were once public utilities to the private sector, and the internationalisation of these markets means that the success of its fuel poverty agenda now rests largely on its ability to steer the commercial activity of competing multinational energy corporations, and plugging failures to do so with a patchwork of targeted supports. Meanwhile, Dwyer, in Chapter Eight, showed how moves to boost economic competitiveness (and reduce social expenditure) by increasing labour market participation have been central to an increase in conditionality that has fundamentally affected the governance of social rights. The chapters by Horsfall and Finch et al (One and Two) included an examination of activation strategies, noting that they have become increasingly central to many –although not all – welfare systems. Yet, as these chapters showed, activation and conditionality can be combined with stronger – or weaker – social protections: processes of change can be complex and multi-dimensional. Taken together, these chapters unpack some of the complex ways in which the governance of welfare has adapted in response to intensified global competition, sometimes protecting social rights, sometimes reformulating social rights, sometimes working against social rights.

Cognition

Irrespective of how far the intensification of economic globalisation is 'real', the fact is that so many policy makers act as if it is means that the *idea of globalisation* is having an impact on the ideational frameworks surrounding social policies. The second of our key cross-cutting themes, cognition, was chosen to reflect the view that (the idea of) intensified competition has reframed how social policy is conceptualised in key ways. Once again, our authors approach this theme from a number of different angles.

Firstly, the ways in which *competition is used as narrative to justify reform* is a central issue that a number of authors discussed. Chapters by Kühner (Ten), Horsfall (One), Farnsworth and Irving (Eleven), Dwyer (Eight) and Roumpakis and Papadopoulos (Three) all discussed ways in which the narrative of competition has been used to justify or sell social policy reforms. At the broadest level, Kühner's systematic review of manifestos on which governments have secured election in a dozen countries over a period of over 40 years demonstrated that the core messages of Left parties in government have altered in response to global competition, with the need for greater public sector efficiency becoming increasingly central to their agendas. At the same time, however, we should note that he found many Right parties of government shifting towards the centre on social policy issues, a reminder once again that we should avoid drawing overly simplistic conclusions about the impact of competition on welfare. Data limitations mean that Kühner's review does not capture the picture since the global economic crisis hit, and he concluded by asking whether this economic shock might have unsettled this move towards the political centre ground. Farnsworth and Irving (Chapter Eleven) picked up the story from here; they highlighted that the crisis provided a window for some older ideas about how the welfare state might boost the economy to come back into the debate, but underlined that the notion of 'austerity' seems to have provided an even stronger and more urgent 'global competition' argument to bolster the rhetoric of those looking to slim social rights further. As they concluded, the future of social policy across many high-income countries now rests on how far this austerity argument resonates with electorates.

This feeds into another angle explored by our authors: whether and how competition has shifted public attitudes to welfare. While changing political discourse can reflect changing societal values, political discourse can also lead public opinion. Likewise, public attitudes are shaped by the social and economic context of the times. In Chapter One Horsfall argued that structural changes in society may have fostered a more receptive mood for an austerity and retrenchment pitch, the shift from Fordist modes of production to a dominance of the service sector potentially weakening many of the bonds of solidarity on which national welfare states were built and supported. Lowe suggested in Chapter Four that increases in homeownership, in part facilitated by a pro-global competition loosening of mortgage markets, may also have served to foster individualism. He pointed to a complex set of interrelated trends, including a move towards asset-based welfare whereby the majority of homeowning households may begin to view the equity in their property as an alternative (more reliable?) source of security to that provided by the (welfare) state. This, in turn, he suggests, may push the electorate further towards parties offering economic security and stability over those offering greater provision of welfare.

A third angle explored by our authors is more subtle, and a step removed in terms of abstraction, concerned with *how (the notion of) intensified competition has reshaped broader social policy discourse* as the search for greater efficiency and/or economic competitiveness has resulted in new concepts and ideas coming to the fore of social policy debate. Brown's Chapter Nine provided a good example here. While at first sight the notion that social policy ought to prioritise supporting the most vulnerable appears almost to be common sense, she documented how, in the context of increasingly scant resources, vulnerability frameworks are often being used to ration resources, creating a race to 'demonstrate' vulnerability, with groups or individuals not deemed vulnerable losing access to support. The debate here is layered, with the meaning of key policy principles evident only when placed in the context of the wider discourse it operates in. Dwyer's Chapter Eight offered similar insights on the continued rhetoric of competition and responsibility and the use of value-loaded dichotomies such as workers vs shirkers that has normalised the notion of a limited welfare state that stresses work first. As he noted, the conditionality and sanctions approach is rooted in the 'nudge' thinking of behaviourial economics, not only an attempt to incentivise work but a wider strategy to alter the way in which citizens behave and, ultimately, think. For Dwyer, conditionality has helped to individualise and de-socialise the causes of poverty, vulnerability and disability.

Conditionality

This links to the third and final of the overarching themes, which is conditionality. The casting of individuals as integral elements of a nation's economic competitiveness has seen the relationship between the state and citizens recast in many countries as part of a rewriting of the social contract, with a citizen's social rights increasingly being contingent on their contribution to the state's own efforts to maximise competiveness in the global marketplace. Once again, our authors approached this issue from a number of different angles.

The first captured suggestions from policy makers that greater *conditionality is needed in order to make individuals more 'competitive' in a labour market that is deemed to be tougher because of intensified economic competition.* Dwyer (Chapter Eight), Farnsworth and Irving (Chapter Eleven), Finch et al (Chapter Two) and Horsfall (Chapter One) all noted that the last quarter of a century or so has seen seen increased pressure on individuals to work and the tightening of regulations to ensure that protections are conditional on this pursuit. Protective services are increasingly being restricted and offered conditionally on this engagement as many countries look to maximise labour market participation. A number of chapters argued that one of the ways in which welfare states have been reconfigured in response to perceived competition pressures is through a rewriting of social contracts in order to de-emphasise social rights and place a stronger emphasis on individual responsibilities. For Brown (Chapter Nine), Dwyer (Chapter Eight), Horsfall (Chapter One), and Lowe (Chapter Four) it is the drive for increased economic competitiveness that provides the context for recasting of the rights and responsibilities mix.

A second angle explored in the book was that, *in weakening central planks of the welfare state settlement, competition may have sown the seeds for greater public support for conditional entitlements.* Indeed, Dwyer (Chapter Eight) went so far as to argue that we have witnessed a coming together of money and morals that has turned the principle of welfare states on its head: where once the notion of social justice was used to endorse claims to public welfare, Dwyer contended that it is now used to deny them, with a consensus emerging around the need for greater responsibilities, backed by sanctions. We have noted already the possible impacts of competition on cognition, and the arguments are similar here – although with an emphasis on coalitions of interest as much as on ideas, the increased pressure on public sector resources (irrespective of whether in response to real or perceived economic threats arising from global competition) posing risks for traditional coalitions of support for social policy as entitlements are slimmed back or targeted to save money. This formed one of the key planks of Horsfall's Chapter One, and we have already discussed his argument that structural changes in wider socio-economic institutions may have weakened some of the bonds of social solidarity. Lowe's arguments in Chapter Four about the rise of (private) asset-based welfare are of importance here too, not least his suggestion that there is a trade-off between welfare state spending and home-ownership rates that has grown more pronounced as the 'financialisation of everyday life' has gathered pace. But, again, we should avoid simple linear conclusions here: all three authors highlight countervailing trends, be they cross-national variations in practice or shifts in trends that have taken place following the global financial crisis.

A third, more nascent, angle was explored in the chapters too, which is that *intensified competition is creating pressure for conditional social policy supports targeted not at shifting the behaviour of citizens but influencing the behaviours of competing welfare states.* Roumpakis and Papadopoulos (Chapter Three) explored this most directly, showing how European governance mechanisms, particularly those around competition, are now being used to steer key aspects of social policy in particular directions, with increased power to censure states for failing to adhere.

For some states, the global financial crisis has created a situation where there is de facto sanctioning of essential financial support for failure to adhere to the rules of the game.

Towards future research agendas

In drawing together arguments from across the book we have necessarily simplified our contributors' arguments, and done so further by summarising them within the confines of the three themes of competition, cognition and conditionality. We should stress that this is a heuristic device that captures the key foci of our agenda in parsimonious manner, but in practice there is no clear separation between these three interconnected themes. Nonetheless, this has allowed us to identify nine key ways in which intensified global competition and social policy are intertwined:

1. global competition placing (perceived?) downward pressure on the social wage;
2. social policy provisions being used to feed into national competitiveness;
3. economic competition as a driver of new social policy governance mechanisms;
4. competition as a narrative to justify social policy reform;
5. competition as a cause/driver of shifting public attitudes to welfare;
6. competition as a key concept underpinning shifts in broader social policy discourse;
7. competition creating pressure for a conditionality-based social contract in order to make individuals more 'competitive' in the labour market;
8. policy feedback loops, meaning that competition may have sown the seeds for greater public support for less-expansive/more conditional social rights;
9. intensified competition creating pressure for conditional social policy supports targeted not at shifting the behaviour of citizens but influencing the behaviours of competing welfare states.

As this list demonstrates, the chains of 'causation' or influence are often complex, long rooted, multi-directional and multi-faceted. Across the book we have tried to highlight complex non-linear, multi-directional linkages between social policy and intensified competition. The space available within each chapter has often restricted the extent to which authors could tease out the complexity of such processes in depth –

the topic of each chapter could span a book in its own right – but all have made clear that there is no simple deterministic argument about the impact of 'competition' on social policy that can be offered. At the same time, the chapters have shown that major pressures for change have unfolded; arguing that intensified competition has had little impact on welfare states seems also to be an untenable position.

Theoretically rooted analyses must be at the core of such an agenda. We have drawn on ideas from many disciplines in this book, including those with origins in political science, political economy, international relations, geography, health studies, business studies, economics, law, sociology, social psychology, environmental studies and urban studies, as well, of course, as social policy. We believe that this inter-pollination/cross-fertilisation of ideas is important in developing an understanding of the complex and multi-faceted ways in which competition is influencing (and been influenced by) welfare states. But, while theory is central to this agenda, it must also be rooted in detailed empirical analysis. All of the authors in this collection are social policy specialists who bring engagement with policy detail to their analysis. In looking to transcend the competition state/welfare state dichotomy, this interplay between theory and evidence is key, and where we believe theoretically rooted social policy analysts can add particular value to current debates.

Although space has naturally restricted the range of themes we could explore in this text – for example, we have focused primarily on teasing out the ways in which competition processes are reshaping welfare states, and less on the impacts of these processes on key policy outcomes – we have nonetheless highlighted a rich and wide-ranging agenda for future research that presents major theoretical, conceptual and methodological challenges and draws together a wide range of substantive topics rarely considered alongside one another.

References

Aalbers, M. (2008) 'The financialization of home and the mortgage market crisis', *Competition & Change*, vol 12, no 2, pp 148–66.

Aassve, A., Cottini, E. and Vitali, A. (2013) *Youth vulnerability in Europe during the Great Recession*. Dondena Working Paper No. 57, Dondena Centre for Research on Social Dynamics. Milan: Italy.

Abbott, P. and Wallace, C. (1992) *Family and the New Right*, London: Pluto Press.

Aggarwal, A. (2007) *Impact of special economic zones on employment, poverty and human development*, Working Paper no 194, New Delhi: Indian Council for Research on International Economic Relations.

Aitken, R. (2007) *Performing capital: Toward a cultural economy of popular and global finance*, New York: Palgrave Macmillan.

Allan, J.P. and Scruggs, L. (2004) 'Political partisanship and welfare state reform in advanced industrial societies', *American Journal of Political Science*, vol 48, no 3, pp 496–512.

Anderson P. (2011) *The new old world*, London: Verso.

André, S. and DeWilde, C. (2016) 'Home ownership and support for government redistribution', *Comparative European Politics*, vol 14, no 3, pp 319–48.

Ansell, B. (2013) *The political economy of ownership: Housing markets and the welfare state*, working paper, University of Minnesota.

Appleton, J.V. (1999) 'Assessing vulnerability in families', in McIntosh, J. (ed) *Research issues in the community*, Basingstoke: Macmillan.

Ares, E. (2014) *Carbon Price Floor*, House of Commons Library Briefing (Science and Environment Section).

Armingeon, K. (2013) 'Breaking with the past? Why the Global Financial crisis led to austerity policies but not to the modernization of the welfare state', in C. Pierson, F.G. Castles, and I.K. Naumann (eds) *The Welfare State Reader*, 3rd edn, Cambridge: Polity.

Armingeon, K. and Baccaro, L. (2012) 'Political economy of the sovereign debt crisis: the limits of internal devaluation', *Industrial Law Journal*, vol 41, no 3, pp 254–75, doi: 10.1093/indlaw/dws029.

Armingeon, K., Isler, C., Knöpfel, L. and Weisstanner, D. (2015) *Supplement to the Comparative Political Data Set – Government Composition 1960–2013*, Bern: Institute of Political Science, University of Berne.

Arora, S., Charlesworth, A., Kelly, E. and Stoye, G. (2013) *Understanding competition and choice in the NHS, IFS Public payment and private provision: The changing landscape of health care in the 2000s*, London: Institute for Fiscal Studies.

Bacon, R. and Eltis, W. (1976) *Britain's economic problem: Too few producers*, London: Macmillan.

Baker, W. (2011) *Reaching the fuel poor: Making the Warm Home Discount work*, Consumer Focus.

Bambridge, J. (2013) 'Healthcare: 15 mega-hospital projects', *Construction Week-Online*, 31 May.

Bank of England (2007) 'Financial Stability Report', 15 October. Available at: www.bankofengland.co.uk/publications/fsr.

Bankoff, G., Frerks, G. and Hilhorst, T. (eds) (2004) *Mapping Vulnerability: Disasters, Development and People*, London: Earthscan.

Barbier, J.-C. (2012) 'Tracing the fate of EU "social policy": Changes in political discourse from the "Lisbon Strategy" to "Europe 2020"', *International Labour Review*, vol 151, no 4, pp 377–99, doi: 10.1111/j.1564-913X.2012.00154.x.

Barker, N. and Lamble, S. (2009) 'From social security to individual responsibility: sanctions, conditionality and punitiveness in the Welfare Reform Bill 2009 (part one)', *Journal of Social Welfare and Family Law*, vol 31, no 3, pp 321–32.

Barnes, C. (1992) 'Institutional discrimination against disabled people and the campaign for anti-discrimination legislation', *Critical Social Policy*, vol 12, no 1, pp 15–22.

Bauman, Z. (1998) *Work, consumerism and the new poor*, Buckingham: Open University Press.

BBC (2013a) 'Target winter fuel benefit to pay for elderly care' (January), http://www.bbc.co.uk/news/health-20887547.

BBC (2013b) 'Ed Miliband: Labour would freeze energy prices', http://www.bbc.co.uk/news/uk-politics-24213366.

BBC (2015) 'Give Ofgem new powers on energy bills – Ed Miliband' (11 January), http://www.bbc.co.uk/news/uk-politics-30766452.

Beatty, C. and Fothergill, S. (2013) *Hitting the poorest places hardest: The local and regional impact of welfare reform*, http://www.shu.ac.uk/research/cresr/sites/shu.ac.uk/files/hitting-poorest-places-hardest_0.pdf (accessed 12 May 2014).

Beck, U. (1992) *Risk society: Towards a new modernity*, London: Sage.

Beck, U. (2009) *World at risk*, Cambridge: Polity Press.

Bermeo, N. and Pontusson, J. (eds) (2012) *Coping with crisis: Government reactions to the Great Recession*, New York, NY: Russell Sage Foundation.

Betzelt, S. and Bothfeld S. (eds) (2011) *Activation and labour market reforms in Europe: Challenges to social citizenship*, Basingstoke: Palgrave.

Bird, G. and Mandilaras, A. (2013) 'Fiscal imbalances and output crises in Europe: will the fiscal compact help or hinder?', *Journal of Economic Policy Reform*, vol 16, no 1, pp 1–16, doi: 10.1080/17487870.2013.765081.

Blair, T. (1998) *The Third Way: New politics for a new century*, Fabian Society pamphlet no 588, London: Fabian Society.

Blyth, M. (2013) *Austerity: The history of a dangerous idea*, Oxford: Oxford University Press.

BMA (British Medical Association) (2013) 'Understanding the reforms … Choice and any qualified provider', BMA briefing, April 2013.

Boardman, B. (2012) 'Fuel poverty synthesis: Lessons learnt, actions needed', *Energy Policy*, vol 49, pp 143–8.

Bobbio, N. (1996) *Left and Right: The significance of a political distinction*, Cambridge: Polity Press.

Bobeva, D. (2013) 'The new EU Macroeconomic Imbalances Procedure and its Relevance for the Candidate Countries', *Journal of Central Banking Theory and Practice*, vol 2, no 1, pp 69–88.

Bolton/House of Commons Library (2014) Energy Prices – Commons Library Standard Note, http://www.parliament.uk/business/publications/research/briefing-papers/SN04153/energy-prices

Bonefeld, W. (2015) 'European economic constitution and the transformation of democracy: On class and the state of law', *European Journal of International Relations*, vol 21, pp 867–86.

Bonoli, G. (2012) 'Active labour market policy and social investment: a changing relationship', in Morel, N., Palier, B., Palme, J. (eds) (2012) *Towards a social investment welfare state? Ideas, policies and challenges*, Bristol: Policy Press.

Bonoli, G. (2013) *The origins of active social policy: Labour market and childcare policies in a comparative perspective*, Oxford: Oxford University Press.

Bonoli, G. and Natali, D. (2012) 'The politics of "new" welfare states: analysing reforms in Western Europe', in G. Bonli and D. Natali (eds) (2012) *The politics of the new welfare state*, Oxford: Oxford University Press.

Bradshaw, S. (2013) *Gender, development and disasters*, Cheltenham: Edward Elgar.

Bräutigam, D. and Xiaoyang, T. (2011) 'African Shenzhen: China's special economic zones in Africa', *Journal of Modern African Studies*, vol 49, no 1, pp 27–54.

Brenner, N., Jessop, B., Jones, M. and Macleod, G. (eds) (2003) *State/Space: A Reader*, Oxford: WileyBlackwell.

Brenner, N., Peck, J. and Theodore, N. (2014) 'New constitutionalism and variegated neo-liberalization', in Gill, S. and Cutler, A.C. (eds) *New constitutionalism and world order*, Cambridge: Cambridge University Press, pp 126–42.

Brown, K. (2013) 'The concept of vulnerability and its use in the care and control of young people', PhD thesis, University of Leeds.

Brown, K. (2014) 'Questioning the Vulnerability Zeitgeist: Care and control practices with 'vulnerable' young people', *Social Policy and Society*, vol 13, no 3, pp 371–87.

Brown, K. (2015) *Vulnerability and young people: Care and social control in policy and practice*, Bristol: Policy Press.

Buck, R., Phillips, C.J., Main, C.J., Barnes, M.C., Aylward, M. and Waddell, G. (2006) *Conditionality in context: Incapacity benefit and social deprivation in Merthyr Tydfil*, http://www.epolitix.com/NR/rdonlyres/03C6EAF4-BACB-40A2-9461-7775C7742ABC/0/ConditionalityinContext.pdf

Budge, I., Klingemann, H.-D., Volkens, A. and Bara, J. (2001) *Mapping policy preferences I. Estimates for parties, electors, and governments, 1945–1998*, Oxford: University Press.

Burney, E. (2005) *Making People Behave: Anti-Social Behaviour, Politics and Policy*, Cullompton: Willan.

Burrows, R. and Loader, B. (eds) (1994) *Towards a post-Fordist Welfare State?*, London: Routledge.

Busch, K., Hermann, C., Hinrichs, K. and Schulten, T. (2013) *Euro crisis, austerity policy and the European Social Model: How crisis policies in Southern Europe threaten the EU's social dimension*, Berlin: Friedrich Ebert Stiftung.

Butler, J. (2004) *Precarious life: The powers of mourning and violence*, London: Verso.

Butler, J. (2012) 'Bodily vulnerability, coalitions and street politics' in Kuzma, M., Lafuente, P., and Osborne, P (eds) *The State of Things*, London: Office for Contemporary Art Norway and Koenig Books.

CAB (Citizens Advice) (2015) 'You can't switch energy supplier because of a debt', https://www.citizensadvice.org.uk/consumer/energy-supply/problems-switching-energy-suppliers/you-can-t-switch-energy-supplier-because-of-a-debt/

Cahn, A. and Clemence, M. (2011) *The Whitehall entrepreneur: Oxymoron or hidden army?*, London: Institute for Government.

Cameron, D. (2012) 'David Cameron hails historic moment of Welfare Reform', Official email from the Prime Minister, https://www.gov.uk/government/news/prime-ministers-message-on-welfare-reform.

Campbell, A. (1991) 'Dependency revisited: the limits of autonomy in medical ethics' in Brazier, M. and Lobjoit, M. (eds) *Protecting the Vulnerable: Autonomy and Consent in Healthcare*, London: Routledge, pp 101–13.

Carmel, E. (2005) 'Governance and the constitution of a European social', in J. Newman (ed), *Remaking governance: Peoples, politics and the public sphere*, Bristol: Policy Press, pp 39–58.

Carr, H. (2013) 'Housing the vulnerable subject: The English context', in Fineman, M. and Grear, A. (eds) *Vulnerability: Reflections on a new ethical foundation for law and politics*, Farnham: Ashgate, pp 13–29.

Carr, H. and Hunter, C. (2008) 'Managing vulnerability: homelessness law and the interplay of the social, the political and the technical', *Journal of Social Welfare and Family Law*, vol 30, no 4, pp 293–307.

Casper, S., Lehrer, M. and Soskice, D. (1999) 'Can high-technology industries prosper in Germany? Institutional frameworks and the evolution of the German software and biotechnology industries', *Industry and Innovation*, vol 6, no 1, pp 5-24.

Castells, M. (2000) *The Rise of the Network Society*, Oxford: Blackwell.

Castells, M. (2010) *The Rise of the Network Society* (2nd edn with revised preface), Oxford: Blackwell.

Castles, F.G. (1998) *Comparative public policy: Patterns of post-war transformation*, Cheltenham: Edward Elgar.

Castles, F.G. (2005) 'The Kemeny Thesis revisited', *Housing, Theory and Society*, vol 22, no 2, pp 84-86.

Castles, F.G. (2010) 'Black swans and elephants on the move: the impact of emergencies on the welfare state', *Journal of European Social Policy*, vol 20, no 2, pp 91–101.

Cerny, P. (1990) *The changing architecture of politics: Structure, agency and the future of the state*, London: Sage.

Cerny, P. (1997) 'Paradoxes of the competition state: the dynamics of political globalization', *Government and Opposition*, vol 32, no 2, pp 251–74.

Cerny, P. (2010) 'The competition state today: from raison d'etat to raison du monde', *Policy Studies*, vol 31, no 1, pp 5–22.

Cerny, P. and Evans, M. (1999) *New Labour, globalization and the competition state*. Boston: Harvard CES Working Paper Series 70. .

Cerny, P. and Evans, M. (2003) 'Globalization and social policy', in Ellison, N. and Pierson, C. (eds) (2003) *Developments in British Social policy 2*, Basingstoke: Palgrave Macmillan Press.

Cerny, P. and Evans, M. (2004) 'Globalisation and public policy under New Labour', *Policy Studies*, vol 25, no 1, pp 51–65.

Chakrabortty, A. (2015) 'The £93bn handshake: businesses pocket huge subsidies and tax breaks', *Guardian*, 7 July.

Chambers, R. (1989) 'Vulnerability, coping and policy', *Institute of Development Studies (IDS) Bulletin*, vol 37, no 4, pp 33–40.

Chanda, R. (2002) 'Trade in health services', *Bulletin of the World Health Organization*, vol 80, pp 158–63.

Chester, L. (2010) 'Conceptualising energy security and making explicit its polysemic nature', *Energy Policy*, vol 38, no 2, pp 887–95.

Choi, D. and Kim, P. (2014) 'Promoting a policy initiative for nation branding: The case of South Korea', *Journal of Comparative Asian Development*, vol 13, no 2, pp 346–68.

Cityam (2014) 'There is a problem in the UK's energy market – but it's the regulator's fault', http://www.cityam.com/1404232720/there-problem-uk-s-energy-market-it-s-regulator-s-fault

Clarke, H.D., Borges, W., Stewart, M.C., Sanders, D. and Whiteley, P. (2013) 'The politics of austerity; modeling British attitudes towards public spending cuts', in N. Schofield, G. Caballero and D. Kselman (eds) *Advances in Political Economy*, Springer Berlin Heidelberg, pp 265–87.

Clarke, J. and Newman, J. (2012) 'The alchemy of austerity', in *Critical Social Policy*, vol 32, no 3, pp 299–319.

Clifton, J. and Díaz-Fuentes, D. (2008) 'The new public service transnationals: consequences for labour', *Work Organisation, Labour & Globalisation*, vol 2, no 2, pp 23–39.

CMA (Competition and Markets Authority) (2014) *Energy Market Investigation*, https://www.gov.uk/cma-cases/energy-market-investigation

Coalition Government (2011) 'Innovation, health and wealth', https://www.gov.uk/government/news/accelerating-adoption-of-innovation-in-the-nhs

Conant, L. (2002) *Justice contained: Law and politics in the European Union*, Ithaca and London: Cornell University Press.

Conlon, G., Litchfield, A. and Sadlier, G. (2011) 'Estimating the value to the UK of education exports', BIS Research Paper no 46.

Conway, P., Janod, V. and Nicoletti, G. (2005) 'Product market regulation in OECD countries: 1998 to 2003', OECD Economics Department Working Papers, no 419, Paris: OECD Publishing, doi: 10.1787/783417550348.

Council of Europe (2008) *Housing policy and vulnerable social groups: Report and guidelines*, Strasbourg: Council of Europe Publishing.

Cox, R.H. (1998) 'The consequences of welfare reform: How conceptions of social rights are changing', *Journal of Social Policy*, vol 27, no 1, pp 1–16.

CPAG (2007) 'The Welfare Reform Act 2007', *Welfare Rights Bulletin 198*, London: Child Poverty Action Group.

CPAG (2016) 'Changes in the Welfare Reform and Work Act 2016', *Welfare Rights Bulletin No 252*, June 2016, London: Child Poverty Action Group, http://www.cpag.org.uk/content/changes-welfare-reform-and-work-act-2016

Cremers, J. (2014) 'Letter-box companies and abuse of the posting rules: how the primacy of economic freedoms and weak enforcement give rise to social dumping', ETUI Policy Brief no 5.

Crespy, A. and Menz, G. (eds) (2015) *Social policy and the Eurocrisis: Quo vadis Social Europe*, Basingstoke: Palgrave Macmillan.

Crouch, C. (2009) 'Privatised Keynesianism: an unacknowledged policy regime', *The British Journal of Politics and International Relations*, vol 11, pp 383–99.

Crouch, C. (2011) 'The strange non-death of neoliberalism', Cambridge: Polity Press.

Crouch, C. (2015) *Governing social risks in Post-Crisis Europe*, Cheltenham: Edward Elgar.

Crouch, C. (2015a) 'The social investment welfare state: the missing theme in British social policy debates', *Policy & Politics Blog*, 12 March, http://policyandpoliticsblog.com/2015/03/12/the-social-investment-welfare-state-the-missing-theme-in-british-social-policy-debates/

Crouch, C. (2015b) 'The social investment welfare state: the missing theme in British social policy debates', Plenary Lecture delivered to the 2015 Social Policy Association Annual Conference, Belfast, 8 July 2015.

Cusack, T.R. and Engelhardt, L. (2002) 'The PGL file collection: file structures and procedures', available at http://www.wzb.eu/alt/ism/people/misc/cusack/d_sets.en.htm

Daily Mail (2014) 'Gas costs you three times what the companies pay: Millions of households being ripped off after wholesale cost halves in six months', 1 September, http://www.dailymail.co.uk/news/article-2739304/Gas-costs-THREE-times-energy-firms-pay-Millions-households-ripped-wholesale-cost-halves-six-months.html

Daniel, B. (2010) 'Concepts of adversity, risk, vulnerability and resilience: a discussion in the context of the "child protection system"', *Social Policy and Society*, vol 9, no 2, pp 231–41.

Davey, E. (2014) 'Speech by Energy Secretary, Edward Davey MP, to the Economist Energy Summit on the UK's energy security', https://www.gov.uk/government/speeches/uk-energy-security-active-government-smart-intervention

De Grauwe, P. and Ji, Y. (2013) *The legacy of austerity in the Eurozone*, Brussels: Centre for European Policy Studies.

De Grauwe, P. and Ji, Y. (2014) *Disappearing government bond spreads in the Eurozone: back to normal?*, Centre for European Policy Studies.

de la Porte, C. and Heins, E. (2015) 'A new era of European integration? Governance of labour market and social policy since the sovereign debt crisis', *Comparative European Politics*, vol 13, pp 8–28.

Deacon, A. (1994) 'Justifying workfare: the historical context of the workfare debates', in M. White (ed) *Unemployment and public policy in a changing labour market,* London: PSI.

Deacon, A.J. (2005) 'An ethic of mutual responsibility? Toward a fuller justification for conditionality in welfare', in L.M. Mead and C. Beem (eds) *Welfare reform and political theory*, New York: Russell Sage Foundation.

Dean, H., Bonvin, J., Vielle, P. and Faraque, N. (2005) 'Developing capabilities and rights in welfare-to-work policies', *European Societies*, vol 7, no 1, pp 3–26.

DECC (2013a) *Energy Act policy briefs*, https://www.gov.uk/government/publications/energy-bill-policy-briefs

DECC (2013b) *Fuel poverty report*, https://www.gov.uk/government/uploads/system/uploads/attachment_data/file/199833/Fuel_Poverty_Report_2013_FINALv2.pdf

DECC (2014) *The future of the Energy Company Obligation*, https://www.gov.uk/government/uploads/system/uploads/attachment_data/file/342178/The_Future_of_the_Energy_Company_Obligation_Government_Response.pdf

DECC (2015a) *Statement by Edward Davey on the publication of the Fuel poverty strategy for England*, https://www.gov.uk/government/speeches/fuel-poverty-strategy-for-england

DECC (2015b) *Household Energy*, https://www.gov.uk/government/policies/helping-households-to-cut-their-energy-bills

Deeming, C. and Smyth, P. (2015) 'Social investment after neoliberalism: policy paradigms and political platforms', *Journal of Social Policy*, 44, pp 297–318.

DEFRA/DTI (2001) *UK Fuel Poverty Strategy*, London: DEFRA and DTI.

Degryse, C., Jepsen, M. and Pochet, P. (2013) *The Euro crisis and its impact on national and European social policies*, Brussels: European Trade Union Institution.

Department for Communities and Local Government (2012) *Policy update: Housing for older and vulnerable people*, accessed online at: www.gov.uk/government/policies/providing-housing-support-for-older-and-vulnerable-people

Dinnie, L. (2010) 'Repositioning the Korea Brand to a global audience: challenges, pitfalls, and current strategy', 2010 Academic Paper Series on Korea, Korea Economic Institute, vol 3, pp 95–104.

DoH (2010) *Equity and excellence: Liberating the NHS*, White Paper, London: DoH.

Dolan, P., Hallsworth, M., Halpern, D., King, D. and Vlaev, I. (2010) *MINDSPACE: Influencing behaviour through public policy*, London: Cabinet Office/Institute for Government.

Drake, R.F. (2000) 'Disabled people, New Labour, benefits and work', *Critical Social Policy, Special Issue: Disability and the Restructuring of Welfare: Employment, Benefits and the Law*, vol 20, no 3, pp 421–39.

Duhigg, C. and Barboza, D. (2012) 'In China, human costs are built into an iPad', *New York Times*, 25 January, http://www.nytimes.com/2012/01/26/business/ieconomy-apples-ipad-and-the-human-costs-for-workers-in-china.html?pagewanted=all&_r=0

Dunn, M., Clare, I. and Holland, A. (2008) 'To empower or protect? Constructing the "vulnerable adult" in English law and public policy', *Legal Studies*, vol 28, no 2, pp 234–53.

DWP (Department for Work and Pensions) (2008) *No one written off: Reforming welfare to reward responsibility*, London: DWP.

DWP (2011a) *Localising Crisis Loans and Community Care Grants Impact Assessment*, accessed online at: www.parliament.uk/documents/impact-assessments/IA11-022AO.pdf.

DWP (2011b) *Extra push for jobseekers as mandatory work activity placements come on-stream for those who need more focus*. Press Release, 17 May 2011, London: Department for Work and Pensions, available at https://www.gov.uk/government/news/extra-push-for-jobseekers-as-mandatory-work-activity-placements-come-on-stream-for-those-who-need-more-focus

DWP (2012) *Employment and Support Allowance (Sanctions) (Amendment) Regulations 2012 Equality Analysis*, London: DWP, available at: https://www.gov.uk/government/uploads/system/uploads/attachment_data/file/175120/eia-esa-sanctions-regs-2012.pdf.pdf.

DWP (2013) *Overview of revised sanctions regime*, London: DWP, http://statistics.dwp.gov.uk/asd/workingage/esa_sanc/overview_of_revised_sanctions_regime.pdf

DWP (2014) *Households Below Average Income: An analysis of the income distribution 1994/95–2012/13*, London: DWP.

DWP (2014) 'Million new ESA claimants found fit for work', DWP Press Release, 27 January, London: DWP, https://www.gov.uk/government/news/million-new-esa-claimants-found-fit-for-work.

DWP (2015a) Winter Fuel Payment, https://www.gov.uk/winter-fuel-payment/what-youll-get.

DWP (2015b) *Jobseeker's Allowance and Employment and Support Allowance sanctions: decisions made to December 2014*, London: DWP, https://www.gov.uk/government/statistics/jobseekers-allowance-and-employment-and-support-allowance-sanctions-decisions-made-to-december-2014.

DWP (2016) *Universal Credit: Transition Rollout Schedule – April 2017 to September 2018*. London: DWP (November).

Dwyer, P. (1998) 'Conditional citizens? Welfare rights and responsibilities in the late 1990s', *Critical Social Policy*, vol 18, no 4, pp 519–43.

Dwyer, P. (2000) *Welfare rights and responsibilities: Contesting social citizenship*, Bristol: Policy Press.

Dwyer, P. (2004) 'Creeping conditionality in the UK: from welfare rights to conditional entitlements', *Canadian Journal of Sociology*, vol 29, no 2, pp 265–87.

Dwyer, P. (2008) 'The conditional welfare state', in M. Powell (ed) *Modernising the welfare state: the Blair legacy*, Bristol: Policy Press.

Dwyer, P. (2010) *Understanding social citizenship: Issues for policy and practice* (2nd edn), Bristol: Policy Press.

Dwyer, P. (2016) 'Citizenship, conduct and conditionality: sanction and support in the 21st century UK welfare state', in *Social Policy Review 28*, Bristol: Policy Press/Social Policy Association.

Dwyer, P. and Ellison, N. (2009) 'Work and welfare: the rights and responsibilities of unemployment in the UK' in M. Giugni (ed) *The politics of unemployment in Europe: Policy responses and collective action*, London: Ashgate, pp 53-66.

Dwyer, P. and Wright, S. (2014) 'Universal credit, ubiquitous conditionality and its implications for social citizenship', *Journal of Poverty and Social Justice*, vol 22, no 1, pp 27–36.

Ebico (2012) 'Done badly collective switching will increase fuel poverty', https://www.ebico.org.uk/blog/2012/05/11/done-badly-collective-switching-will-increase-fuel-poverty/

EC (European Commission) (2008) 'A renewed commitment to social Europe: Reinforcing the open method of coordination for social protection and social inclusion. Communication from the Commission to the European Parliament, the Council, the European Economic and Social Committee and the Committee of the Regions', European Commission.

EC (2012) Treaty on Stability, Coordination and Governance – Eurozone (2012).

EC (2014) Statistical Annex of Alert Mechanism Report 2014: European Commission.

EC (2015) *Climate Policies*, http://ec.europa.eu/clima/policies/ets/index_en.htm

Ecclestone, K. and Goodley, D. (2014) 'Political and educational springboard or straightjacket?: theorizing post/humanist subjects in an age of vulnerability', *Discourse: Studies in the Cultural Politics of Education*, doi: 10.1080/01596306.2014.927112.

Ecclestone, K. and Lewis, L. (2014) 'Interventions for resilience in educational settings: challenging policy discourses of risk and vulnerability', *Journal of Education Policy*, vol 29, no 2, pp 195–216.

ECSR (European Committe of Social Rights) (2013) Conclusions (2013) Strasbourg: Council of Europe.

Edwards, N. (2013) 'Britain's healthy export: How to sell the NHS', *The Economist*, 3 August.

Ekins, P. and Lockwood, M. (2011) *Tacking fuel poverty during the transition to a low carbon economy*, York: Joseph Rowntree Foundation, http://www.jrf.org.uk/publications/tackling-fuel-poverty-low-carbon-economy.

Emmel, N. and Hughes, K. (2014) 'Vulnerability, inter-generational exchange, and the conscience of generations', in Holland, J. and Edwards. R. (eds) *Understanding families over time: Research and policy*, Basingstoke: Palgrave, pp 161–75.

Energy Saving Trust (2015) *Green Deal and ECO*, http://www.energysavingtrust.org.uk/domestic/content/green-deal-and-eco.

Erturk, I., Froud, J., Johal, S., Leaver, A. and Williams, K. (2007) 'The democratisation of finance? Promises, outcomes and conditions', *Review of International Political Economy*, vol 36, pp 51–77.

Esping-Andersen, G. (1990) *The three worlds of welfare capitalism*, Cambridge: Polity Press.

Esping-Andersen, G. (2002) *Why we need a new welfare state*, Oxford: Oxford University Press.

Estevez-Abe, M., Iversen, T. and Soskice, D. (2001) 'Social protection and the formation of skills: a reinterpretation of the welfare state', in Hall, P.A. and Soskice, D. (eds) (2001) *Varieties of capitalism: The institutional foundations of comparative advantage*, Oxford: Oxford University Press.

Evans, M. (2010) 'Cameron's competition state', *Policy Studies*, vol 31, no 1, pp 95–116.

Evans, M. and Davies, J. (1999) 'Understanding policy transfer: a multi-level, multi-disciplinary perspective', *Public Administration*, vol 77, pp 361–85.

Ewing, K.D. and Hendy, J. (2010) 'The dramatic implications of Demir and Baykara', *Industrial Law Journal,* vol 39, no 1, pp 2–51, doi: 10.1093/indlaw/dwp031.

Fairclough, N. (2001) 'Critical discourse analysis as a method in social scientific research' in Wodak, R. and Meyer, M. *Methods of critical discourse analysis*, London: Sage.

Fairclough, N. (2003) *Analysing discourse*, London: Routledge.

Farnsworth, K. (2012) *Social versus corporate welfare: Comparing needs and interests within the welfare state*, Basingstoke: Palgrave MacMillan.

Farnsworth, K. and Fooks, G. (2015) 'Corporate taxation, corporate power, and corporate harm', *Howard Journal*, vol 54, no 1, pp 25–41.

Farnsworth, K. and Irving , Z. (eds) (2011a) *Social policy in challenging times: Economic crisis and welfare systems*, Bristol: Policy Press.

Farnsworth, K. and Irving, Z. (2011b) 'Varieties of crisis', in K. Farnsworth and Z. Irving (eds) *Social policy in challenging times: economic crisis and welfare systems*, Bristol: Policy Press, pp 1–30.

Farnsworth, K. and Irving, Z. (2012) 'Varieties of crisis, varieties of austerity: Social policy in challenging times', *Journal of Poverty and Social Justice*, vol 20, no 2, pp 135–49.

Farnsworth, K. and Irving, Z. (2015) *Social policy in times of austerity: Global economic crisis and the new politics of welfare*, Bristol: Policy Press.

Farnsworth, K. and Irving, Z. (2015) 'Austerity: more than the sum of its parts', in K. Farnsworth and Z. Irving (eds) *Social policy in times of austerity: Global economic crisis and the new politics of welfare*, Bristol: Policy Press, pp 9–41.

Fawcett, B. (2009) 'Vulnerability: questioning the certainties in social work and health', *International Journal of Social Work*, vol 52, pp 473–84.

Feeley, M. and Simon, J. (1992) 'The new penology: notes on the emerging strategy of corrections and its implications', *Criminology*, vol 30, no 4, pp 452–74.

Finch, N. (2006) 'Childcare and parental leave', in J. Bradshaw and A. Hatland (eds) *Social policy, employment and family change in comparative perspective*, Cheltenham: Edward Elgar.

Fineman, M. (2008) 'The vulnerable subject: anchoring equality in the human condition', *Yale Journal of Law and Feminism*, vol 20, no 1, pp 1–23.

Fineman, M. (2013) 'Equality, autonomy and the vulnerable subject in law and politics' in Fineman, M. and Grear, A. (eds) *Vulnerability: Reflections on a new ethical foundation for law and politics*, Farnham: Ashgate, pp 13–29.

Fineman, M. and Grear, A. (eds) (2013) *Vulnerability: Reflections on a new ethical foundation for law and politics*, Farnham: Ashgate.

Flint, J. (2006) 'Housing and the new governance of conduct' in Flint, J. (ed) *Housing, urban governance and anti-social behaviour: Perspectives, policy, practice*, Bristol: The Policy Press, pp 19–36.

Flint, J., Jones, A. and Parr, S. (2011) *An evaluation of the sanction of Housing Benefit*, Research Report no 728, London: Department for Work and Pensions.

Foucault, M. (1972) *The archaeology of knowledge* (trs. A.M. Sheridan Smith), New York: Pantheon Books.

Foucault, M. (1984) 'The order of discourse', in Shapiro, M. (ed.) *The Language of Politics*, Oxford: Blackwell.

Fougner, T. (2006) 'The state, international competitiveness and neoliberal globalisation: is there a future beyond "the competition state"?', *Review of International Studies*, vol 32, pp 165–85.

Freud, D. (2007) *Reducing dependency, increasing opportunity: Options for the future of welfare to work*, an independent report to the Department for Work and Pensions, London: Department for Work and Pensions.

Friedman, M. (2002 [1962]) *Capitalism and freedom*, Chicago: University of Chicago Press.

Froud, J., Haslam, C., Johal, S. and Williams, K. (2000) 'Shareholder value and financialization: consultancy promises and management moves', *Economy and Society*, vol 29, pp 80–110.

Gamble, A. (1994) *The free economy and the strong state: The politics of Thatcherism* (2nd edn), Basingstoke: Palgrave Macmillan.

Gamble, A. (2009) *The spectre at the feast: Capitalist crisis and the politics of recession*, Basingstoke: Palgrave Macmillan.

Garland, D. (2001) *The culture of control*, Oxford: Oxford University Press.

Garthwaite, K. (2011) 'The language of shirkers and scroungers? Talking about illness, disability and Coalition welfare reform', *Disability and Society*, vol 26, no 3, pp 369–72.

Gash, T., Panchamia, N., Sims, S. and Hotson, L. (2013) *Making public services markets work: Professionalising government's approach to commissioning and market stewardship*, Institute for Government.

Genschel, P. (2002) 'Globalization, tax competition and the welfare state', *Politics & Society*, vol 30, pp 244–74.

Genschel, P. and Seelkopf, L. (2015) 'The competition state: the modern state in a global economy', in S. Leibfried, E. Huber, M. Lange, J.D. Levy, F. Nullmeier and J.D. Stephens, *The Oxford handbook of transformations of the state*, Oxford: Oxford University Press, pp 237–52.

Genschel, P., Kemmerling, A. and Seils, E. (2011) 'Accelerating Downhill: How the EU shapes corporate tax competition in the Single Market', *Journal of Common Market Studies*, vol 49, no 3, pp 585–606.

Gentleman, A. (2013) 'Fitness for work tests are unfair, tribunal says', *Guardian*, 23 May, p 18.

Gereffi, G. and Lee, J. (2012) 'Why the world suddenly cares about global supply chains', *Journal of Supply Chain Management*, vol 48, no 3, pp 24–32.

Giddens, A. (1998) *The Third Way: The renewal of social democracy*, Cambridge: Polity Press.

Giger, N. and Nelson, M. (2011) 'The electoral consequences of welfare state retrenchment: Blame avoidance or credit claiming in the era of permanent austerity?', *European Journal of Political Research*, vol 50, no 1, pp 1–23.

Gill, S. (1998) 'European governance and new constitutionalism: economic and monetary union and alternatives to disciplinary neoliberalism in Europe', *New Political Economy*, vol 3, no 1, pp 5–26.

Gill, S. and Cutler, A.C. (eds) (2014) *New constitutionalism and world order*, Cambridge: Cambridge University Press.

Girouard, N. (2010) 'Housing and mortgage markets: An OECD perspective', in Smith, S.J. and Searle, B.A. (eds) *The Blackwell companion to the economics of housing: The housing wealth of nations*, Chichester: Wiley-Blackwell.

Gopalakrishnan, S. (2007) 'Negative aspects of special economic zones in China', *Economic and Political Weekly*, vol 42, no 17, pp 1492–4.

Gorsky, M. (2008) 'The British National Health Service 1948–2008: a review of the historiography', *Social History of Medicine*, vol 21, no 3, pp 437–60.

Gough, I. (1979) *The political economy of the welfare state*, Basingstoke: Macmillan.

Gough, I. (2011) 'From financial crisis to fiscal crisis', in K. Farnsworth and Z. Irving (eds) *Social policy in challenging times: Economic crisis and welfare systems*, Bristol: Policy Press, pp 49–64.

Goul Andersen, J., Clasen, J., van Oorschot, W. and Halvorsen, K. (2002) (eds) *Europe's new state of welfare: Unemployment, employment policies and citizenship*, Bristol: Policy Press.

Grace, C. and Simpson, J. (2009) 'Challenging behaviour', in K. Kerswell and S. Goss (eds) *Challenging behaviour*, London: SOLACE.

Gray, D. (2014) 'Coherence and stability in the conduct of regulatory policies', Speech to the Regulatory Policy Institute Conference, 25 April 2014.

Green, R.K. and Wachter, S.M. (2010) 'The housing finance revolution', in S.J. Smith and B.A. Searle (eds) *The Blackwell companion to the economics of housing: The housing wealth of nations*, Chichester: Wiley-Blackwell.

Greenspan, A. and Kennedy, J. (2005), *Estimates of home mortgage originations, repayment and debt on one-to-four family residences*, Finance and Economics Discussion Series, Division of Research & Statistics and Monetary Affairs, 41, Washington DC: Federal Reserve Board.

Gregg, D. (2008) *Realising potential: A vision for personalised conditionality and support – An independent report to the Department for Work and Pensions*, London: Department for Work and Pensions.

Gregory, S., Dixon, A. and Ham, C. (2012) *Health policy under the Coalition Government*, London: The King's Fund.

Griggs, J. and Evans, M. (2010) *Sanctions within conditional benefit systems: A review of the evidence*, York: Joseph Rowntree Foundation.

Gross, D.A. and Sigelmann, L. (1984) 'Comparing party systems: A multidimensional approach', *Comparative Politics*, vol 16, no 4, pp 463–79.

Grover, C. and Piggott, L. (2013) 'Disability and social (in)security: emotions, contradictions of inclusion and Employment Support Allowance', *Social Policy and Society*, vol 12, no 3, pp 369–80.

Guardian (2013) 'Energy firms expected to increase prices by 8%: Rise could take average annual bill to £1,500, with companies likely to blame environmental levies', http://www.theguardian.com/money/2013/sep/20/energy-firms-increase-prices

Guardian (2014a) 'Energy industry needs to accept tougher regulation, says SSE chief', 3 April, http://www.theguardian.com/business/2014/apr/03/energy-industry-regulation-sse-alistair-phillips-davies

Guardian (2014b) 'British Gas hit by £11m Ofgem fine for energy efficiency delays', http://www.theguardian.com/business/2014/dec/04/british-gas-hit-by-11m-ofgem-fine-for-energy-efficiency-delays

Guardian (2014c) 'Scottish Power faces fine and warning sales operation could be suspended', http://www.theguardian.com/money/2014/nov/14/scottish-power-fine-sales-operation-suspended-ofgem

Guardian (2014d) 'Energy firms under pressure to cut bills after sharp drop in wholesale costs', http://www.theguardian.com/money/2014/jun/10/energy-firms-gas-electricity-pressure-cut-bills-sharp-drop-wholesale-costs-ofgem)

Guardian Datablog (2013) 'Energy price increases: how do the big six compare?', http://www.theguardian.com/news/datablog/2013/nov/19/energy-price-bills-increase-big-six-compare#data

Guertler, P. (2012) 'Can the Green Deal be fair too? Exploring new possibilities for alleviating fuel poverty', *Energy Policy*, vol 49, pp 91–7.

Gurney, C. (1999) 'Pride and prejudice: discourses of normalisation in public and private accounts of home ownership', *Housing Studies*, vol 14, pp 163–83.

Hacker, B. (2013) 'The end of the European Social Model as we have envisioned it? Political economy principles in europe may be changed by the economic crisis governance', paper presented at the conference "Beyond Austerity vs. Growth: The future of the European political economy", Halifax Hall, University of Sheffield, 1–3 July 2013.

Hall, P.A. and Soskice, D. (eds) (2001) *Varieties of capitalism: The institutional foundations of comparative advantage*, Oxford: Oxford University Press.

Hall, S. (2011) 'The march of the neoliberals', *Guardian*, 12 September, http://www.theguardian.com/politics/2011/sep/12/march-of-the-neoliberals

Hamnett, C. (1991) 'A nation of inheritors? Housing inheritance, wealth and inequality in Britain', *Journal of Social Policy*, vol 20, no 4, pp 509–36.

Hancké, B. (2009) *Debating varieties of capitalism*, Oxford: Oxford University Press.

Handler, J. (2004) *Social citizenship and workfare in the United States and Western Europe: The paradox of inclusion*, Cambridge: Cambridge University Press.

Hanefeld, J., Horsfall, D., Lunt, N. and Smith, R. (2013) 'Medical tourism: a cost or benefit to the NHS?', *PLoS ONE*, vol 8, no 10, e70406.

Hantrais, L. (2007 [1995]) *Social policy in the European Union* (3rd edn), Basingstoke: Palgrave Macmillan.

Harrington, M. (2010) *An independent review of the Work Capability Assessment*, London: TSO.

Harrington, M. (2012) *An independent review of the Work Capability Assessment – Year Three*, London: TSO.

Harrison, M. and Sanders, T. (2014) *Social policies and social control: New perspectives on the not-so-big society*, Bristol: Policy Press.

Harvey, D. (2005) *A brief history of neoliberalism*, Oxford: Oxford University Press.

Harvey, D. (2011) *The enigma of capital: And the crises of capitalism*, London: Profile Books.

Häusermann, S., Picot, G. and Geering, D. (2013) 'Rethinking party politics and the welfare state – recent advances in the literature', *British Journal of Political Science*, vol 43, no 1, pp 221–40.

Hay, C. (2004) 'Re-stating politics, re-politicising the state: neo-liberalism, economic imperatives and the rise of the competition state', *The Political Quarterly*, vol 75, no 1, pp 38–50.

Hay, C. and Wincott, D. (2012) *The political economy of European welfare capitalism*, Houndmills: Palgrave Macmillan.

Healthcare UK (2015) *Healthcare UK: Overview and annual review 2014/15*, London: UK Trade and Investment.

Heenan, D. (2002) '"It won't change the world but it turned my life around": participants' views on the personal advisor scheme in the New Deal for Disabled People', *Disability and Society*, vol 17, no 4, pp 383–401.

Hegewisch, A. and Gornick, J. (2011) 'The impact of work–family policies on women's employment: a review of research from OECD countries', *Community, Work & Family*, vol 14, no 2, pp 119–38.

Heichel , S., Pape, J. and Sommerer, T. (2005) 'Is there convergence in convergence research? An overview of empirical studies on policy convergence', *Journal of European Public Policy*, vol 12, no 5, pp 817–40.

Heidenheimer, A. J., Heclo, H. and Adams, T.C. (1990) *Comparative public policy, The politics of social choice in America, Europe and Japan*, New York: St Martin's Press.

Hewitt, M. (1999) 'New Labour and social security', in M. Powell (ed) *New Labour, new welfare state? The third way in British social policy*, Bristol: Policy Press, pp 149–70.

Hillebrand, E. (ed) (2013) *Euro crisis, austerity policy and the European Social Model: How crisis policies in Southern Europe threaten the EU's social dimension*, Berlin: Friedrich-Ebert-Stiftung, International Policy Analysis.

Hills, J. (2012) *Getting the measure of fuel poverty: Final Report of the Fuel Poverty Review*, CASE Report 72.

Hirst, P. and Thompson, G. (1999) *Globalization in question* (2nd edn), Cambridge: Polity Press.

HM Government (2011) *Laying the Foundations: A Housing Strategy for England*, London: HM Government.

HM Treasury (2001) *Institutional investment in the United Kingdom: A Review* [Myners Report, 2001], London: HM Treasury.

HM Treasury (2002) *Selling into wider markets: A policy note for public bodies*, London: HM Treasury Enterprise & Growth Unit.

Hoggett P., Wilkinson H. and Beedell, P. (2013) 'Fairness and the politics of resentment', *Journal of Social Policy*, vol 42, no 3, pp 567–85.

Hollomotz, A. (2011) *Learning difficulties and sexual vulnerability: A social approach*, London: Jessica Kingsley.

Höpner, M. and Schäfer, A. (2007) *A new phase of european integration: Organized capitalisms in post-Ricardian Europe*, MPIfG Discussion Paper 07/4.

Höpner, M. and Schäfer, A. (2010) *Polanyi in Brussels? Embeddedness and the three dimensions of european economic integration*, MPIfG Discussion Paper 10/8.

Horsfall, D. (2010) 'From competition state to competition states?' *Policy Studies*, vol 31, no 1, pp 57–76.

Horsfall, D. (2013a) 'There and back again: convergence towards the competition state plan', *Policy Studies*, vol 34, no 1, pp 53–72.

Horsfall, D. (2013b) 'A fuzzy set ideal-type approach to measuring the competition state', *Policy and Society*, vol 32, no 4, pp 345–56.

House of Commons Library (2015) *Syrian refugees and the UK*, Accessed online at: www.parliament.uk/business/publications/research/briefing-papers/SN06805/syrian-refugees-and-the-uk.

Huber, E. and Stephens, J.D. (2001) *Development and crisis of the welfare state*, Chicago: Chicago University Press.

Hudson, J. (2012) 'Welfare regimes and global cities: a missing link in the comparative analysis of welfare states?', *Journal of Social Policy*, vol 41, pp 455–73.

Hudson, J. and Kühner, S. (2009) 'Towards productive welfare? A comparative analysis of 23 countries', *Journal of European Social Policy*, vol 19, pp 34–46.

Hudson, J. and Kühner, S. (2013), 'Qualitative comparative analysis and applied public policy analysis: New applications of innovative methods', *Policy and Society*, 32, pp 279–87.

Hudson, J. and Medrano, A. (2013) 'Nation-state global city tensions in social policy: the case of Mexico City's rising social city-zenship', *Journal of International and Comparative Social Policy*, vol 29, pp 1–14.

Hurst, S.A. (2008) 'Vulnerability in research and health care: describing the elephant in the room', *Bioethics*, vol 22, no 4, pp 191–202.

Hutchinson, S. (2013) 'Disability benefit assessments "unfair" says ex-worker', *BBC News*, 16 May, http://www.bbc.co.uk/news/uk-22546036

Hutton, J. (2007) *Improving employability for disadvantaged groups*, speech to the Welfare to Work seminar organized by Institute for Public Policy Research North, Manchester, 2 March.

Huws, U. (2008) 'The new gold rush: the new multinationals and the commodification of public service work', *Work Organisation, Labour and Globalisation*, vol 2, no 2, pp 1–8.

Hyde, M. (2000) 'From welfare to work? Social policy for disabled people of working age in the UK in the 1990's', *Disability and Society*, vol 15, no 2, pp 327–41.

IAGS (2015) *Independent Annual Growth Survey*, 3rd Report, December, http://www.iags-project.org/documents/iags_report2015.pdf

ICFTU (2004) *Behind the brand names: Working conditions and labour rights in export processing zones*, International Federation of Free Trade Unions, http://www.newunionism.net/library/internationalism/ICFTU%20-%20Working%20Conditions%20amd%20Labour%20Rights%20in%20Export%20Processiong%20Zones%20-%202004.pdf (accessed 15 April 2014).

ILO (2010) *Report of the Committee of Experts on the Application of Conventions and Recommendations. Report III (Part 1A)*, paper presented at the International Labour Conference, 99th Session, Geneva.

ILO (2015) *Global Wage Report, 2014/15 wages and income inequality*, Geneva: ILO.

IMF (2012) *World Economic Outlook: Coping with high debt and sluggish growth*, Washington DC: International Monetary Fund.

Iversen, T. and Soskice, D. (2006) 'Electoral institutions and the politics of coalitions: Why some democracies redistribute more than others', *American Political Science Review*, vol 100, no 2, pp 165–81.

Jahn, D. (2010) 'Left and Right in comparative politics: a deductive approach', *Party Politics*, vol 17, no 6, pp 745–65.

James, A. and James, A. (2008) *Key concepts in childhood studies*, London: Sage.

Janssen, R. (2011) *Why Europe needs a fairness pact and not a competitiveness pact*, Economic Discussion Paper 2011/07, Brussels: ETUC.

Jansz, A. and Guertler, P. (2012) *The impact on the fuel poor of the reduction in fuel poverty budgets in England*, London: Association for the Conservation of Energy.

Jappens, M. and Van Bavel, J. (2012) 'Regional family norms and child care by grandparents in Europe', *Demographic Research*, vol 27, no 4, pp 85–120.

Jenson, J. (2010) 'Diffusing ideas after neoliberalism: the social investment perspective in Europe and Latin America', *Global Social Policy*, vol 10, no 1, pp 59–84.

Jeong, H.S. (2011) 'Korea's national health insurance-lessons from the past three decades', *Health Affairs*, vol 30, no 1, pp 136–44.

Jessop, B. (2000) 'From the KWNS to the SWPR', in G. Lewis, S. Gewirtz and J. Clarke (eds) *Rethinking social policy*, London: Sage, pp 171-84.

Jessop, B. (2002) *The future of the capitalist state*, Cambridge, MA: Polity.

Jessop, B. (2013a) 'The North Atlantic financial crisis and varieties of capitalism: a Minsky moment and/or a Marx moment? And perhaps Weber too?', in S. Fadda and P. Tridico (eds) *Financial crisis, labour markets and institutions*, London: Routledge, pp 40–59.

Jessop, B. (2013b) 'The complexities of competition and competitiveness: challenges for competition law and economic governance in variegated capitalism', in M.W. Dowdle, J. Gillespie and I. Maher (eds) *Asian capitalism and the regulation of competition: Towards a regulatory geography of global competition law*, New York: Cambridge University Press, pp 96–120.

Jessop, B. (2015) 'Neo-liberalism, Finance-dominated accumulation, and enduring austerity: A cultural political economy perspective', in K. Farnsworth and Z. Irving (eds) *Social policy in times of austerity: Global economic crisis and the new politics of welfare*, Bristol: Policy Press, pp 87–111.

Jessop, B., Kastendiek, H., Nielsen, K. and Pedersen, O. (eds) (1991) *The politics of flexibility, restructuring state and industry in Britain, Germany and Scandinavia*, Aldershot: Edward Elgar.

Johnsen, S. and Fitzpatrick, S. (2010) 'Revanchist sanitisation or coercive care? The use of enforcement to combat begging, street drinking and rough sleeping in England', *Urban Studies*, vol 47, pp 1703–23.

Johnson, A. (2005) 'Fit for purpose- welfare to work and incapacity benefit', speech by the Secretary of State for Work and Pensions, Cardiff University, 7 February, London: Department of Work and Pensions.

Jonasson, E., Pettersson, L. and Södersten, B. (eds) (2004) Employment and non-employment: a study of the Swedish labour market', in *Globalization and welfare states*, Basingstoke: Palgrave Macmillan, pp 172–94.

Jones, M.R. (1997), 'Spatial selectivity of the state? The regulationist enigma and local struggles over economic governance', *Environment and Planning A*, vol 29, no 5, pp 831–64.

Jurgens, J., Naumann, K. and Rupp, J. (2000) 'Shareholder value in an adverse environment: the German case', *Economy and Society*, vol 29, pp 54–79.

Katsapaou, C. (2013) *Response to vulnerability in asylum*, Budapest: United Nations High Commissioner for Refugees, Regional Representation for Central Europe.

Kazepov, Y. (2010) 'Rescaling social policies towards multilevel governance in Europe: Some reflections on processes at stake and actors involved', in Y. Kazepov (ed) *Rescaling social policies: Towards multilevel governance in Europe*, Farnham: Ashgate, pp 35-72.

Keat, R. and Abercrombie, N. (eds) (1991) *Enterprise culture*, London: Routledge.

Keating, M. (2001) *Nations against the state: The new politics of nationalism in Quebec, Catalonia and Scotland* (2nd edn), Basingstoke: Palgrave.

Keating, M. (2009) 'Spatial rescaling, devolution and the future of social welfare', in K. Rummery, I. Greener and C. Holden (eds) *Social Policy Review 21*, Bristol: Policy Press.

Kelly, P. (2006) 'The entrepreneurial self and "youth at-risk": exploring the horizons of identity in the twenty-first century', *Journal of Youth Studies*, vol 9, no 1, pp 17–32.

Keman, H., Paloheimo, H. and Whiteley, P. (1987) *Coping with economic crisis: Alternative responses to economic recession in advanced industrial societies*, London: Sage.

Kemeny, J. (1981) *The myth of home ownership: public versus private choices in housing tenure*, London: Routledge.

Kemeny, J. (1995) *From public housing to the social market*, London: Routledge.

Kemeny, J. (2006) 'Corporatism and housing regimes', In *Housing, Theory and Society*, vol 23, no 1, pp 1–18.

Kennedy, S. (2015) *Welfare Reform and Work Bill* [Bill 51 of 2015–16], House of Commons Briefing Paper Number 07252, 16 July, London: House of Commons.

Kenway, J. and Fahey, J.C. (2009) *Globalizing the research imagination*, Abingdon: Routledge.

Kern, F., Kuzemko, C. and Mitchell, C. (2014) 'Measuring and explaining policy paradigm change: the case of UK energy policy', *Policy & Politics*, vol 42, no 4, pp 513–30.

Kim, K-H. and Renaud, B. (2009) 'The global house price boom and its unwinding: an analysis and a commentary', *Housing Studies*, vol 24, no 1, pp 7–24.

Kim, S., Lee, J. and Jung, J. (2013) 'Assessment of medical tourism development in Korea for the achievement of competitive advantages', *Asia Pacific Journal of Tourism Research*, vol 18, no 5, pp 421–45.

King, P. (2004) 'What do we mean by responsibility? The case of UK housing benefit reform', *Journal of Housing and the Built Environment*, vol 21, no 2, pp 111–25.

Kirby, P. (2006) *Vulnerability and violence: The impact of globalisation*, London: Pluto Press.

Klein, R. (1989) *The politics of the NHS* (2nd edn), London: Longman.

Klingemann, H.D., Volkens, A., Bara, J., Budge, I. and McDonald, M. (2006) *Mapping policy preferences II: Estimates for Parties, electors, and governments in Eastern Europe, the European Union and the OECD, 1990–2003*, Oxford: Oxford University Press.

Kraemer, K., Linden, G. and Dedrick, J. (2011) *Capturing value in global networks: Apple's iPad and iPhone*, working paper, http://pcic.merage. uci.edu/papers/2011/Value_iPad_iPhone.pdf

Krugman, P. (2012) 'Europe's austerity madness', *New York Times*, 28 September.

Kühner, S. (2010) 'Do party governments matter after all? Executive ideology, constitutional structures and their combined effect on welfare state change', *Journal of Comparative Policy Analysis: Research and Practice*, vol 12, no 4, pp 395–415.

Kühner, S. (2015) 'Government ideology, veto players and their combined effect on productive and protective welfare policy: do parties still matter after all?', paper presented at the SPA Annual Conference 2015: Social Policy in the Spotlight: Change, Continuity and Challenge, Belfast Metropolitan College, 6–8 July 2015.

Lambert, J. (2013) *Draft Report on Access to Care for Vulnerable Groups*, Committee on Employment and Social Affairs, European Parliament.

Laver, M. and Hunt, W.B. (1992) *Policy and party competition*, New York: Routledge.

Lees, C. (2012) *UK trade performance across markets and sectors*, BIS Economics Paper 17.

Leonard, P. (2012) 'All aboard for NHS exports?', *Health Service Journal*, 28 November.

Levien, M. (2011) 'Special economic zones and accumulation by dispossession in India', *Journal of Agrarian Change*, vol 11, no 4, pp 454–83.

Lévy-Vroelant, C. (2010) 'Housing vulnerable groups: the development of a new public action sector', *International Journal of Housing Policy*, vol 10, no 4, pp 443–56.

Lijphart, A. (1999) *Patterns of democracy: Government forms and performance in thirty-six countries*, New Haven: Yale University Press.

Lindsay, C. and Houston, D. (2013) (eds) *Disability benefits, welfare reform and employment policy*, Basingstoke: Palgrave Macmillan.

Lindstrom, N. (2010) 'Service liberalization in the enlarged EU: A race to the bottom or the emergence of transnational political conflict?', *Journal of Common Market Studies*, vol 48, no 5 (Nov), pp 1307–27.

Lipsky, M. (1980) *Street-level bureaucracy: The dilemmas of the individual in public service*, New York: Russell Sage Foundation.

Lister, R. (1998) 'From equality to social inclusion: New Labour and the welfare state', *Critical Social Policy*, vol 18, no 55, pp 215–25.

Lowe, S. (1990) 'Capital accumulation in home ownership and family welfare', in Manning, N. and Ungerson, C. (eds) *Social Policy Review 1989–90*, Harlow: Longman, pp 44-66.

Lowe, S. (1992) 'The social and economic consequences of the growth of home ownership', in Birchall, J. (ed) *Housing policy in the 1990s*, London: Routledge, pp 68-90.

Lowe, S. (2004) *Housing policy analysis: British housing in cultural and comparative context*, Houndmills: Palgrave Macmillan.

Lowe, S. (2011) *The housing debate*, Bristol: Policy Press.

Lowe, S. and Watson, S. (1989) *From first-time buyers to last-time sellers: An appraisal of the social and economic consequences of equity withdrawal from the housing market, 1982–1988*, York: Joseph Rowntree Memorial Trust/University of York.

Lowe, S., Smith, S. and Searle, B. (2011) 'From housing wealth to mortgage debt: the emergence of Britain's asset-shaped welfare state', *Social Policy & Society*, vol 11, no 1, pp 105–16.

Lundvall, B-A. and Lorenz, E. (2012) 'Social investment in the globalising learning economy: A European perspective', in N. Morel, B. Palier and J. Palme (eds) *Towards a social investment welfare state? Ideas, policies and challenges*, Bristol: Policy Press, pp 235-60.

Lunt, N. and Horsfall, D. (2013) 'New Zealand's reform of sickness benefit and invalid's benefit', in C. Lindsay and D. Houston (eds) *Disability benefits, welfare reform and employment policy*, Basingstoke: Palgrave Macmillan, pp 216–32.

Lunt, N., Horsfall, D. and Hanefeld, J. (eds) (2015) *Handbook on medical tourism and patient mobility*, Cheltenham: Edward Elgar.

Lunt, N., Exworthy, M., Hanefeld, J. and Smith, R. (2014) 'International patients within the NHS: A case of public sector entrepreneurialism', *Social Science & Medicine*, vol 124, pp 338–45.

Lunt, N., Hanefeld, J., Smith, R.D., Exworthy, M., Horsfall, D. and Mannion, R. (2013) 'Market size, market share and market strategy: three myths of medical tourism', *Policy & Politics*, vol 42, no 4, pp 597–614.

Lupton, D. (1999) *Risk*, London: Routledge.

Lyons, H. (2014) 'Should all NHS organisations be selling their services internationally?' https://healthcareuk.blog.gov.uk/2014/05/02/nhs-in-world-wide-demand/ (accessed 3 December 2014).

Mackenzie, C., Rogers, W. and Dodds, S. (2014) *Vulnerability: New essays in ethics and feminist philosophy*, Oxford: Oxford University Press.

McLaughlin, K. (2012) *Surviving identity: Vulnerability and the psychology of recognition*, London: Routledge.

Mahon, R. (2013) 'Socialinvestment according to the OECD/DELSA: a discourse in the making', *Global Social Policy*, vol 4, no 2 pp 150–9.

Marmott Review Team (2011) *The health impacts of cold homes and fuel poverty*, Friends of the Earth/Marmot Review Team.

Marsh, S. (2012) 'Welfare to fare well', *Journal of Poverty and Social Justice*, vol 20, no 2, pp 219–21.

Marshall, T.H. (1950) *Citizenship and social class and other essays*, Cambridge: Cambridge University Press.

Marshall, T.H. (1992) *Citizenship and social class*, London: Pluto.

Martinsen, D.S. (2011) 'Judicial policy-making and Europeanization: the proportionality of national control and administrative discretion', *Journal of European Public Policy*, vol 18, no 7, pp 944–61, doi: 10.1080/13501763.2011.599962.

Mason, P. (2015) *Post-Capitalism*, London: Allen Lane.

Mause, K. (2009) *Contracting out the state in the OECD world: What do we (not) know*, Paris: OECD.

May, C. (2014) 'The rule of law as the *Grundnorm* of the new constitutionalism', in S. Gill and A.C. Cutler (eds) *New constitutionalism and world order*, Cambridge: Cambridge University Press, pp 63–74.

Mazzucato, M. (2013) *The entrepreneurial state: Debunking public vs. private sector myths*, London: Anthem Press.

McCallum, J.K. (2011) *Export processing zones: Comparative data from China, Honduras, Nicaragua and South Africa*, Working Paper no 21, Geneva: ILO.

Meers, J. (2014) 'The downward drag of Pereira: Ongoing disputes with vulnerability' *Critical Urbanists* blog: https://criticalurbanists. wordpress.com/category/housing-law/.

Meers, J. (2015) 'The downward drag of Pereira: The assessment of vulnerability under s.189 Housing Act 1996', *Journal of Social Welfare and Family Law*, vol 37, no 4, pp 473–5.

Megginson, W.L. and Netter, J.M. (2001) 'From state to market: A survey of empirical studies on privatisation', *Journal of Economic Literature*, vol 39, no 2, pp 321–89.

Milanovic, B. (2015) Twitter status, 26 July, https://twitter.com/ brankomilan/status/625219413227274240.

Miles, D. (2004) *The Miles review of the UK mortgage market: Taking a long-term view*, Final Report, London: HMSO/HM Treasury.

MindfulMoney (2013) 'Energy regulator Ofgem slammed by MPs for "failing consumers"', accessed at http://www.mindfulmoney. co.uk/uncategorized/energy-regulator-ofgem-slammed-by-mps-for-failing-consumers/#sthash.1r6McRiQ.dpuf, 6 July.

Mirowski, P. (2014) *Never let a serious crisis go to waste*, London: Verso.

Misztal, B.A. (2011) *The challenges of vulnerability: In search of strategies for a less vulnerable social life,* Houndmills: Palgrave Macmillan.

Molina, O. and Rhodes, M. (2007) 'The political economy of adjustment in mixed market economies: a study of Spain and Italy', in B. Hancké, M. Rhodes and M. Thatcher (2007), *Beyond varieties of capitalism: Conflict, contradictions, and complementarities in the European economy*, Oxford: Oxford University Press.

Morel, N., Palier, B. and Palme, J. (eds) (2012a) *Towards a social investment welfare state? Ideas, policies and challenges*, Bristol: Policy Press.

Morel, N., Palier, B. and Palme, J. (2012b) 'Beyond the welfare state as we knew it?', in N. Morel, B. Palier and J. Palme (eds) *Towards a Social Investment Welfare State? Ideas, policies and challenges*, Bristol: Policy Press, pp 1–32.

Morel, N., Palier, B. and Palme, J. (2012c) 'Social investment: a paradigm in search of a new economic model and political mobilisation', in N. Morel, B. Palier and J. Palme (eds) *Towards a social investment welfare state? Ideas, policies and challenges*, Bristol: Policy Press, pp 353–76.

Morgan, K.J. (2012) 'Promoting social investment through work-family policies: which nations do it and why?', in Morel, N., Palier, B. and Palme, J. (eds) *Towards a social investment welfare state? Ideas, policies and challenges*, Bristol: Policy Press, pp 153–80.

Morris, S. (2011) ' Government round up', *Journal of Poverty and Social Justice*, vol 19, no 2, pp 193–8.

Moschella, M. (2014) 'Monitoring macroeconomic imbalances: is EU surveillance more effective than IMF surveillance?' *JCMS: Journal of Common Market Studies*, doi: 10.1111/jcms.12136.

Mosley, H. and Mayer, A. (1999) *Benchmarking national labour market performance: A radar chart approach, WZB Discussion Paper*, No. FS I 99–202.

Muellbauer, J. (2008) *Housing, credit and consumer expenditure*, CEPR Discussion Paper no 6782.

Muellbauer, J. and Murphy, A. (2008) 'Housing markets and the economy: the assessment', *Oxford Review of Economic Policy*, vol 24, no 10, pp 1–33.

Muncie, J. (2006) 'Governing young people: coherence and contradiction in contemporary youth justice', *Critical Social Policy*, vol 26, no 4, pp 770–93.

NAO (National Audit Office) (2013) *The role of major contractors in the delivery of public services*, Report by the Comptroller and Auditor General, Comptroller and Auditor General, HC 810, Session 2013–2014, National Audit Office, 8 November 2013.

NEA (National Energy Action) (2014) *Fuel Poverty Monitor*, http://www.nea.org.uk/policy-and-research/publications/2014/monitor-2014

Newbery, D.M. (1997) 'Privatisation and liberalization of network utilities', *European Economic Review*, vol 41, pp 357–83.

Newman, J. (2001) *Modernizing governance: New Labour, policy and society*, London: Sage.

Newton Dunn, T. and Ashton, E. (2012) 'Workers not shirkers: Osborne gets tough on the economy. Benefit blitz to aid struggling families', *Sun*, 6 December, http://www.thesun.co.uk/sol/homepage/news/politics/4683376/George-Osborne-gets-tough-over-the-economy.html

Ngai, P. (2004) 'Women workers and precarious employment in Shenzhen special economic zone, China', *Gender & Development*, vol 12, no 2, pp 29–36.

Nicoletti, G. and Scarpetta, S. (2006) 'Regulation and economic performance: product market reforms and productivity in the OECD', in T.S. Eicher and C. Garcia-Penalosa (eds) *Institutions, Developments, and Economic Growth*, Massachusetts: Massachusetts Institute of Technology Books.

Nicoletti, G., Scarpetta, S. and Boylaud, O. (2000) *Summary indicators of product market regulation with an extension to employment protection legislation*, Paris: OECD.

Nikolai, R. (2012) 'Towards social investment? Patterns of public policy in the OECD world', in N. Morel, B. Palier and J. Palme (eds) *Towards a social investment welfare state? Ideas, policies and challenges*, Bristol: Policy Press, pp 91–116.

O'Neill, J. (2001) 'Building better global economic BRICs', Global Economics Paper no 66, Goldman Sachs.

O'Neill, J. (2013) 'Who you calling a BRIC', Bloomberg, 13 November.

OECD (2012) *Restoring Public Finances, 2012 Update*, Paris: OECD.

OECD (2013a) Product Market Regulation Database, www.oecd.org/economy/pmr

OECD (2013b) *Report on integrated service delivery for vulnerable groups*, Paris: OECD.

OECD (2014a) *Employment outlook*, Paris: OECD.

OECD (2014b) *Focus on inequality and growth – December 2014*, Paris: OECD.

OECD (2014c) *The scope and comparability of data on labour market programmes*, Paris: OECD.

OECD (2014d) *Health: Key Tables*, Paris: OECD.

OECD (2014e) *Social Expenditure Update: Social spending is falling in some countries, but in many others it remains at historically high levels, Insights from the OECD Social Expenditure database (SOCX)*, November, Paris: OECD.

OECD (2015) *Tax and Benefit Systems: OECD Indicators*, Paris: OECD.

OECD (2015a) Social Expenditure Database, Paris: OECD.

OECD (2015b) Employment Database, Paris: OECD.

OECD (2015c) Tax Database, Paris: OECD.

Ofgem (2002) 'Ofgem Factsheet: New Electricity Trading Arrangements (NETA) – One Year Review', https://www.ofgem.gov.uk/ofgem-publications/64113/1109-factsheet110224july.pdf

Ofgem (2013) 'Ofgem Fines SSE £10.5 for misspelling', https://www.ofgem.gov.uk/ofgem-publications/76232/sse-press-release.pdf.

Ofgem (2014a) 'Ofgem calls on suppliers to explain prices to consumers', https://www.ofgem.gov.uk/publications-and-updates/ofgem-calls-suppliers-explain-prices-consumers

Ofgem (2014b) 'E.ON to pay £12 million package following Ofgem mis-selling investigation', https://www.ofgem.gov.uk/publications-and-updates/e.-pay-£12-million-package-following-ofgem-mis-selling-investigation

Ofgem (2014c) 'EDF Energy to pay £3 million following Ofgem investigation into the company's complaints handling arrangements', https://www.ofgem.gov.uk/publications-and-updates/edf-energy-pay-£3-million-following-ofgem-investigation-companys-complaints-handling-arrangements

Ofgem (2015a) 'The renewables obligation', https://www.ofgem.gov.uk/environmental-programmes/renewables-obligation-ro

Ofgem (2015b) 'The feed-in tariff', https://www.ofgem.gov.uk/environmental-programmes/feed-tariff-fit-scheme

Ofgem (2015c) 'Warm Home Discount', https://www.ofgem.gov.uk/environmental-programmes/social-programmes/warm-home-discount

Ofgem/CMA (2014) 'State of the market assessment', https://www.ofgem.gov.uk/ofgem-publications/86804/assessmentdocumentpublished.pdf

Ofgem/DECC (2011) 'Smart metering implementation programme', https://www.gov.uk/government/uploads/system/uploads/attachment_data/file/42742/1475-smart-metering-imp-response-overview.pdf

Ohmae, K. (1990) *The borderless world*, London: Collins.

Oliver, M. and Barnes, C. (1998) *Disabled people and social policy: From exclusion to inclusion*, London: Longman.

Ong, A. (2000), 'Graduated sovereignty in South East Asia', *Theory, Culture & Society*, vol 17, no 4, pp 55–75.

Osborne, G. and Thaler, R. (2010) 'We can make you behave', *Guardian*, 28 January.

Page, R. (1997) 'Caring for strangers: can an altruistic welfare state survive?', paper presented at the 'Citizenship and welfare: fifty years of progress?' conference, Ruskin College Oxford, December.

Papadopoulos, T. and Roumpakis, A. (2012) 'The Greek welfare state in the age of austerity: anti-social policy and the politico–economic crisis', in Kilkey, M., Ramia, G. and Farnsworth, K. (eds) *Social Policy Review 24: Analysis and debate in social policy*, Bristol: Policy Press, pp 205–30.

Papadopoulos, T. and Roumpakis, A. (2013a) 'The meta-regulation of European industrial relations: power shifts, institutional dynamics and the emergence of regulatory competition among Member States', *International Labour Review*, vol 152, no 2, pp 255–74.

Papadopoulos, T. and Roumpakis, A. (2013b) 'Familistic welfare capitalism in crisis: social reproduction and anti-social policy in Greece', *Journal of International and Comparative Social Policy*, vol 29, no 3, pp 204–24.

Papadopoulos, T. and Roumpakis A. (2015) 'Democracy, austerity and crisis: Southern Europe and the decline of the European Social Model', in S. Romano and G. Punziano (eds) *The European Social Model Adrift*, Aldershot: Ashgate, pp 189–212.

Patrick, R. (2011) 'Disabling or enabling: the extension of work-related conditionality to disabled people', *Social Policy and Society*, vol 20, no 3, pp 309–20.

Patrick, R. (2012) 'All in it together? Disabled people the Coalition and welfare to work', *Journal of Poverty and Social Justice*, vol 20, no 3, pp 307–22.

Pauly, L.W. and Grande, E. (2005) 'Reconstituting political authority: Sovereignty, effectiveness, and legitimacy in a transnational order', in E. Grande and L.W. Pauly (eds) *Complex sovereignty: Reconstituting political authority in the twenty-first century*, Toronto: University of Toronto Press, pp 3–21.

Peck, J. and Tickell, A. (1994), 'Jungle law breaks out: Neoliberalism and global-local disorder', *Area*, vol 26, no 4, pp 317–26.

Peroni, L. and Timmer, A. (2013) 'Vulnerable groups: the promise of an emergent concept in European Human Rights Convention law', *International Journal of Constitutional Law*, vol 11, no 4, pp 1056–85.

Pierson, P. (1994) *Dismantling the welfare state? Reagan, Thatcher and the policies of retrenchment*, Cambridge: Cambridge University Press.

Pierson, P. (1996) 'The new politics of the welfare state', *World Politics*, vol 48, no 2, pp 143–79.

Pierson, P. (1998) 'Irresistable forces, immovable objects: Post–industrial welfare states confront permanent austerity', *Journal of European Public Policy*, vol 5, no 4, pp 539–60.

Pierson, P. (ed) (2001) *The new politics of the welfare state*, Oxford: Oxford University Press.

Pierson, P. (2004) *Politics in time: History, institutions and social analysis*, Princeton, NJ: Princeton University Press.

Piketty, T. (2013) *Capital in the twenty-first century*, Cambridge: Harvard University Press.

Plantenga, J. and Hansen, J. (1999) 'Assessing equal opportunities in the European Union', *International Labour Review*, vol 138, no 4, pp 351–79.

Plimmer, G. (2014a) 'UK outsourcing spend doubles to £88bn under coalition', ft.com, 6 July .

Plimmer, G. (2014b) 'British outsourcing groups dominate public sector contracts', ft.com, 19 November.

Polanyi, K. (1944 [2002]) *The great transformation; The political and economic origins of our time*, London: Beacon Press.

Pollitt, M.G. (2012) *The role of policy in energy transitions: Lessons from the energy liberalization era*, Electricity Policy Research Group Working Paper 1208, University of Cambridge.

Porter, M. (1990) *The competitive advantage of nations*, London: Macmillan.

PSE (Poverty and Social Exclusion) (2013) 'MPs warn over fuel poverty', http://www.poverty.ac.uk/editorial/mps-warn-over-fuel-poverty.

Powell, M. (ed) (1999) *New Labour, new welfare state? The third way in British social policy*, Bristol: Policy Press.

Reinhart, C.M. and Rogoff, K.S. (2009) *This time is different: Eight centuries of financial folly*, Princeton, NJ: Princeton University Press.

Renaud, B. and Kim, K-H. (2007) 'The global housing price boom and its aftermath', *Housing Finance International*, vol 22, no 2, pp 3–15.

Republic of Turkey Ministry of Health (2013a) 'Health tourism in Turkey from past to future', http://saglik.gov.tr/SaglikTurizmi/belge/1–24205/ingilizce-saglik-turizmi-ozet-bilgi-2013.html (accessed 15 November 2014).

Republic of Turkey Ministry of Health (2013b) 'Evaluation Report on medical tourism in Turkey 2013', http://www.saglik.gov.tr/SaglikTurizmi/dosya/1-91774/h/evaluaton-report-on-medical-tourism-in-turkey-2013.pdf (accessed 15 November 2014).

Richards, A. (2011) 'The problem with "radicalisation": The remit of "Prevent" and the need to refocus on terrorism in the UK', *International Affairs*, vol 87, no 1, pp 143–52.

Roberts, J. (1991) 'A medical malaise in hospital: private medicine: the NHS's safety valve', *BMJ*, vol 203, pp 163–5.

Rodger, J. (2008) *Criminalising social policy: Anti-social behaviour and welfare in a de-civilised society*, Cullompton: Willan.

Rolfe, H. (2012) 'Requiring the long-term unemployed to train: is benefit conditionality effective?' *National Institute Economic Review*, no 219, January.

Romano, S. and Punziano, G. (2015) *The European Social Model adrift: Europe, social cohesion and the economic crisis*, Oxon: Routledge.

Roulstone, A. and Prideaux, S. (2012) *Understanding Disability Policy*, Bristol: Policy Press.

Roulstone, A. and Sadique, K. (2013) '"Vulnerability" and the fight for legal recognition', in Roulstone, A. and Mason-Bish, H. (eds) *Disability, hate crime and violence*, Abingdon: Routledge.

Sadler, R.J. (2000) 'Corporate entrepreneurship in the public sector: the dance of the chameleon', *Australian Journal of Public Administration*, vol 59, no 2, pp 25–43.

Sassen, S. (1991) *The global city: New York*, London, Tokyo, Princeton, NJ: Princeton University Press.

Sassen, S. (2001) *The global city: New York* (2nd edn), London, Tokyo, Princeton, NJ: Princeton University Press.

Sassen, S. (2005) 'The global city: introducing a concept', *Brown Journal of World Affairs*, vol 11, pp 27–43.

Sauvé, P. (2002) 'Trade, education and the GATS: what's in, what's out, what's all the fuss about?', OECD Trade Directorate, Paris, Paper prepared for the OECD/US Forum on Trade in Educational Services.

Save the Children (2010) *Measuring severe child poverty in the UK*, Policy briefing, Save the Children.

Schäfer, A. and Streeck, W. (2013) *Politics in the age of austerity*, Cambridge: Polity.

Scharpf, F.W. (1999) *Governing in Europe: Effective and democratic?* Oxford: Oxford University Press.

Scharpf, F.W. (2013) 'Monetary union, fiscal crisis and the disabling of democratic accountability', in A. Schäfer and W. Streeck (eds) *Politics in the age of austerity*, Cambridge: Polity, pp 108-42.

Scheil-Adlung, X. and Kuhl, C. (2011) *Social security for all: Addressing inequities in access to health care for vulnerable groups in countries of Europe and Central Asia*, Geneva: International Labour Organisation (ILO).

Schelke, W. (2012) 'In the spotlight of crisis: how social policies create, correct, and compensate financial markets', *Politics & Society*, vol 40, pp 3–8.

Schiantarelli, F. (2008) 'Product market regulation and macroeconomic performance: a review of cross-country evidence', *Boston College Working Papers in Economics*, no 623, Boston: Boston College Department of Economics.

Schmidt, V. (2002) *The futures of European capitalism*, Oxford: Oxford University Press.

Schrank, A. (2001) 'Export processing zones: Free market islands or bridges to structural transformation?', *Development Policy Review*, vol 19, no 2, pp 223–42.

Schütz, H., Speckesser, S. and Schmid, G. (1998) *Benchmarking labour market performance and labour market policies: Theoretical foundations and applications*, WZB Discussion Paper No. FS I 98-205.

Schwartz, H.M. and Seabrooke, L. (2008) 'Varieties of residential capitalism in the international political economy: old welfare states and the new politics of housing', *Comparative European Politics*, vol 6, pp 237–61.

Scruggs, L. and Allan, J.P. (2006) 'Welfare-state decommodification in 18 OECD countries: A replication and revision', *Journal of European Social Policy*, vol 16, no 1, pp 55–72.

Seymour, R. (2014) *Against austerity: How we can fix the crisis they made*, London: Pluto Press.

Siaroff, A. (1999) 'Corporatism in 24 industrial democracies: meaning and measurement', *European Journal of Political Research*, vol 36, no 2, pp 175–205.

Simonin, B.L. (2008) 'Nation branding and public diplomacy: challenges and opportunities', *The Fletcher Forum of World Affairs*, vol 32, no 3, pp 19–34.

Skocpol, T. (1992) *Protecting soldiers and mothers: The political origins of social policy in the United States*, Cambridge, MA: Harvard University Press.

Smith, S.J. and Searle, B.A. (2010) 'Housing wealth as insurance: insights from the UK', in S.J. Smith and B.A. Searle (eds) *The Blackwell companion to the economics of housing: The housing wealth of nations*, Chichester: Wiley-Blackwell.

Snell, C. and Thomson, H. (2013) 'Energy policy under the Coalition government: green deal or no deal', *Social Policy Review 25*, Bristol: Policy Press.

Snell, C., Bevan, M. and Thomson, H. (2014) 'Disabled people, fuel poverty and welfare reform', www.eagacharitabletrust.org

Social Enterprise UK (2012) *The shadow state*, Social Enterprise UK.

Sovacool, B.K. and Mukherjee, I. (2011) 'Conceptualising and measuring energy security: a synthesized approach', *Energy Policy*, vol 36, no 8, pp 5343–55.

Starke, P., Kaasch, A., Hooren, F.V. and Van Hooren, F. (2013) *The welfare state as crisis manager: Explaining the diversity of policy responses to economic crisis*, Basingstoke: Palgrave Macmillan UK.

Stern, N. (2006) *The economics of climate change: The Stern review*, Cambridge: Cambridge University Press.

Stockton, H. and Campbell, R. (2011) *Time to reconsider UK energy and fuel poverty policies?*, York: Joseph Rowntree Foundation.

Streeck, W. (2014) *Buying time: The delayed crisis of democratic capitalism*, London: Verso.

Streeck, W. and Schafer, A. (2013) *Politics in the age of austerity*, Cambridge: Polity.

Supiot, A. (2012a) 'Under Eastern eyes', *New Left Review*, vol 73, pp 29–36.

Supiot, A. (2012b) *The spirit of Philadelphia: Social justice vs the total market*, London and New York: Verso.

Swank, D. (2002) *Global capital, political institutions and policy change in developed welfare states*, Oxford: Oxford University Press.

Szyszczak, E. (2009) 'United Kingdom', in R. Blanpain and A.M. Światkowski (eds), *The Laval and Viking cases: Freedom of services and establishment v. industrial conflict in the European Economic Area and Russia*, Alphen aan den Rijn Kluwer Law International, pp 167–76.

Tangian, A. (2007) 'European flexicurity: concepts, methodology and policies', *Transfer: European Review of Labour and Research Winter 2007*, vol 13, no 4, pp 551–73.

Tangian, A. (2010) *Not for bad weather: Macroanalysis of flexicurity with regard to the crisis*, Working Paper 2010.06, Brussels: European Trade Union Institute.

Taylor, M.Z. (2007) 'Empirical evidence against varieties of capitalism's theory of technological innovation', in B. Hancké (ed) *Debating varieties of capitalism*, Oxford: Oxford University Press.

Taylor, P. (1994) 'The state as container: territoriality in the modern world system', *Progress in Human Geography*, vol 18, no 2, pp 151–62.

Taylor, P. (2005) 'Leading world cities: empirical evaluations of urban nodes in multiple networks', *Urban Studies*, vol 42, pp 1593–608.

Taylor-Gooby, P. (2013) *The double crisis of the welfare state and what we can do about it*, Basigstoke: Palgrave.

Taylor-Gooby, P., Gumy, J. and Otto, A. (2015) 'Can "new welfare" address poverty through more and better jobs?' *Journal of Social Policy*, vol 44, pp 83–104.

TC Kalkınma Bakanlığı (2013) *Onuncu Kalkınma Planı (2014–2018)*, http://www.kalkinma.gov.tr/Lists/Yaynlar/Attachments/518/Onuncu%20Kalk%C4%B1nma%20Plan%C4%B1.pdf (accessed 14 November 2014).

Telegraph (2015) 'George Osborne: "Falling oil and gas prices should bring cheaper household bills"', 6 January, http://www.telegraph.co.uk/news/shopping-and-consumer-news/11328776/George-Osborne-Falling-oil-and-gas-prices-should-bring-cheaper-household-bills.html

The Economist Intelligence Unit (2014) *Healthcare in Saudi Arabia: Increasing capacity, increasing quality?*, London: Economist Group.

Thaler, R. and Sunstein, C. (2009) *Nudge: Improving decisions about health, wealth and happiness*, New Haven, CT: Yale University Press.

TheEnergyShop (2015) *Deregulation history*, https://www.theenergyshop.com/HomeEnergy/advice-guides-deregulationHistory#.VUiiTJ1waUl.

Timmer, A. (2013) 'A quiet revolution: vulnerability in the European Court of Human Rights', in Fineman, M. and Grear, A. (2013) *Vulnerability: Reflections on a new ethical foundation for law and politics*, Farnham: Ashgate, pp 147–71.

Tovar, M.A. (2012) 'The structure of energy efficiency investments in the UK households and its average monetary and environmental savings', *Energy Policy*, vol 50, pp 723–35.

Tsebelis, G. (2002) *Veto players: How political institutions work*, Princeton, NJ: Princeton University Press).

TUC and NEF (Trades Union Congress and the New Economics Foundation) (2015) *Outsourcing public services*, TUC and NEF.

Turner, B. (2006) *Vulnerability and human rights*, Pennsylvania: The Pennsylvania State University Press.

Tyler, I. (2013) *Revolting subjects: Social abjection and resistance in neoliberal Britain*, London: Zed Books.

Ulmestig, R. (2013) 'Incapacity benefits – change and continuity in the Swedish welfare state', in C. Lindsay and D. Houston (eds) *Disability benefits, welfare reform and employment policy*, Basingstoke: Palgrave Macmillan, pp 178–98.

United National Development Programme (UNDP) (2014) *Human Development Report 2014: Sustaining human progress: reducing vulnerabilities and building resilience*, New York: UNDP.

United Nations Department of Economic and Social Affairs (2003) *Report on the World Social Situation 2003, Social vulnerability: Sources and challenges*, New York: United Nations.

UtilityWeek (2014) 'Ofgem answers its critics' (interview/statement by Ofgem chairman David Gray 24/09/2014), http://www.utilityweek. co.uk/news/ofgem-answers-its-critics/1054862#.VUjn0Z1waUk

van Berkel, R. (2013) 'From Dutch disease to Dutch fitness? Two decades of disability crisis in the Netherlands', in C. Lindsay and D. Houston (eds) *Disability benefits, welfare reform and employment policy*, Basingstoke: Palgrave Macmillan, pp 199–215.

van der Zwan, N. (2014) 'Making sense of financialization', *Socio-Economic Review*, vol 12, pp 99–129.

van Ham, P. (2001) 'The rise of the Brand State: the postmodern politics of image and reputation', *Foreign Affairs*, September/October, pp 2–6.

van Kersbergen, K. (1995) *Social capitalism. A study of Christian Democracy and the welfare state*, London: Routledge.

van Kersbergen, K., Vis, B. and Hemerijck, A. (2014) 'The great recession and welfare state reform: Is retrenchment really the only game left in town?', *Social Policy and Administration*, vol 48, no 7, pp 883–904.

Vis, B. (2010) *Politics of risk-taking: Welfare state reform in advanced democracies*, Amsterdam: Amsterdam University Press.

Volkens, A., Lehmann, P., Merz, N., Regel, S. and Werner, A. (2014) *The Manifesto Data Collection. Manifesto Project (MRG/CMP/MARPOR)*, Version 2014b, Berlin: Wissenschaftszentrum Berlin für Sozialforschung (WZB), https://manifestoproject.wzb.eu/information/information

Wacquant, L. (2009) *Punishing the poor: The neoliberal government of social insecurity*, London: Duke University Press.

Wakabayashi, D. (2014) 'Apple considered firing longtime ad agency TBWA', *Wall Street Journal*, 4 April, http://online.wsj.com/news/articles/SB10001424052702303847804579481883007501484.

Wallbank, J. and Herring, J. (eds) (2013) *Vulnerabilities, care and family law*, London: Routledge.

Waldfogel, J. (2006) 'What do children need?', *Public Policy Research*, vol 13, no 1, pp 26–34.

Walker, G. and Day, R. (2012) 'Fuel poverty as injustice: integrating distribution, recognition and procedure in the struggle for affordable warmth', *Energy Policy*, vol 49, pp 69–75.

Walsh, J. (2013) 'Social policy and special economic zones in the Greater Mekong subregion', *International Journal of Social Quality*, vol 3, no 1, pp 44–56.

Walters, W. (1997) 'The active society: new designs for social policy', *Policy & Politics*, vol 25, no 3, pp 221–34.

Ward, H. and Samways, D. (1992) 'Environmental policy', in D. Marsh and R.A.W. Rhodes (eds) *Implementing Thatcherite policies*, Buckingham: Open University Press.

Watson, M. (2009) 'Planning for a future of asset-based welfare? New Labour, financialized economic agency and the housing market', *Planning, Practice and Research*, vol 24, no 1, pp 2009, pp 41–56.

Watts, B. (2014) 'Homelessness, empowerment and self-reliance in Scotland and Ireland: The impact of legal rights to housing for homeless people', *Journal of Social Policy*, vol 43, pp 793–810.

Watts, M.J. and Bohle, H.G. (1993) 'The space of vulnerability: the causal structure of hunger and famine', *Progress in Human Geography*, vol 17, no 1, pp 43–67.

Webster, C. (2002) *The National Health Service: A political history*, Oxford: Oxford University Press.

Webster, D. (2015) 'Briefing: the DWP's JSA/ESA sanctions statistics release', 18 February, http://www.cpag.org.uk/david-webster.

WEF (2006) *The Global Competitiveness Report 2006–2007*, Cologny: World Economic Forum.

WEF (2008) *The Global Competitiveness Report 2008–2009*, Cologny: World Economic Forum.

WEF (2014) *The Global Competitiveness Report 2014–2015*, Cologny: World Economic Forum.

WHO and Ministry of Health and Welfare (2012) Health Service Delivery Profile Republic of Korea, WHO/MoHW.

Wilcox, S. (2010) *Financial barriers to home ownership*, Genworth Financial and Centre for Housing Policy, University of York.

Wilding, P. (1992) 'The British welfare state: Thatcherism's enduring legacy', *Policy & Politics*, vol 20, no 3, pp 201–12.

Wilensky, H.L. (1975) *The welfare state and equality: Structural and ideological roots of public expenditure*, Berkeley, CA: University of California Press.

Williams, F. (1989) *Social policy: A critical introduction*, Cambridge: Polity Press.

Williams, F. (2015) 'Towards the welfare commons: contestation, critique and criticality in social policy', in Z. Irving, M. Fenger, and J. Hudson (eds) *Social Policy Review 27: Analysis and debate in social policy,* Bristol: Policy Press.

Wincott, D. (2003) 'Beyond social regulation? New instruments and/ or a new agenda for social policy at Lisbon?' *Public Administration*, vol 81, no 3, pp 533–53.

Wisner, B. and Adams, J. (eds) (2002) *Environmental health in emergencies and disasters: A practical guide*, Geneva: World Health Organisation.

Wishart, G. (2003) 'The sexual abuse of people with learning difficulties: do we need a social approach model approach to vulnerability?', *The Journal of Adult Protection*, vol 5, no 3, pp 14–27.

Wood, L. and Kroger, R. (2000) *Doing discourse analysis*, London: Sage.

Woolfson, C. and Sommers, J. (2006) 'Labour mobility in construction: Europeanimplications of the Laval un Partneri dispute with Swedish Labour', *European Journal of Industrial Relations*, vol 12, pp 49–68.

Woolfson, C. and Sommers, J. (2016) 'Austerity and the demise of Social Europe: the Baltic Model versus the European Social Model', *Globalizations*, vol 13, pp 78–93.

World Bank (2005) *World Development Report 2000–2001, Attacking poverty: Opportunity, empowerment and security*, Washington DC: The World Bank.

World Bank (2008) *Special economic zones: Performance, lessons learned, and implications for zone development*, Washington DC: The World Bank.

Wright, S. (2011) 'Steering with sticks, rowing for rewards: The new governance of activation in the UK', in R. van Berkel, W. de Graaf and T. Sirovatka (eds) *The governance of active welfare states in Europe*, Basingstoke: Palgrave, pp 85–109.

Wright, S. (2012) 'Welfare to work, agency and personal responsibility', *Journal of Social Policy*, vol 41, no 2, pp 309–28.

Yu, J-Y. and Ko, T. (2012) 'A cross-cultural study of perceptions of medical tourism among Chinese, Japanese and Korean tourists in Korea', *Tourism Management*, vol 33, no 1, pp 80–5.

Zheng, Y. (2007) *De facto federalism in China: Reforms and dynamics of central-local relations*, London: World Scientific.

Index

Note: Page numbers in *italics* indicate figures, tables and boxes. Page numbers followed by 'n' refer to end-of-chapter notes.